My first reaction to this book was "Wow"! My continued response is still "Wow!" My fuller consideration does lead me to the question: What kind of person would know all this information? And, be brave and honest enough to write this book? My appraisal of Bernard Stephenson, after fellowshipping in a variety of divine appointments and opportunities is that he is one of few writers that could and has lived out many of the restorative steps of God's plan. His life's focus over these years of birthing "Steps to Wholeness" has also been sharpened by real life experiences. This manual has readable and applicable steps for each stage of the restoration process. The person, who will pursue this material honestly, will be able to see measurable steps of progress. This progress will continue to manifest in new and improved lives and relationships for today and forever. It is my pleasure to commend the author first and then to congratulate him on this masterpiece on God's full plan of restoration for individuals, families, churches and indeed the broader society that will hear it. The Lord bless all who read this book!

Rev. Ralph Glagau,
Senior Pastor, Humberlea Church of God,
Toronto ON Canada

Steps to Wholeness is a helpful guide to the path of personal healing and restoration. Using many Biblical examples, Bernard Stephenson explains how to have the right relationship with God that will set you free. This book will help you chart a new direction for your life.

Grant Mullen M.D.,
Author of Emotionally Free
drgrantmullen.com

Without a doubt we live in a very broken world. As we face the uncertainty of our troubled generation, we cannot afford to turn away from the counsel of the word of God. In a very penetrating manner, Dr. Bernard Stephenson, in his book, "Steps to Wholeness", establishes principles to restore hope, restoration and wholeness. It is the path for both individuals and the nations of the world to come back into alignment with their Creator. Author Bernard Stephenson clearly shares the journey back to full restoration. The author deals with the issues plaguing humanity but also God's remedy. This is a must read and get ready for you are about to embark on an incredible journey of truth to freedom.

Rev. Bob Johnston,
Lead Pastor, Global Kingdom Ministries,
Toronto, ON Canada

I love this kind of books! The practical working of becoming like Jesus is the best journey any follower of Jesus can take. God has given us His Holy Spirit to help us to put off stuff we don't need, and then put on all the character of Jesus and fruit of the Spirit. Bernard's four steps to wholeness are very practical, as well as, life giving steps based on solid Bible examples. As you get to know Bernard through this book, you will see his heart for seeing everyone on this journey into wellness.

Steve Long,
Senior Leader, Catch the Fire Toronto,
Author of My Healing Belongs to Me,
On the Run,
The Faith Zone

Bernard Stephenson is a man of character and excellence who has a heart to see all come into their God given destiny including through wholeness and healing of past wounds.

Through Biblical lessons occurring in Gilgal, Bethel, Jericho and the Jordan River and using creative writing and stories, Bernard shows how freedom can be obtained. The importance of morality and living God's best is outlined on a personal and corporate scale in this work as we see the consequences of actions taken - for good or destruction. "Steps to Wholeness" leads one into hope for change. Indeed, our past does not need to be an excuse for our future as the power of the cross of Jesus Christ has paid it all. May all who read this work experience transformation.

Rev. Patricia Bootsma,
Sr. Leader Catch the Fire Canada,
Director Canadian Prophetic Council,
Leader, Canadian National House of Prayer

STEPS

TO

WHOLENESS

By **Bernard Stephenson,**
M.Div., MD

Steps to Wholeness

ISBN: 978-1-9995040-0-7

Cover design by Rev. Adauto Rezende
Inside graphics by Oswald OCSDesign
Printing by Printing Icon, Toronto, ON Canada

DEDICATION

I dedicate this book to my Lord and Heavenly Father who has inspired me to write this book. As well, I dedicate it to all His people who will benefit from its knowledge that will vindicate and encourage them. I also dedicate it to my wife, my children, my parents and all who prayed for and encouraged me, in so many ways, to stand firm with our God and Savior, for truth and for the common good.

CONTENTS

ACKNOWLEDGEMENTS

First, my thanks go to my Heavenly Father and His Holy Spirit, without which this work would have been impossible. He moved me to press on when so many times I wanted to quit.

I am so grateful to my wife and children who had to tolerate the seven years of my sitting behind my computer toiling away at a book that never seemed could be completed and to my parents for their support.

My sincere thanks to Rev. Adauto Rezende for the amazing Book Cover, Oswald Ocsdesign, who was instrumental in creating the graphics inside, Patricia King Edwards for the editing, and to the many who contributed to this book in some major or minor way whether through prayers, encouragement or advice.

PREFACE

As an ex-physician, I have learned from studying the natural order that we all must fully integrate into it or else we will suffer the consequences. As the world was intelligently designed, we cannot hope to succeed at anything if we do not know and follow life's requirements. "*My people are destroyed for lack of knowledge, laments the Lord.*" (Hosea 4:6a) Most people go through life without a clue that all things work together to maintain or restore order and unity (wholeness) in the individual and in the environment. Therefore, this book, Steps to Wholeness, will shed light on God's natural model for life, in which, truth is tied to righteousness, loving-kindness, peace and wellness, and on its restorative paths to wholeness.

God has a roadmap for geo-social wholeness: to restore everything, including people, who have lost their way in life, including their relationship with Him. There is a restorative path of justice for every path of injustice. Thus, we can learn from Elijah's last journey of the phases of God's restorative and redemptive plan to move us from enslavement to freedom, from brokenness to wholeness, and from enmity with God to falling in love with Him -- both individually and as a society.

As you can imagine, it is God who will complete the process of being "*made a new creature in Christ Jesus*":

> *"This means that anyone who belongs to Christ has become a new person. The old life is gone; a new life has begun! And all of this is a gift from God, who brought us back to himself through Christ. And God has given us this task of reconciling people to him. For God was in Christ, reconciling the world to himself, no longer counting people's sins against them. And he gave us this wonderful message of reconciliation. So we are Christ's ambassadors; God is making his appeal through us. We speak for Christ when we plead, "Come back to God!" For God made Christ, who never sinned, to be the offering for our sin, so that we could be made right with God through Christ." (II Corinthians 5:17-21, NLT)*

This book will illuminate specific growth principles that will enable individuals as well as corporate institutions to be restored so they can thrive in the Kingdom of God on Earth.

This hour of power word is for such a time as ours when governments are compelling everyone to align with their politically (in)correct stance, their human rights agendas and action plans regarding climate change. God's program involves healing a land that is hurting, a fact that is fuelling conversations around water fountains and dinner tables across the globe regarding climate change. A cry is going up from the land for society to turn back from Nature's breaking point and the brink of disaster and come back to the Way. As we earnestly await our Lord's return in this hostile, toxic environment, the teachings of this book will enable us all to remove barriers to unity, correct injustices, restore the natural balance, while promoting growth and restoring divine order. This divine revelation will restore all our trust in God's rule and re-energize our love for God and our search for truth and learning.

This book, in bringing together both faith and science, vindicates Christian values as natural, and proves that moral values are not optional, but essential for wholeness and wellbeing. You will see that as God, the Creator, wisely embedded His values into Nature, you cannot reject (or accept) one without rejecting (or accepting) the other. Thus, it will strengthen and encourage leaders to stand firm with -- rather than against their God and Lord, help everyone understand the essence of Natural Law, as well as the need to remain systemically integrated, within the normal range (narrow way); not the politically correct 'normal', or what people consider to be 'normal', but within God's and nature's true normal.

I hope the reader will catch this vision that the Lord has revealed and, by it, may step out upon their own journey back to life, rise in divine oneness to go forth in turn to benefit others and the environment, and bring joy to their Heavenly Father.

Bernard Stephenson,
M.Div., MD

Author's note: Yahweh, whenever used, is the name of the God of Israel and our Heavenly Father.

INTRODUCTION

I had once thought that serial killers had no chance of rehabilitation or salvation until I heard Aldo Nascimento's story, which changed my thinking. It made me even more amazed at God's awesome unconditional power and love for us all.

He had grown up in the Assemblies of God Church in Brazil. His mother was a strong believer, but his dad was not. At the age of 6, like many his age, he was a hyperactive child. One day, while travelling with his mother, Aldo decided to pull a prank on her and hide in the train station's washroom. After fruitlessly searching for him and seeing a little boy that looked just like her own enter the train, she boarded hoping he was onboard. The train left while Aldo was still in hiding. After a while, he began to look for his mom, but she was nowhere to be found. Scared and alone, he was now a street kid having to fend for himself on the fearsome and brutal streets.

Later, he was adopted by a witch, who would groom this church-going child to become one of Brazil's foremost Satanists, even while he was still a teenager. He thrived in the entertainment world providing satanic services to the TV industry's actors and actresses. According to Aldo, he would kidnap and ritually murder children then offer their blood to Satan, to dedicate a soap opera. While still a young man, he was finally arrested as a serial killer and sentenced to life in prison.

Even though he was dying of terminal cancer, Aldo was euthanized in the jail's hospital, after two failed attempts, despite his profuse protesting and not before he had cried out to the God of his mother to save him. You see, after almost two decades, Aldo had an unfulfilled urge to find his mother. Finally, he was pronounced dead, was issued a death certificate and his body was removed to the morgue. There, God miraculously brought him back to life. He was rushed back to the hospital, where he fully recovered; and under the guidance of the Prison Chaplain, he repented of his past sins and reconciled with God.

After acknowledging that Aldo had fulfilled his sentence by death and seeing his amazing transformation from serial killer and Satanist to 'born again' transformed Christian, he was released from prison into the custody of the kind chaplain, who took him in, helped him find and reconciled him with his mother. Eighteen years had passed since that ill-fated day. The chaplain then groomed him to become an ordained pastor. You can hear the testimony of this completely transformed ex-Satanist, in greater detail, on YouTube (but only in Portuguese).

How can this happen, you ask? What do you have to do? I have entitled this book Steps to Wholeness and consider this a very important timely topic. When God created our world, everything worked together as one, so much so, that he was pleased with His masterpiece, concluding that it was "*very good*". It is only when humanity fell, that even our earth, never mind our own selves, became corrupted, as we veered away from God and polluted our earth with our rebellious ways. God's desire is to move us back by taking us along His journey to wholeness and restoration of our lives. I have thus taken advantage of the template of Elijah's journey going from Gilgal to the Jordan River to show God's plan and purpose for how this restoration to wholeness should take place. However, first we must look at the definition of wholeness.

According to **the Oxford Dictionary,** the definition of 'Wholeness' is the state of forming a complete and harmonious whole; unity. Again, according to t**he Free Dictionary**, wholeness implies that all components are complete, not divided or disjoined; not wounded, injured or impaired; sound or unhurt. As each transgressed, became wounded and/ or broken and fell away from the wholeness that once existed when the Creator pronounced that everything He created was "very good", we need to be restored to that wholeness. Christians often say, "I am whole in Christ," or "Christ has made me whole." What does this mean? It means that we are being brought back into the whole -- physically, emotionally, mentally, spiritually -- through Christ. In other words, we need to, once again, align with and be integrated into the unity of the kingdom of God and of His ecosystem. Then, they will be able to experience the goodness of God and of His creation, "lacking nothing".

Through the life of Elisha, on his journeys through Gilgal, Bethel, Jericho and the Jordan River and interspersed with my own testimony, and Biblical passages, I have attempted to outline the various life phases that God planned for us all to go through on our way to heaven. It is truly God's steps back to wholeness and to life.

So, let the Lord reveal to you 'the hidden manna' of this revelation knowledge how to find freedom, deal with the critical aftermath of years of abuse and attain physical and emotional wellbeing. Anyone can obtain a new lease on life with a new identity, new wholesome labels and a renewed hope -- if they surrender to the Lord of all life and take up His ordained journey for their lives. Let this book identify the steps that God calls us all to go through on our way back to wholeness and life.

START YOUR STEPS TO WHOLENESS AND RESTORATION

STEP ONE

GILGAL:
TO RID THE SHAME OF PAST MISTAKES

For those of us who have fallen short of the glorious and abundant life and have become disjointed from the whole – the kingdom of God and of the ecosystem -- one must find how to take that very first step on the journey back to wholeness. We must first restore our inner spiritual balance, before we can embark on restoring the rest towards wholeness. However, before we start out on this journey, we must ask ourselves these probing questions:

Is there any hope for me?
If I had the opportunity to start over again, would I take it?
If I had a second chance at life, what would I do differently?
Can I recover from the calamity and horrendous abuse that I endured in the past?
Can I forgive the person(s) who offended me?
Can I rid myself of the shame and stigma of the past?

Can I get rid of the shackles of addiction and mental health issues that have kept me chained for such a long time?
Will my loved ones or society ever forgive me for my past mistakes?
Can I ever forgive myself?
Can I regain my lost freedom, self-esteem, health and integrity?
Can I ever enjoy life again?

The answer to all these questions is a definite resounding **YES**!!! In the Bible Old Testament story, Israel was in just such a situation. They cried out for help and received it. Like the Israelites, we can all be restored to enjoy life again.

Elijah's last journey (and our restoration) begins at Gilgal, which was located on the eastern border of Jericho (Joshua 4:19) just west of the Jordan River. It was the place where the Israelites encamped immediately after crossing the Jordan River for the first time. An altar of 12 stones, each representing a tribe, was set up at Gilgal. Joshua was told to circumcise the people as this younger generation had not been. Their parents, apart from Joshua and Caleb, had all died in the desert. Upon seeing their obedience, *GOD said to Joshua, "Today I have rolled away the reproach of Egypt."* (Joshua 5:1-12, MSG). Thus, began the journey back to normalcy.

Let's look at the journey from Elisha's perspective. *"Just before GOD took Elijah to heaven in a whirlwind, Elijah and Elisha were on a walk out of Gilgal.*" (2 Kings 2:1-17, MSG)

Elisha's Reflections on His Journey with Elijah

"Do you need me anymore, Elijah? I asked.
"No, you can go to bed, Elisha", he replied.

I sensed that he was going to sleep. I had already given him his bed-time tea. I was tired and wanted to go to bed. An excitement was in the air as there was talk among the others that something fantastic was about to happen. Some even said that Elijah would be leaving us, for good. I myself felt that the Lord had been preparing me to take over from Elijah as His Prophet to Israel. I wondered if the others knew. Elijah had never said anything to me. So, I wondered… Anyway, I trusted in the Lord's choice, whoever He was.

Over the past few years, I had been having many great and wonderful experiences with the Lord. I had been reading the Torah over and over, ever since I had learned to read. God's Word had been consuming me night and day… every spare moment I had. I felt as if I was walking on clouds, I was so full of joy. The Lord spoke to me often – sometimes comforting me when I felt that I couldn't handle Elijah's overbearing attitude, sometimes revealing the hearts of our ancestors, such as, Moses, or just, filling me with words that I myself didn't understand. I just knew that God loved me and was very pleased with me. I felt special, very special. I understood how Moses had felt. I even understood my Rabbi, Elijah. My confidence had grown a great deal ever since Elijah had called me to be his disciple.

This night, I was especially tired, so I went straight to bed. I had to pack our stuff because Elijah had said that the Lord had told him to go to Bethel. The funny thing was that he hadn't said "we" but "I". I hadn't bothered to question him about it as I was too tired. Anyway, I would see about that in the morning. As I lay there with my eyes closed, I thought about Gilgal and what it meant for Israel and for me. I had visited the pile of twelve stones that Joshua had the people build on the Lord's instructions. Some of them had fallen away from the pile and were just lying there next to it. The pile symbolized the unity and wholeness that the Lord wished for Israel. Even though my people were divided into twelve tribes, we were to act as one people; but, like the rocks that had fallen away, Israel had also fallen away from that unity and wholeness.

I began to imagine the joy and relief that the people must have felt as they stood there, finally, in the Promised Land. Freedom! Rescued! Saved! Redeemed! Delivered! Safe again! Happy! Alive! God had done it. He had fulfilled His promise. Most significantly, He had proven His ability to redeem an entire nation from under the tyranny of slavery to the Egyptians. Amazingly, He had done it in spectacular fashion forcefully wrenching them out of Pharaoh's hands, inflicting numerous plagues on the nation and its people, even killing all their firstborn, both of people and of animals, on Passover night. What a terrifying night it turned out to be, but greater still, what an amazing deliverance for all those who believed. They had submitted to God, obeying His every instruction and painted the doorposts with the lambs' blood just as He had instructed Moses. Moreover, God did not send the people away empty-handed, for He instructed the people to ask for jewelry and other valuable stuff from their neighbors who, amazingly, handed it all generously over to them. Thus, they plundered the Egyptians before leaving. Praise be to God!

God led them miraculously across the Red Sea on dry ground and when the Egyptian army attempted to do the same, they drowned when the walls of water came crashing down on the soldiers and horses alike. Like a compassionate Shepherd, He guided and cared for the entire group of Israelites on through the dangerous and relentless desert, feeding them with His own creation, manna, and with quail in abundance. Even their shoes did not wear out! Only those, who rejected His instructions and did not submit to His leadership, wore out and died on that epic journey. Gilgal was the end of a long journey from slavery to freedom. It was the turning point in Israel's history -- a new beginning for my people in the land that God had promised our ancestors: Abraham, Isaac and Jacob; the land that has been ours now for the past 550 years.

Soon after arriving at Gilgal, Joshua had everyone circumcised, even those who had not previously been. I imagined that was necessary as the whole generation of children who were born in the desert were not, so God had told Joshua to have the people fulfill the covenant He had made with them before. This practice was not yet established at its beginning as it is now. My thoughts went all the way back to my own circumcision, which I was told occurred just after my birth. I had been covenanted with the Lord. I was an adolescent when I reaffirmed my commitment to God. I had told Him that, as He was my God and my Lord, whatever He wanted me to do, I would do and wherever He wanted me to go, I would go. Thus, when Elijah called me to be his disciple, I readily accepted. It was an easy decision. I left everything and followed him.

Then, as usual, after seeing the people's obedience, came God's blockbuster declaration: "*Today I have removed the disgrace (shame) of Egypt from you", God said to Joshua"* (Joshua 5:9); which gives us the name Gilgal, which means '*rolled away*'.

I understood what this all meant for me and my people and, even more so, God's role and importance in it. It was our God, the God of Israel, who had rolled away the disgrace. He had rolled mine away and that of everyone who had submitted to Him. He was our Savior. What a salvation! My people had been severely mistreated and humiliated as slaves in Egypt. Every family in Israel had loved ones who had died as a direct result of the mistreatment. Tears came to my eyes as I thought of their suffering and shame. I too could have been born into slavery… God had graciously redeemed and delivered my people from the humiliation of subjugation. I was glad that the Lord was my God. I shall not be afraid of my enemies even if I fall into their hands because He is my God and Deliverer. *"Thank you, Lord!"*

The people had been physically damaged because of all the maltreatment they had endured, so the Lord had healed them and taken away this aspect of the disgrace. Even if I was hurt because of persecution from God's enemies; I trust in my Lord to heal me, if He so wishes. They were also emotionally unstable from all the abuse they had endured. Again, the Lord healed them after they had obeyed His instructions to renounce anger, hatred, grudges against the Egyptians and refrained from going back into the past to remember the abuse. I myself had to forgive the Egyptians for what they had done to my people, and love them and all the foreign people, who lived among us. The Lord had confronted me before about my anger, especially, towards foreigners. I had thought it was alright to have fits of rage when people hurt my feelings. God, however, said it was not alright and that I had to forgive quickly, control myself and not allow my anger to boil over. Now, I am much better at controlling myself and haven't had a fit of rage in a while. You see, the Lord had also revealed that I was afraid of being abused and that I had no reason to be afraid since He was always with me. If I remained faithful, loving, fearing and obeying Him, I had no reason to be fearful. So, I disciplined myself not to be afraid and constantly reminded myself of God's faithfulness to me and mine to Him. I have even helped people who were emotionally unstable by reminding them of these same instructions the Lord gave to Israel and to me.

"Thank you, Lord, for healing and restoring me
to emotional stability!
Thank you, Lord, for removing the stigma
and shame of mental disease from over me!"

Then the people celebrated the Passover, which was the 40th anniversary of their Exodus from Egypt and the source of the shame of it all. I have celebrated the Passover many times, but I wished I had been there with my people at that time as it must have been special! Oh, what a joy it must have been to remember the goodness of the Lord in delivering us from our enemies and redeeming us from the scourge of slavery. He covered our sins by shedding the blood of the Passover lamb, which we painted on the doors of every believer's house. This showed His special care and love for His Son, Israel. Yes, I am glad that He is my God. What great and wonderful things He has done for Israel and has done and will do for me! Hallelu-Jah! What a deliverance! I couldn't help but smile.

After the celebration was over, the people had to get accustomed to their new situation. They were no longer slaves nor travelers in the desert. Food was no longer scarce, but abundant. Life was no longer difficult, but easy. The manna and quail had stopped as the people were no longer in the desert, so didn't require God's daily provision of food. I wonder how this might have affected the people, at that time for, like children, they had received everything, but now they had to fend for themselves; even though, it was in a land of plenty. I hoped they all would adapt quickly, grow up and move to a higher maturity level, where they could begin to take advantage of the fertile land and enjoy this new phase of their life, without grumbling.

I awoke sometime during the night with the Lord speaking to me -- "*Elisha, you are to go with Elijah to Bethel. Do not be afraid for I am sending you. Do not leave Elijah alone; follow him wherever he goes for He will soon be going home.*" I was filled with joy as I broke out in prophesying to the Lord. I must have fallen asleep again as I awoke with the sunlight streaming through the tiny gaps in the walls. The shadows danced on the ground and walls as the wind rustled the leaves of the fig and date trees outside. I felt refreshed as I got up quickly to prepare for the journey to Bethel. I heard Elijah walking about in the adjacent room. Suddenly, he appeared in the doorway and said, *"Stay here, for the LORD has told me to go to Bethel.*" I quickly replied. *"As surely as the LORD lives and you yourself live, I will never leave you"*. (2 Kings 2:2) He did not say a word. So, after we had eaten, we set out for Bethel.

I felt different. I had a renewed sense of purpose. I had heard from the Lord. Previously, I had suspected, but now I knew that I was His chosen one. I belonged. I was no longer just

Elijah's servant, but God's chosen vessel. I felt at peace. I felt one with the Lord, the God of Israel. He was my God.

YOUR JOURNEY
--THE LIFE LESSONS--

Setting the captives FREE

At Gilgal, Israel was called to repent and to renew its covenant with the Lord. Israel had committed mistakes in life for which they had suffered the harsh consequences. They had left the highway and had sinned against Nature, themselves, others and their God, by engaging in the same sins as the Egyptians, who worshipped many different gods, which gave them no benefit, except the misery of enslavement. They had abandoned their God, Yahweh, the Fountain of the Water of Life and had "*dug for themselves cracked cisterns that can hold no water at all*" (Jeremiah 2:13). Indeed, Israel needed to covenant to repent and turn back to the way of righteousness and shalom.

In any covenant between two parties there must be a commitment from both sides, especially as the plan is for One to save the other. Gilgal is about our commitment to **forsake all**, **repent** and **enthrone** Jesus as Savior and King before the Lord circumcises our hearts and proclaims that we have been **enlivened** -- set **F.R.E.E.**

Forsaking All

The Israelites had been slaves in Egypt. That was their starting point. We must ask ourselves what is our own starting point?

What is yours? Are you a slave, (a bonded or forced laborer), in a bad marriage, a child or sex slave, a child soldier, an addict to sex, drugs, alcohol or gambling, or are you just feeling an overwhelming sense of emptiness and that something is missing in your life? Are you bitter with lots of hatred towards someone or something? Do you have an extreme (or just a simple) dissatisfaction with your life or the way it is going? Have you ever thought of committing suicide? Well, you don't have to kill yourself, but you can take the steps to surrender your broken life to Jesus Christ and be willing to give up everything that He asks you to. In return, He will give you a new life, new attitude and a new heart. He will place His Holy Spirit within you, who will give you the will to choose righteousness. In other words, surrender this life of sin and brokenness and choose God's offer of a new righteousness-loving life.

It was Israel's extreme dissatisfaction with the status quo that drove them to cry out to the Lord day and night for deliverance. They cried out to many gods, but only the Lord God of Israel, responded and sent a savior, Moses, who showed them the way out of their misery. The Lord will also show you the way out of yours. He sent Jesus Christ to be your own personal Savior and Lord. Are you crying out to Jesus? I recall a young man who was fascinated with the Gothic lifestyle, who called out to a demon god that he had heard of to save him from oppression by evil spirits. Obviously, the situation got worse. It was only when he cried out to Jesus Christ and rebuked the evil spirits in His name that he was delivered.

Forsaking Your Comfort Zone

The decision to abandon the life you know, which you may have been living for years, if not decades, is not an easy one. It will take a lot of courage to abandon the only life you know; even though, that life is one of seemingly endless pain, guilt, misery and sorrow. It took a lot of courage for the Israelites to abandon their life of slavery. They knew what it meant to run away from their slave masters. It could mean death if they were caught. They could lose their meager rations of food. They would have to abandon their homes, their friends, the temples where they practiced witchcraft, and the slave conditions in which they had worked and where they had seen many of their friends and relatives die. You might wonder why they would not want to abandon those conditions. Well, it was their lifestyle. It was what they had been accustomed to all their lives. It had been the lot of their parents, their grandparents and their great grandparents before them. It was their comfort zone, even if it was cold. What is your comfort zone? It doesn't matter what form of bondage you are in -- it has been your 'cold comfort' zone for a long time and it is time to forsake it.

Jesus encourages us all to '*deny*' ourselves, pick up our cross and abandon this 'cold comfort' in order to seek freedom and a new life of joy, satisfaction and hope in Him. Just as He did for the Israelites, He will also do for us. He will defend us against our enemies and nurture us back to life. Therefore, we are not to be afraid to forsake it all. Why should we continue to hang on to such a life? It will only continue to offer more pain, suffering, guilt, despair and misery. Furthermore, the status quo is never static, but it will continue to get worse each day we remain in it. Today, like the Israelites almost thirty-five hundred years ago, we can walk away. First, we must be willing to deny ourselves by forsaking our comfort zone. You will not regret leaving yours.

I witnessed an amazing testimony by Mike W. who came to my church on Thanksgiving Sunday (2010) when I was on the Pastoral Team. That Sunday, I gave everyone the opportunity to give God thanks. This young man, whom I had never seen before, was the first to jump up and say how thankful he was to God for saving him. He had been desperate to get out of depression, alcoholism and illicit drug abuse, so one night, at around midnight, he determined to seek God until he found peace. He prayed and read all the verses in his Gideon Bible that pertained to his situation until about 4 a.m. when he finally felt peace. He was so happy but was concerned that this experience might be short lived. However, his peace and inner joy remained. He later had an inner urge to find a church, which was why he was there. There, he was guided through the steps to wholeness, has remained faithful and has since married a beautiful and God-fearing young woman.

It is wise to seek help from the experts -- from our Heavenly Father and His representatives: pastors, prophets, Christian counselors, etc. and have a submissive attitude in following their advice. Seeking their help and not fully following their advice is unwise. So....**forsake all** and...

Repent

"Therefore repent and return, so that your sins may be wiped away, in order that times of refreshing may come from the presence of the Lord; and that He may send Jesus, the Christ appointed for you" (Acts 3:19-20, NASB)

The first step to freedom is repentance. There is no freedom without first turning away from the very wrongdoing that placed you in that miserable situation to begin with. Repentance goes beyond regret or remorse. Regret does not imply admission of guilt nor responsibility. Remorse does imply admission of guilt and personal responsibility and is accompanied by emotional pain and anguish. Neither regret nor remorse imply change, but repentance goes further and implies a decision of the will to change. So, one must repent rather than just being regretful or remorseful. You must conclude that enough is enough and that there needs to be a dramatic change in your life. Whoever works with drug addicts knows how important this little detail is. Unless a person wants to be helped, is willing to collaborate in their own process and is ready to abandon their bad habits, they cannot be helped. They must first hate the addiction and all the pain it is causing and decide to change. They must not only regret and be remorseful, but they must make the decision to turn away from their sinful ways and return all the way to the normal range.

To achieve victory at Gilgal, we are to commit ourselves to turning away from all that ruined our lives -- from all the sinful, harmful, evil ways that we once walked in. Our Savior said, *"If anyone would come after me, let him deny himself and take up his cross and follow me. For whoever wants to save his life will lose it, but whoever loses his life for me will find it."* (Matthew 16:24-25 ESV) Yes, all of us first must let go of what is broken and ready to be discarded and offer it to Jesus, the Savior, so He can fix it and give us new life.

While repentance is a priority when you are the offender, what about when you are the one that has been offended?

The Priority of Reconciliation -- Forgiveness

Principle: Forgive, forget, reconcile and move on in order to heal

To walk in freedom, there must be the willingness to forgive, forget and let go of past offenses. We are not to wait on the perpetrator to ask for forgiveness as they might never do so or even repent. We are to just leave a post-dated cheque of forgiveness, as Jesus did, and move on. Forgiveness can only be 'cashed' when the person repents of wrongdoing in the same way that you were only able to 'cash' in on Jesus' forgiveness, when you repented of your sins. You will do yourself an enormous favor by just leaving that cheque of forgiveness and getting on with your life. Only then, will you be able to walk away free from the baggage of bitterness and hate. The alternative is waiting, hanging on to the forgiveness without giving it, and experiencing its transformation into bitterness, rage, depression, and other emotional and physical ailments. So, sincerely, we are to forgive all those who have sinned against us.

In the Lord's Prayer, Jesus revealed its importance by including the principle that being forgiven by the Father is conditional on our forgiving others: *"Forgive us as we forgive others."* (Matthew 6:12) In the Parable of the Unforgiving Servant, Jesus told us the story of the person who was forgiven a large debt, but who was unwilling to forgive a much lesser debt owed to him by someone and he even had him thrown in jail. The forgiveness that had been extended to him was then withdrawn and he was thrown in jail. *"So also my Heavenly Father will do to every one of you, if you do not forgive your brother from your heart."* (Matthew 18:21-35) Jesus' counsel to '*forgive from your heart*' means to forgive sincerely and passionately, with all your heart. Many of us have heard of the stories of Corrie Ten Boom and Phan Thị Kim Phúc, mostly known as Kim Phúc, who were both survivors of the horrible atrocities of war -- Corrie, of the 2nd World War and Kim, of the Vietnam War.

Corrie, immortalized in her autobiography, The Hiding Place, and in the movie of the same name, witnessed the death of her father and sister in the Nazi concentration camps. She, herself had suffered detention at the infamous Ravensbruck Concentration Camp in the Netherlands. Even though she was a born-again Christian, she harbored hatred towards those who committed the atrocities. After surviving both the war and the concentration camps, Corrie spoke of her ordeal and how she had dealt with it. After one of the many meetings at which she spoke, she came face to face with one of the Nazi guards. She wrote:

> "*Even as the angry vengeful thoughts boiled through me, I saw the sin of them. Jesus Christ had died for this man; was I going to ask for more? Lord Jesus, I prayed, forgive me and help me to forgive him.... Jesus, I cannot*

> *forgive him. Give me your forgiveness... And so, I discovered that it is not on our forgiveness any more than on our goodness that the world's healing hinges, but on His. When He tells us to love our enemies, He gives along with the command, the love itself.*" "*Forgiveness is an act of the will, and the will can function regardless of the temperature of the heart.*" "*And for all these people alike, the key to healing turned out to be the same. Each had a hurt he had to forgive.*" (Corrie ten Boom, The Hiding Place).

Yes, thank God, for He indwells us and gives us both the will and the strength to do the very things that He demands of us -- things that benefit us enormously because they complete our healing and as you will see later, they restore balance.

Kim Phuc's story, like Corrie's is no different. Her story, that of 'The Girl in the Picture', became etched in our minds in the book and movie of the same name. She was horribly burned when a South Vietnamese Air Force pilot mistakenly napalm-bombed her group, killing two of her cousins and two other villagers. The Pulitzer Prize winning photo of Kim Phuc running naked and crying turned out to be one of the most haunting and defining images of the Vietnam War. She stated:

> "*Forgiveness made me free from hatred. I still have many scars on my body and severe pain most days, but my heart is cleansed. Napalm is very powerful, but faith, forgiveness, and love are much more powerful. We would not have war at all, if everyone could learn how to live with true love, hope, and forgiveness. If that little girl in the picture can do it, ask yourself: Can you?*" (Kim Phuc)

As the previous stories suggest, forgiveness and reconciliation are not only necessary when it is between individuals, but they are also imperative when it is between individuals and corporate bodies or between corporate bodies.

Corporate Forgiveness

Many, like the Israelites, must also deal with the consequences of abuse by corporate bodies: governments and their institutions, ethnic groups, religious groups, including churches, and commercial and charitable organizations. Inter-religious strife is all too common in this 21st Century, but government abuses against minority religions, most notably against Christians and Jews, are still very common in majority Communist, Islamic, Hindu, Buddhist and even secular atheistic nations.

> "*Around the world, presidents, state officials, police, religious warriors, radicals, terrorists and even ordinary citizens are trying to stop the spread of the Christian faith. "I will stop Christianity in this country," said Iranian President Mahmoud Ahmadinejad in 2007.*" (The Persecuted Church Global Report, 2011).

Today, there are numerous accounts of genocide -- some in the distant past, such as the Armenian Genocide of about 1.5 million Christian men, women and children by the Muslim Turks in 1915; the Holodomor, or Ukrainian Genocide by forced starvation of millions of Ukrainians by Stalin in the 1930s; and still others more recently, such as the Rwandan Genocide of about 1 million Tutsis by the majority Hutu tribe in 1994. Church abuse is quite common, unfortunately. The Inquisitions within the Roman Catholic Church, which began in the 12th and continued up to the 19th Century, were the cause of much bitterness. More recently, there are stories from India and Pakistan where whole villages, such as, Gojra, with their churches, have been burned to the ground with many people martyred. Further to this, my editor owned a Christian Publishing House in India that was burned to the ground by

Hindu extremists in April 2017. She lost 150,000 Christian books -- the proceeds of which were going to support Indian indigenous pastors. Again, closer to home, the victims, and their descendants, of the Residential Schools in Canada are still dealing with their bitterness towards the Roman Catholic Church and the Canadian government. Today, while not at the same level and intensity as during the Inquisitions, persecution of so-called heretics continues across Christianity and in every religious group.

Whatever the abuse, the need to deal with the trauma of it remains a reality today. The consequences of chronic emotional, mental and physical imbalance are passed down from generation to generation, often within the same family line, so the children suffer from a past life that they had nothing to do with. This still requires the very same solution as at the individual level -- the need of the corporate body to repent and reconcile with their victims on the one hand (which often is not even close to ever happening) and the abused one to forgive, forget, reconcile and move on, on the other. While it is hard to repent and apologize or forgive and forget, at the individual level, it is even more difficult and complex at the corporate level. Corporate bodies are groups of individuals that function as one. Therefore, making decisions are not simple. They all have different decision-making processes holding them back, such as, unanimity, wherein every individual member must agree; the preponderance of members, wherein, the majority, at least two-thirds, must agree; and, simple majority, wherein half plus one must concur. So, don't wait for an apology from a corporate body as it may never happen but, leave a post-dated cheque of forgiveness and move on.

Some corporate bodies have acknowledged the abuse, but many have not. Even when a public apology was given, it was done many years or decades, even centuries, later. In the past few decades since the end of World War II, many church groups have officially apologized to the Jewish people for the role of their governments and church organizations in actively and passively ignoring the plight of Jews who were fleeing the Holocaust. In late 2010, a 50-member delegation of Amish groups in Idaho went to Israel to apologize on behalf of the entire Amish people *"For our collective sin of pride and selfishness by ignoring the plight of the Jewish people and the Nation of Israel."* The Catholic Church in France apologized for their role in passively, and sometimes actively, supporting the arresting and placing of Jews in local concentration camps and of deporting many to concentration camps, such as, Auschwitz.

While corporate apologies are welcome, individuals must still know how to deal with this issue at a personal level. Individuals, such as Corrie and Kim Phuc, had to contend, not only with their bitterness and hatred towards specific individuals, but also with people groups, nations, organizations and even churches. The Lord, knowing of the danger of not being able to forgive, commanded the Israelites not to hate the Egyptians: "*Do not despise an Egyptian, because you resided as foreigners in their country.*" (Deuteronomy 23:7b) One may argue that they were abused and enslaved by the Egyptians so were thus justified to harbor bitterness and hatred. As the inability to forgive leads to bitterness, which in turn has physical, emotional and spiritual adverse effects, it is not justified for us to hurt ourselves over and beyond the hurt that has already been inflicted. It is, therefore, wise to forgive quickly, forget the issue, reconcile with the perpetrator and move on, so as not to suffer greater emotional and spiritual adversities. Furthermore, we are commanded to love, not hate, our enemies as this is essential to quality life both in our natural world and in God's Kingdom. I will discuss this further in Step 4. To experience full restoration, it is not enough to forgive; we must also commit ourselves to forgetting the abuse.

Forget

Even as God forgets our sins, we must also forget those of others. He said, *"For I will forgive their wickedness and will remember their sins no more."* (Hebrews 8:12) This is a long, hard process, but to be restored, you must commit to forgetting and not keep reliving the memories. Whenever you find yourself reliving any offense, just stop, push it out of your mind, and occupy your mind with something else: *"Fix your thoughts on what is true, and honorable, and right, and pure, and lovely, and admirable. Think about things that are excellent and worthy of praise." (*Philippines.4:8, NLT) This takes time, perhaps months and even years; so, don't give up but keep striving towards the goal of forgetting.

Don't try to forget without first forgiving; that would be a mistake. It does not work that way. It only takes a voice or sight of something or someone or a thought that can trigger a flashback and a flood of painful memories. Planning not to forget is also a mistake as the painful memories will persist longer thus prolonging your suffering. Besides, the constant distraction of reliving the abuse or thinking about the abuser will disturb your day-to-day life. It can hurt your job; distract you while operating dangerous machines; and endanger your life or the lives of others. No wonder Jesus warned us that *"No one who puts a hand to the plow and looks back is fit for service in the Kingdom of God."* (Luke 9:62) Looking back while plowing is a temptation that can cause you to miss the rock in the ground and potentially break the plow. We must always pay full attention to what we are doing in the present. Constant looking back into the past will only distract you and hamper your effectiveness in carrying out your responsibilities in the present. So, forgive **and** forget.

Reconcile

The third component of forgiving is reconciliation, as it restores balance and community life. The goal and purpose of forgiveness is reconciliation, if possible. I say, 'if possible', because reconciliation must be avoided in certain cases, such as, with an unrepented sexual offender or murderer, as these will repeat the abuse when given the chance. Holding onto un-forgiveness places barriers, which are detrimental to community. Community, common unity, or interdependence can only occur when there are no barriers to the flow of give and take. If a barrier exists to this exchange, such as the barrier put up due to offenses -- *"I don't want anything from you"," I will not give you anything"* or *"I don't want anything to do with you"* – then both parties suffer and wholeness is lost. Good social or interpersonal skills are dependent on one's ability to effectively socialize within the boundaries without being limited by the barriers erected because of unforgiven offenses. We will explore further in the 4th step how reconciliation is necessary for overall balance and wholeness.

Jesus drove home the priority of reconciling and of completing the entire process when he said:

> *"Therefore, if you are offering your gift at the altar and there remember that your brother or sister has something against you, leave your gift there in front of the altar. First go and be reconciled to them; then come and offer your gift. "Settle matters quickly with your adversary who is taking you to court. Do it while you are still together on the way, or your adversary may hand you over to the judge, and the judge may hand you over to the officer, and you may be thrown into prison. Truly I tell you, you will not get out until you have paid the last penny."* (Matthew 5: 23-26)

In those days, there was only one centralized House of God. Many had to travel great distances to get there. So, Jesus' command to leave your gift at the altar and, first, go back to solve any outstanding issues, before returning to complete your dealings with the Lord, speaks, loud and clear, regarding the priority of forgiveness, reconciliation and community. All barriers between people must be broken down just as there must be no barriers between you and God.

You can only let go of the bitterness and move on, if you first forgive, literally and intentionally put it out of your mind, and, reconcile. Only then can that chapter of your life close, freeing you to begin another chapter, this time, free of the chains of bitterness that once bound you.

Let Go of the Past, Move on -- Do Not Look Back

Now that you have closed this chapter related to the offense, you can literally move forward unfettered by it. God Himself says, "*as far as the east is from the west, so far has he removed our transgressions from us.*" (Psalm 103:12) Therefore it doesn't make any sense to bring the memory back to the forefront of what has been relegated to the past. In the book of Isaiah, we read, *"Do not remember the past events, pay no attention to things of old." (*Isaiah 43:18, HCS) Therefore, avoid contemplating on your past with all its hardships, mistakes, traumas and heartaches. It is wise to not look back in life to the things that only caused you pain, whether they were self-inflicted or caused by others. Rather, walk in your new freedom with confidence, gratefulness and happiness. You are NOT a slave any longer. You are FREE! You thought as a slave. You lived as a slave. You behaved as a slave. Others treated you as a slave and you expected to be treated as one. But now, you must think, live and behave as a freed person and expect to be treated as one. You would be living on false expectations if you were to expect anything different in your new reality. The truth is that you have been freed and saved by God's immense grace.

Believe in this truth, with all your heart. Focus all your efforts on aligning your entire life, including your thought sphere, with this new reality; and, live it out, with all confidence and gratefulness. Enjoy your new reality.

However, you must overcome the awkward and uncomfortable feelings that stem from living a new reality. Everything is new; therefore, everything will feel uncomfortable at the beginning until the new reality sets in and becomes normal and comfortable. Remember that your old life with all its mistakes, traumas, pain and misery was what constituted your 'comfort' zone. It was what you were accustomed to. It was your 'normal', not God's or nature's normal, and for this very reason, the results were disastrous. So, don't be fooled by the awkwardness that you are feeling, but trust in the ***rightness*** of your decision and actions that are solely based on truth. This truth will be illuminated throughout the rest of this book.

Making the mental shift from everything related to the offense and, hence, moving out of the past and into the present, is a very important part of cementing yourself in your new healthy lifestyle. You will reap the benefit of "*quietness and confidence*" the sooner you do so; and, you will avoid harvests of unnecessary anguish, pain and sorrow. How much effort you put into aligning yourself with your new reality and the intentional forgetting of the past will determine how fast you make the transition. Memories take time to fade, but the forgetting happens at a faster rate the more you avoid thinking about it. When you find yourself thinking about a specific episode of the past, intentionally stop and think about something different. Those of you suffering from some form of PTSD (Post Traumatic Stress Disorder) -- this is the prescription for your full recovery. It's the turning away from what is in the past that will save you and allow you to live in quietness and confidence -- *"In turning away and resting is your salvation, in quietness and confidence is your strength."* (Isaiah. 30:15 (PP) Again, *"And this (rightness) will bring peace. Yes, it will bring quietness and confidence forever."* (Isaiah.32:17 NLT)

Remember, "*As far as the east is from the west, so far has He removed our transgressions from us.*" (Psalm 103:12 KJV) So, when we give over our lives to God and fully repent, He removes all our past life from us.

But, in moving on …

Don't Transfer the Offense of the Past onto Others

'Transference' according to Mosby's Medical Dictionary: *is 'an unconscious defense mechanism whereby feelings and attitudes originally associated with important people and events in one's early life are attributed to others in current interpersonal situations, including psychotherapy.'*

This is a common unconscious temptation that must be avoided. The saying, '*Once bitten, twice shy*', applies here if one has been hurt before, as it is common to put safety mechanisms in place to avoid being hurt a second time. While these mechanisms are valid, it is unhealthy, when transference is added. These mechanisms become unhealthy when they have been broadened to include others, which is not only unjust, but damaging to community.

For example, the temptation, for the Israelites, was to transfer the offense of those Egyptians who had enslaved and mistreated them, onto all, as well as, future generations of Egyptians and onto any foreigner. Hence, we have the Lord's warning to "*not despise an Egyptian, because you resided as foreigners in their country."* (Deuteronomy 23:7b) As they had been foreigners in Egypt, the Israelites should be grateful to them for receiving and treating them well in the time of Joseph and thus be tolerant of any foreigners living among them. In other words, they must treat others in the same right way that they would want to be treated.

If you were offended, don't transfer this offense onto others. For example, as I had been offended by my dad, I became rebellious against those in authority. I expected people in authority to be just as faulty as my dad had been, which was both unfair and false. When my dad had repented and reconciled, it would have been unfair of me to perceive and treat him as if he was the same person that had offended me in the past. Others often transfer the offense of their dads to their husbands when they become fathers, and even onto all men; or, to their wives and all women, if the offender was their mom. Similarly, rape victims may transfer onto all males or females. One or two corrupt politicians becomes transferred into "all politicians are corrupt". The scenarios are endless. So, we are to discipline ourselves to observe, without voicing or labelling people with the original offense, because once we do so, we are transferring. The person in your present is NOT the person in your past.

The curse of the original offense can live on indefinitely and ruin many relationships around you; if you do not break the cycle. You have probably heard of long-standing feuds, such as, with the Hatfields and McCoys, the War of Roses, Israel and the Palestinians/Arabs, the Koreas etc. An important step in breaking the cycle, whether it is between individuals or clans or nations, is to forgive; and, as was mentioned before, to forget, reconcile and move on -- all the while being careful not to transfer the original offense onto others. Community is hurt whenever this process is incomplete and must be restored. So, repent, as often as is necessary, until reconciliation and restoration can be completed, and justice is victorious.

When you make the decision to forsake your old lifestyle, it includes the decision to turn away from wrongdoing. Jesus tells us to 'deny' or humble ourselves. Begin, therefore, to curtail your wrong desires. Self-control is an essential virtue because it helps you return to the normal range. Exercise self-control so as not to be excessive or deficient, but 'just right'; say "No!" to temptation and "Yes!" to the right behavior. Remember that if you do not control yourself, somebody else must control you, whether it is the justice system placing you in custody or the Mental Health workers placing you in a strait jacket. God's life system always has a way to bring you under control, one way or another.

So, *'take up (your) cross'* of repentance or turn away, in the same way that Jesus walked with His cross to his death. Pick up your cross of wrongdoing, mistakes, bitterness, anger, hatred, temper tantrums, wild behavior, negative labels, self-condemnation and all the unrighteous and unjust ways and walk with it, dying to each one, and leave it at His feet. Also, do not pick it up again later. This is the refining process that will make you into pure gold. In order to complete this entire process of repentance and refining, you must enter into the covenant with your Savior, Jesus Christ, as your Lord. It is taking up the cross of this New Covenant, with all its rights and responsibilities, for all eternity. You must enter this covenant with Jesus Christ. He is the only Way, for *"He Himself bore our sins in His body on the cross, so that we might die to sin and live to righteousness; for by His wounds you were healed.*" (1 Peter 2:24, NASB) He is giving you a wonderful opportunity to transform your life of sin and accept his offer of rebirth as a righteousness-loving person. Will you accept His offer? How?

Enthrone Jesus as Savior and Lord

The most important lesson of Gilgal is to give Jesus His rightful position in your life. He is Lord and King. He must be **your** Lord and King in order to be your Savior and lead you to safety for He knows the way. The Lord is the Head and, therefore, the only One who can show and lead you to this new life. He is the only One who can change you on the inside and make you into a new person. He is the only One who can heal and save you and the only One who can help you forsake all and repent. Remember, you cannot do any of this without His help. None of us who have already become Christians could have succeeded without His daily help. This covenant with Him is, therefore, foundational and essential. You are the only one to decide to accept Jesus as your Savior and Lord, and Yahweh as your God and King. In humility, you commit to follow and obey Him. This is the firm foundation on which is built your faith. You are entering a covenantal relationship with the Almighty God because you need Him to be your Heavenly Father.

So, what does it mean to enthrone and accept Jesus as your Lord and Savior?

It means:

- Belonging to God's and Jesus' family;
- Placing yourself in His Divine Order even as the planets are in the Solar Order;
- Announcing your decision to follow Jesus Christ as your Lord, Leader and King;
- Taking the decision to repent and submit to the clean(sing), purifying and sanctifying work of His Indwelling Holy Spirit;
- Entering God’s Kingdom;
- Living by His House and Kingdom rules of righteousness, which as you will see in Step 4, is expressed in Natural Law.

So, enthrone Him!
Pray with me...

“Dear Lord, forgive me all my sins. I commit to turn away from my sinful ways and return to your narrow way of life. I forgive myself and all those who have offended me (name each person or group) even as you now forgive me my sins. I surrender my life to you to be yours and for you to become my

God and Lord. From now on, your will be done in my life even as your will is done in Heaven. I will follow you all the days of my life. This is my decision. I trust you to make me into a new person by giving me a new heart and attitude and your Holy Spirit to indwell me so that you can always be with me.

In the name of Jesus Christ, I pray. Amen!"

Now, cement your resolve by...

Water Baptism

The word baptism comes from the Greek words, '*bapto*' and '*baptizo*', which mean '*to dip in or under*', '*to dye*', '*to immerse*', '*to sink*', '*to drown*', '*to bathe*', '*to wash*'. *Bapto* appears in the New Testament in its literal sense meaning '*to dip*', (Luke 16:24) '*to dye*' (Revelation19:13); and, '*baptizo*' is used in a cultic sense, meaning '*to baptize*'. These words are translations of the Hebrew word '*taval*', which means '*to dip*', '*to plunge*'. None of the other Greek meanings are understood by this Hebrew term (TDNT; The Brown-Driver-Briggs Hebrew and English Lexicon).

The Preponderance of Believer's Baptism

At the time of the Old Testament, water baptism was common place to the Israelites and baptism by immersion was the norm. They were accustomed to the ritual washings that accompanied a trip to the temple or before they offered a sacrifice or in preparation for the Day of Atonement. It was common practice for the priests to immerse themselves in water before entering the temple, especially, on holy days such as Yom Kippur, as part of their ceremonial cleansing. What many did not realize was that with the coming of Jesus and His baptism, it was the dawn of the New Covenant that Jeremiah had prophesied over 600 years prior. (Jeremiah 31:31-34) This new baptism in water held the same spiritual significance that circumcision had under the Old Covenant and, hence, was to be done once. Jesus confirmed this when He Himself asked to be baptized in order to "*fulfill all righteousness*". (Matthew 3:15)

The Jewish practice of proselyte baptism utilized **baptism by immersion** due to the Levitical command to "*bathe the whole body in water*". (Leviticus.15:16) New converts to Judaism had to fulfill one or two of three rituals as part of their initiation -- circumcision (for males) and baptism by immersion in water (for both males and females). The third practice was to offer a sacrifice, which was waived due to the absence of the temple. Thus, baptism was touted as a new birth experience. (Yebamot 22a; 48b; 97b) – (Yebamot is a tractate of the Talmud that includes rules governing conversion to Judaism).

Baptism previously referred to the ritual washing or cleansing of both people and objects. Some common usages in the Old Testament:

> "*Then a man who is ceremonially clean is to take some hyssop, dip it in the water and sprinkle the tent and all the furnishings and the people who were there.*" (Numbers 19:18)
> "*He shall dip his finger into the blood and sprinkle it before the Lord seven times in front of the curtain.*" (Leviticus 4:17)
> "*...Wash and be cleansed! So, (Naaman) went down and dipped himself seven times in the Jordan, as the man of God had told him.*" (2 Kings 5:13-14)

So, we can assume with confidence that the word baptism refers to the act of *dipping* in water. Later, it came to refer to the ritual cleansing or initiation of people in preparation for the coming of the Messiah/Holy Spirit in the New Covenant. Therefore, a believer's baptism is a core Christian ordinance. The evidence even suggests that Jesus was thus baptized in the presence of John. People were baptized by immersion -- the individual dipped himself or was dipped completely, while standing in water in the presence of witnesses. This complete submersion of the body would have been the basis for Paul's baptismal analogy of burial and resurrection with Christ. (Romans 6:3-4)

Our Lord clearly stated that baptism was a requirement for new believers -- *"It should be done, for we must carry out all that God requires."* (Matthew 3:15, NLT**)** A person entered the Old Covenant with the Lord through circumcision and, similarly, baptism symbolizes entry into the New Covenant by the blood of Jesus Christ. Jesus' blood is not only the price of redemption for your soul, but it is also the covering of grace that allows God's Holy Spirit to indwell an unclean place. *Peter replied, "Repent and be baptized, every one of you, in the name of Jesus Christ for the forgiveness of your sins. And you will receive the gift of the Holy Spirit."* (Acts 2:38) Thus, it symbolizes the real baptism – that of the Holy Spirit.

The three symbols of inner cleansing then become present -- water, blood and the fire of the Holy Spirit. Like how water cleans people and things of dirt and other uncleanness, the purpose and symbol of baptism is that it declares your disposition to be cleansed of sinful habits and to put on the white, clean and pure clothes of righteous behavior. It symbolizes your willingness to be cleansed by the purifying and refining influence of the indwelling Holy Spirit and is accomplished through your wholehearted and continuous repentance. This is the process of sanctification to make you holy and pure like Jesus Christ.

The Purpose of Baptism

The purpose of baptism allows one to demonstrate their acceptance and faith in the death and resurrection of God's only Son Jesus. This ceremonial washing by water is symbolic of our being washed by the blood of Jesus and purified by the fire of the Holy Spirit. This cleansing heralds new birth and new life in the Kingdom of God. Paul stated in Titus "*He saved us through the washing of rebirth and renewal by the Holy Spirit.*" (Titus 3:5b) Paul elaborates further, by making baptism a symbol of participation in the death, burial and resurrection of Jesus:

> "*Or don't you know that all of us who were baptized into Christ Jesus were baptized into his death? We were therefore buried with him through baptism into death in order that, just as Christ was raised from the dead through the glory of the Father, we too may live a new life.*" (Romans 6:3-4)

Baptism in water must accompany, or rather, culminate in the inner act of repentance. It is the outward act of what Jesus accomplishes on the inside of us, by our being washed in His blood that He shed on the cross at Calvary. These two elements, blood and water, had long been known as purifying elements in the temple purification rituals. The third element of the cleansing trio would be fire, symbolized by the baptism in the Holy Spirit.

It is done once in obedience to the letter of the Law, but it is the spirit of the Law that really matters. John first makes this purpose all too clear when he called on the people to prepare for the coming of the Messiah by repentance from sinful ways and water baptism. "*Produce fruit in keeping with repentance...The axe is already at the root of the trees, and every tree that does not produce good fruit will be cut down and thrown into the fire.*" (Matthew 3:8, 10) The Israelites would have been told to '*consecrate*' by '*washing*' themselves and their clothes before any appearance of the Lord. (Exodus 19:10-11) The appearance of the dove lighting on Jesus right after his baptism symbolized the coming of the Holy Spirit. (Matthew 3:16-17; Acts 2:38; 3:19-20) Similarly, we prepare for the coming of the Holy Spirit by first consecrating ourselves through baptism in water.

Jesus then went on to command his disciples to baptize the new adherents to this New Covenant -- "*Go, therefore, and make disciples of all peoples, baptizing them in the name of the Father and of the Son and of the Holy Spirit, and teaching them to observe everything I have commanded you;*" (Matthew 28:19-20) and that, *"Whoever believes and is baptized will be saved, but whoever does not believe will be condemned."* (Mark 16:16) Peter confirms this ordinance when he said, "*Repent and be baptized every one of you in the name of Jesus Christ for the forgiveness of sins; and you will receive the gift of the Holy Spirit.*" (Acts 2:38) Then, again, "*Repent, then and turn to God, so that your sins may be wiped out, that times of refreshing may come from the Lord, and that he may send the Christ, who has been appointed for you, even Jesus.*" (Acts 3:19-20) Paul succinctly states the case for repentance, personal transformation and covenant initiation when he said,

> "*For in Christ all the fullness of the Deity lives in bodily form, and you have been given fullness in Christ, who is the head over every power and authority. In him you were also circumcised, in the putting off the sinful chapter, not with a circumcision done by hands of men but with the circumcision done by Christ, having been buried with him in baptism and raised with him through your faith in the power of God, who raised him from the dead.*" (Colossians.2:9-12)

Baptism, as an act of cultic cleansing from sins, was an acknowledgement of the individual's commitment to repent of wrongdoing. This was the spirit of the Law. Baptism signified your commitment to deny yourself, pick up your cross of wrongdoing and follow Jesus all the way to crucifixion at Calvary.

Thus, in conclusion, **Jesus was Himself baptized** to demonstrate his allegiance to this new requirement. He said, "*...It is proper for us to do this in order* ***to fulfill all***

righteousness." (Matthew 3:15) In other words, Jesus is saying that baptism fulfills the requirement of righteousness. It is the right thing to do. And, to confirm the Father's pleasure in His Son's obedience, "*...the heavens opened and he saw the Spirit of God descending like a dove and lighting on him. And a voice from heaven said, "***This is my son, whom I love; in Him, I am well pleased.***" (Matthew 3:16-17)

He told his disciples to baptize new believers. "*All authority in heaven and earth is given me. Therefore go and make disciples of all nations,* ***baptizing*** *them in the name of the Father, and of the Son and of the Holy Spirit;* ***and teaching them to obey everything I have commanded you***." (Matthew 28: 18-20) He not only commanded His disciples to baptize new believers, but he also told them to teach them **everything that He** taught and demonstrated to them.

Baptism came after believing and repenting. When the jailer asked Paul and Silas, "*Sirs, what must I do to be saved?" They replied, "Believe in the Lord Jesus and you will be saved – you and your household ... then immediately* ***he and his family were baptized***." (Acts 16:30-33) Again, while Peter was preaching the gospel to the household of the centurion Cornelius, in Caesarea,

> "*...the Holy Spirit came on all who heard the message. (They) were astonished that the gift of the Holy Spirit had been poured out even on the Gentiles for they heard those speaking in tongues and praising God. Then Peter said, "Can anyone keep these people from being* ***baptized in water****? They have received the Holy Spirit just as we have. So, he ordered that they* ***be baptized in the name of Jesus Christ***." (Acts 10:44-48)

Should people baptized as infants or by other modes other than immersion be baptized again? Loyalty to traditional creeds and doctrines has generally been an obstacle to Christian unity. Historically, this discussion over baptism has been a divisive issue among Christians. It is common knowledge that the Old Covenant required circumcision, which for most Jews, took place usually just eight days after birth. (Luke 2:21) This has been the main justification for the validity of infant-baptism. When the jailer was saved, he and his whole household -- if there could have been children under the age of understanding -- were baptized by Paul and Silas. (Acts 16:33b) The common tradition at the time was that children under the age of understanding i.e., "*before the child knows enough to reject the wrong and choose the right.*" (Isaiah 7:15) could enter covenant with God by the decision of their parents. That could well be the reasoning behind the fact that this subject is never addressed directly in the New Testament.

When all these things are taken into consideration, it is plainly understandable that infant-baptism could be justified, as an exception to the rule. The baptism of a believer is plainly the main thrust of Jesus' and the apostles' teaching for the plain reason that entry into covenant requires one's understanding of, and agreement to, its terms. As Jesus did not give any other instruction other than to baptize in water in the name of the Father and of the Son and of the Holy Spirit, then those who were baptized as infants should not be required to be re-baptized, if they are following the Spirit of the Law.

Baptism by Aspersion – dipping in water and sprinkling the individual. This idea comes from the priestly practice of dipping his finger in water or blood and sprinkling people or things as a means of cultic purification or ritual cleansing. (Numbers 19:18; Lev.4:17)

Baptism by Affusion – water was poured out on the person's head while the person may or may not be standing in water. The idea of pouring comes from the common Jewish practice of pouring water on one's hands as part of washing and ritual cleansing that started in the temple and remained afterwards as a Jewish tradition. Peter also referred to the baptism in the Holy

Spirit as a "*pouring out*" of the Spirit upon the person. "*In the last days I will pour out my Spirit on all people...*" (Acts 2:17, 18) and again, "*He has received from the Father the promised Holy Spirit and has poured out what you now see and hear*" (Acts 2:33); and, "*...the gift of the Holy Spirit had been poured out even on the Gentiles....*" (Acts 10:45, 47)

If we look carefully at the word *dipping*, baptism by immersion would be the acceptable mode. The argument, though, for the other modes would remain when viewed through the lens of actual Temple practices surrounding the central purpose of ritual cleansing or purification. Baptism or ceremonial cleansing of individuals was by total immersion. The priest '*dipped*' his finger in water or blood and '*sprinkled*' crowds of people and large objects, such as, houses and '*poured out*' water or blood on the earth in order to accomplish ritual purification.

The only direction we are given by Jesus was to baptize "*in the name of the Father, and of the Son and of the Holy Spirit.*" (Matthew 28:19) No other specific instructions were given because it would have been common knowledge regarding the whole area of ritual cleansing. The diversity of modes of baptism exists today because Jesus did not give any other instruction except what has just been mentioned. Jesus knew that ceremonial cleansing was practiced in the temple utilizing immersion, "*dipping and sprinkling*" and "*pouring out*" so he could have expanded it, if He thought it necessary. The fact that He only gave us that simple instruction is reason for me not to be intolerant of people who believe in the validity of modes other than immersion or require re-baptism. It would also have been acceptable to baptize children under the age of understanding when whole families were being initiated into the New Covenant like the practice of circumcision; and, not to require their re-baptism when they became of age.

Everyone knew that these only had cultic significance as no one expected *dipping,* or *sprinkling, washing* or *pouring out* of water to literally cleanse from sins. Actual cleansing was instead a legal and spiritual act of God. Only the blood of Jesus and baptism by the Holy Spirit can cleanse a person from sin. In other words, it is the actions of Jesus and the Holy Spirit upon the person that save, not the act of baptism in water. The Holy Spirit convicts us and leads us to repent and follow Christ, which are our covenantal responsibilities. Our obedience and repentance are what constitutes the spirit of, and leads us to fulfill the purposes of, baptism. This is what matters to the Lord and pleases Him. Anything else is vanity.

Therefore, while a believer's baptism by total submersion in the name of the Father and of the Son and of the Holy Spirit is still the most comprehensive, whether you were baptized as an infant or by the other modes, we are all united in one family by one baptism and by One Spirit. The letter of the law, which is to be baptized in water in the name of the Father and of the Son and of the Holy Spirit, once fulfilled, does not need repeating. All that matters now is that you fulfill the spirit of the law which is to repent and be converted. This is the only thing that Jesus asks us to do and to teach. This is what unites the Body of Christ. Anything else is anathema. There will always be diversity of opinions, but this diversity must never come at the expense of our common unity or of the spirit of the law.

It is only after you have committed to denying yourself, picked up the cross of repentance and covenanted with Jesus Christ that you can receive the gift of the Holy Spirit and are ...

Enlivened

At Gilgal, it was only after Israel had committed to enter God's divine order and fulfill their responsibilities in the covenant by being circumcised, that they heard the blockbuster statement: *"Today, I have rolled away the disgrace and shame of (your past) from over you."* This is an amazing statement. It is like the Judge saying, "You are free to go"; or the Physician declaring, "You are healed". When the fire from heaven comes, you are transformed from within. The Spirit of God comes upon you and you become a new person: *"I'll give you a new heart, put a new spirit (attitude) in you. I'll remove the stony heart from your body and replace it with a heart that's God-willed, not self-willed. I'll put my Spirit in you and make it possible for you to do what I tell you and live by my commands."* (Ezekiel 36:26, MSG) You are no longer the same person made of body and soul. Now you are tripartite: body, soul and God's Holy Spirit. Look at this equation:

(body + soul) You (y) + God (G) = Gy

Neither you nor anyone else can declare that you are the same person as before because now you are the temple of the Holy Spirit, the House of the Living God. The previous person with its old labels is now joined to the Lord. Reject and take off the old labels as they no longer apply. The old person is no longer there but a new person has taken its place. The Word says explicitly, "*Therefore, if anyone is in Christ, he is a new creation. The old has passed away; behold, the new has come."(II Corinthians 5:17 ESV)*

You are no more '*good for nothing*', '*insignificant*', '*will never amount to anything in life*', '*wretched*', '*pitiable*', '*poor*', '*blind*', '*naked*', '*prostitute*', '*lazy*', etc. You are now valuable, rich, with great potential, happy, content, well-adjusted, complete, healthy and peaceful because of the Holy Spirit who dwells in you and makes you His. You can walk from Gilgal in newness of life, with a renewed sense of purpose, happy that you have been...

Freed,

Rescued,
Saved,
Redeemed,
Delivered,
Restored,
Healed, and
Renewed.

You are...

Safe at home again,
At peace,
At rest, and
Fortunate.

This is what Peter was referring to in his sermon when he said that "*times of refreshing*" will "*come from the presence of the Lord*" (Acts 3:19) and Mike W., as he publicly expressed his gratitude to the Lord in his testimony. The Lord's plan is to refresh and renew our lives. I hope you are taking or have taken advantage of this amazing opportunity as I have.

My Story

One beautiful Sunday morning in September 1972, I put on my short pants and T-shirt and went around the corner to my new-found friend Jolyon. As usual, it was shaping up to be one of those hot and humid days in Georgetown, Guyana. I was 12 years old and had just graduated to secondary school at one of the prestigious schools in Georgetown: Saint Stanislaus College. It was there I first met Jolyon as we both walked home and discovered that he lived just around the corner from me.

I had been hoping to play, but when I got to his house, he told me that he was going to the church next door. I was very disappointed, but as I did not want to waste my efforts of hanging out with my friend, I decided to hang around with him as he was awaiting the arrival of the Pastor. I recall sitting on the church doorstep waiting as people filed past me to enter the church. Soon the Pastor arrived and passed me by sitting there. Jolyon went inside and as I was about to get up to leave, the Pastor turned around and said, *"Won't you like to come in?"*

I looked at him inquisitively at the same time pointing to my play clothes as if to say, *"I am not dressed appropriately for church."*

He immediately said, *"Don't worry, just come and join us"*.

So, I joined Jolyon as he sat in his Sunday School class and later, in the church service. I was so enraptured by this whole new experience. The pastor, his wife and the people looked so peaceful and kind. Everybody seemed to have a reason to smile. I had no reason except that I was happy to be there. I decided then and there to return the very next week. I did, but this time I was dressed for church.

I became a regular attendee at this little church, Bible Missionary Church, and was amazed at the things I was hearing. I came to the realization that I was not a part of God's covenant family. I had grown up as a baptized and confirmed Roman Catholic going to church probably twice a year but had no sense of commitment to God. Even at that age, I knew what it meant for someone to be my Lord. God was certainly not my Lord and that knowledge scared me. The more I thought about it, the more I realized that I was not ready to hand over my life to God. *'What if I died and went to Hell?'* *'Well', I told myself, 'just before you die you can accept Jesus as Lord and Savior.* But, *'What if I died suddenly and didn't get a chance to pray?'* I struggled with all this, but still I was not willing to let the Lord of Heaven and Earth be my Lord. I couldn't give my all and I knew He wouldn't accept a partial surrender. So, I sat on my decision...

Then, one day, I came to church to hear the shocking news that the Pastor had died by drowning while fishing. I was shocked. I went home dazed after the service. I stayed home the next Sunday and the next and the next... This was my opportunity to avoid that nagging question: "*When are you going to accept Jesus as your Lord?"* I tried to push it out of my mind, but it was always there. I was anxious to go back, but at the same time, I was afraid -- very afraid of making the decision.

One Sunday morning I noticed a family passing by our home. I knew they were heading to the Bible Missionary Church because they were dressed in the same manner as the previous Pastor and his family. I quickly realized this was the new Pastor and he had a rather large family – five or six children. I noticed a boy my size and a very pretty girl also my size. Excitement grew within me and I ran in, put my clothes on and ran to church. I became friends with Daniel and Judith Stracener, the Pastor's two oldest children -- Judith was so pretty. I tried as much as possible to be near her and visited their home often.

I became a regular attendee again, but still avoided answering that nagging question, until the 1974 Easter Week celebration. There was a special speaker giving a sermon series called "*Occupy until I come*". I was so convicted by the message that I decided to answer the altar call and raised my hand. However, when he invited everyone who raised their hands to go up to the front to seal the deal, I couldn't, as I was too embarrassed to do so. I went home worried and scared.

That night, as I laid in bed, I felt as if the Lord was telling me it was okay to ask Jesus to be my Lord and Savior right there in bed. I didn't need to do it in church. So, I prayed and accepted Jesus as my own Lord and Savior. What a relief! Finally, I had done it. I went to bed that night very happy. The next Sunday, I felt no fear and I got up in church to tell the congregation that I had finally accepted Jesus. Everyone was overjoyed. I beamed from ear to ear. I was 14 years old.

However, I had a relapse sometime over the next few weeks, for the Lord confronted me that He was no longer the Lord of my life. It appeared that I had listened to a thought that said it was okay if I kept back some control of my life. I knew that I was not being sincere, but I thought it was still okay for him to have most of my life. I was not committed to Jesus being my Lord 24/7/366. In marriage, even if you are 99.9% committed, it means that you will have an affair once every 1000 days or three and a half years. If the airline industry had a similar commitment to quality, two major passenger airlines would be crashing at an international airport every day (Total Quality Ministry, p.13). This was unacceptable. I repented and re-affirmed my commitment to my Lord. I was now 100% committed. Now that the Lord, the key stone of the solution, was occupying His rightful position in my life, He could now proceed with the rest of my treatment. I was fully committed to carefully listen to and obey every instruction. *"Not my will, Lord, but your will be done!'*

Over the next few weeks and months, I began to observe the changes in my life, the "*times of refreshing from the Lord.*" I was happy, very happy. It seemed as if joy was oozing out of every pore in my body. I wasn't a criminal or had a vice, but I was an emotional wreck with constant nightmares; often getting up in the middle of the night crying and falling off my top bunk bed. So, I was pleasantly surprised when I noticed that there were no more nightmares. *'What happened to the nightmares?'* I thought to myself. '*Wow, they are gone! I don't have them anymore!'* I was a very anxious young man -- sweat would drip from my armpits, hands and feet. I often felt as if there was a bolus in my throat preventing me from breathing properly; and, my mind raced a lot. I recall once thinking and planning to commit suicide by drinking a poison we had in the home: Malathion. However, I was too afraid to carry it out.

I recall the first time the Lord confronted me about my 'baggage' of unforgiveness and hatred. I still hated my dad. The Holy Spirit convicted me that I could not be a part of His family if I chose to hate rather than love and I could not love without first forgiving. After much internal debating, I agreed to forgive my dad. However, there was still the matter of love. I told the Lord that I had no love for my dad. The Lord told me to ask Him for love. As I had no more excuses, I asked the Lord for forgiveness, forgave my Dad, and asked the Lord to pour out His unconditional love into my heart. As time passed, I noticed that I was becoming more loving, not only towards my Dad but to everyone, which spurred me to pray for him and others -- something I wasn't doing.

I also had very low self-esteem, especially, about my body image, which was a significant reason for my constant anxiety. I grew up in a poor and dysfunctional family. My dad, at the time, was addicted to gambling and would occasionally waste his entire paycheck on this vice. So, I was very skinny, not because I was anorexic, but because I did not have much to eat and, at the same time, I was a very active athlete, who was on the school's Track and Field team. I could not pass a mirror or shop window without stopping to look at myself; I hoped I would look 'fatter'. The Lord told me to ignore the urges and stop doing that. So, I made up my mind to obey and eventually stopped worrying about my body image. In summary, He helped me control the anxiety attacks by ignoring and disobeying the obsessive and compulsive urges, whether they were to hyperventilate to overcome the bolus in my chest or to look in the window to see if I was fatter. He reminded me that His Spirit within me was not "*a Spirit of fear but of power, love and a healthy mind.*" (2 Timothy 1:7) He encouraged me to "*be strong and courageous! Do not be afraid or discouraged. For the LORD your God is with you wherever you go."* (Joshua 1:9) Whenever I condemned myself over some mistake, the Lord would remind me "*that God is greater than our hearts, and he knows everything"* (1 John 3:20). This would put my heart at ease. One 'sin' that the Lord confronted me with was rebellion. I knew I was a rebel, so when I read, "*Rebellion is as the sin of witchcraft*", (1Sam.15:23) I was immediately convicted, repented and renounced my rebellious attitude.

I loved to read, so as a new Christian believer, I read biographies of fellow believers. It is always amazing to read about and listen to the testimonies of this Gilgal phase. I can only imagine what the Israelites felt at that moment knowing what they had gone through. They were slaves and now they were FREE, at last!

What a New Beginning!

The month of the first Passover was significant to Israel as it heralded a new life and a new beginning. This one was even more special as it was their 40th. The highlight of the Passover was the first night when they slaughtered the Passover lamb, roasting it and then eating it communally with '*the bread of haste'* (unleavened bread). That very night was when Israel was miraculously delivered from slavery. The Passover began a week of rest, hurrying and eating in a yeast-free environment. The cleansing trio of cultic washing, the blood of the lamb and the purification by fire were all present in this festival.

This same cleansing trio is symbolic of our salvation. We are baptized in water once and cleansed by the blood of Jesus that was shed on the cross once and for all. The Holy Spirit's refining fire then proceeds to complete the process of purification. This process is ongoing, but the first week is crucial. Just as Israel celebrates the Passover for one week with '*the bread of haste*', we too must hurry to heed and follow every urge of the Holy Spirit in the first week of our conversion. Life ahead for you will then be amazing with a new Pilot in your life -- the Holy Spirit. He is Wonderful Counselor and King of Peace (Shalom). So, we must make up our minds to follow Him carefully and sincerely.

"Follow me" is the most important advice that Jesus Christ has given us all. As He is our Savior, we must follow His lead continuously for Him to save us. It's not just beginning the relationship; we must now maintain it to the end. As a physician, I know how important this detail is. I cannot help anyone who is not willing to **fully** collaborate with me until the healing is complete. *"Be perfect, therefore, as your heavenly Father is*

perfect.” (Matthew 5:48) The essence of the meaning of ‘perfect’ is complete. So, make His work easy by fully collaborating with Him till the end rather than resisting and quenching Him.

Tell Others about Your Decision

Telling someone about your decision to follow Christ reinforces the decision in your mind. Your decision must be wholehearted, so do not refrain from telling someone about it, because of shame or embarrassment. *“Whoever acknowledges me before others, I will also acknowledge before my Father in heaven. But everyone who denies me here on earth, I will also deny before my Father in heaven.”* (Matthew 10:33; cf. Romans10:9) The decision to follow Christ must be a firm, rock-solid decision, not subject to winds of change or popularity polls.

When the Celebration is Over

Israel had experienced God’s miraculous deliverance. When this happens to you, you become a changed person living in a completely new environment -- the Kingdom of God. When the celebration or ‘honeymoon time’ ends, expect the ecstatic joy that you felt at the beginning to wane. That ardent desire and hunger to pray, to read your Bible and to congregate with other brothers and sisters may diminish. Now, you must continue to do those same things based on their rightness and necessity rather than on a perceived divine inspiration. Before, the indwelling Spirit moved you miraculously to ‘bond’ with your Lord and God, now you must develop the good habit of having daily devotional times -- reading the Scriptures, praying and meditating. It’s not that the Holy Spirit is no longer moving you; He is always there doing just that. However, the first encounter one has with the Holy Spirit is always ecstatic and mind-boggling because it is so new; after all, it’s the first one. It is almost like drinking coffee for the first time. Subsequent ones don’t have the same effect as that first one.

Therefore, adapt to this new reality – 'the old you' is gone. The new has begun. You are a totally new person led by the indwelling Holy Spirit. As He leads you, His refining fire will continue, and eventually complete, the process of purifying and sanctifying you so that you can be *"a living sacrifice, holy and pleasing to God"* (Romans12:1) and fully integrated into the kingdom of God.

Celebrate the Anniversary of Your Salvation

Passover was the celebration of Israel's deliverance and salvation. Every year, they celebrate its anniversary. At Easter, we remember, together as a Church, the Body of Christ, not only the crucifixion and resurrection of Jesus Christ, but our collective redemption and deliverance from slavery to sin. It's a celebration of the great things that the Lord has done for us. He did it for Israel and He did it for you and me. Therefore, celebrate the anniversary of your salvation and broadcast your testimony to as many as will listen. In so doing, you will be a blessing to '*all the families of the earth*'. Everyone must be encouraged to seek the Lord for their own salvation and deliverance. If He can do it for you, He can also do it for them.

This ushers in a new phase in your relationship with God. As you will see in the next Step, the Lord revealed to Elisha and to us, God's and our rights and responsibilities in this New Covenantal-paternalistic relationship.

CONCLUSION

You have encountered the Savior, Yeshua, who has guided you out of the perilous 'minefield' of your life and given you a second chance at life. Life is fluid, not static, so you must always be moving forward to the goal. You must grasp God's vision of restoring you back to normal; not your idea of 'normal' but the true normal; that is, God's and nature's normal. Now that you have dealt adequately with your past and let go of your 'baggage', you can move on to the new things your Savior has planned for your life as well as conquer those things that have yet to be conquered. The future is bright now that you are no longer 'bogged down' by your past. Thanks be to God your Savior!

As you move forward, remember that your covenant with Christ gives you your new identity. Cherish and hold on tightly to it just as you cherish and hold tightly to your legal ID documents. Reject and take off the old labels, which are no longer applicable. You are a new person with new labels. Move on without looking back. Ignoring and disobeying the urges to do so will help you overcome anxiety, Post-Traumatic Stress Disorder (PTSD), OCD and other disorders. You may still need medical assistance, but don't be afraid to receive it, as we dwell in an unbalanced world which may never attain balance before Jesus returns to restore everything. Follow Him carefully as Gilgal is not the end of the journey; it is only the beginning.

Now, that God is repairing and placing your life back in the fold, He will continue to integrate you into His kingdom by revealing who He is and strengthening that relationship with you at Bethel. He will show you how to fulfill your original purpose in life at Jericho and teach you how to live and succeed at the Jordan River so that you never fail again.

APPENDIX A

Inner Healing -- An Important Resource of Churches Today

The Israelites were abused physically and emotionally in Egypt and many of their friends and relatives had been killed. As they had all been slaves of the Egyptians, their self-esteem was low and shattered. Many would have suffered from emotional and/or mental illnesses, such as, PTSD, anxiety and mood disorders -- depression, unforgiveness, bitterness; as well as other physical ailments. They needed to not only be healed, physically and emotionally, from all those diseases, but they also needed to get rid of all the vices, bad labels and evil spirits that accompanied them.

Today, every believer, adherent and visitor to church comes with their own 'baggage' and, therefore, need healing, help and encouragement on their road to recovery. The Church must be prepared and have ministries in place that facilitate inner healing, which can enable congregants to close the chapter on their past. Then, they can join the community as physically and emotionally healthy people. No one can move on to becoming effective pastors, healers and leaders if they themselves have not first been healed.

APPENDIX B

Ministries that Facilitate Inner Healing:

Eagle Worldwide Ministries
Nicky Gumbel's Alpha and Beta/ Challenging Lifestyle Courses
Neil Anderson's Beta Course
Stephen Ministries
Singing Waters
Ellel Ministries
Cleansing Streams
Soulcare
Dr.Grant Mullen's Transformation Series
Encounter Retreat of G12 Movement
Restoring the Foundations

STEP TWO

BETHEL:
TO EXPERIENCE THE FATHER'S HEART

Now that you have sought, found and experienced the Savior's healing and freedom at Gilgal and finally closed the chapter on your past, you can build on that foundation at Bethel. While God's focus at Gilgal was to roll back the shame of your past mistakes, Bethel is where vertical balance with the Heavenly Father will be restored, so you will experience the Father's Heart and learn about all the rights and responsibilities that come with this paternalistic covenant. Let's look at these texts that help us better understand the nature of Bethel:

> *"As he slept, he dreamed of a stairway that reached from the earth up to heaven. And he saw the angels of God going up and down the stairway. At the top of the stairway stood the LORD, and he said, "I am the LORD, the God of your grandfather Abraham, and the God of your father, Isaac. The ground you are lying on belongs to you. I am giving it to you and your descendants. Your*

*descendants will be as numerous as the dust of the earth! They will spread out in all directions—to the west and the east, to the north and the south. And all the families of the earth will be blessed through you and your descendants. What's more, I am with you, and I will protect you wherever you go. One day I will bring you back to this land. I will not leave you until I have finished giving you everything I have promised you. When Jacob awoke from his sleep, he thought, "Surely the LORD is in this place, and I was not aware of it." He was afraid and said, "How awesome is this place! This is none other than Bethel, (the house of God); this is the gate of heaven." Early the next morning Jacob took the stone he had placed under his head and set it up as a pillar and poured oil on top of it. He called that place Bethel, though the city used to be called Luz." (*Genesis 28:12-19; cf. 10-2, NLT*)*

God said to Jacob, "Arise, go up to Bethel, and live there. Make there an altar to God, who appeared to you when you fled from the face of Esau your brother." Then Jacob said to his household, and to all who were with him, "Put away the foreign gods that are among you, purify yourselves, change your garments. Let us arise and go up to Bethel. I will make there an altar to God, who answered me in the day of my distress, and was with me in the way which I went." They gave to Jacob all the foreign gods which were in their hands, and the rings which were in their ears; and Jacob hid them under the oak which was by Shechem. They traveled, and a terror of God was on the cities that were around them, and they did not pursue the sons of Jacob. So Jacob came to Luz (that is, Bethel), which is in the land of Canaan, he and all the people who were with him. He built an altar there and called the place El Beth El; because there God was revealed to him, when he fled from the face of his brother. God said to him, "Your name is Jacob. Your name shall not be Jacob any more, but your name will be Israel." He named him Israel. God said to him, "I am El Shaddai. Be fruitful and multiply. A nation and a company of nations will be from you, and kings will come out of your body. The land which I gave to Abraham and Isaac, I will give it to you, and to your descendants after you will I give the land." God went up from him in the place where he spoke with him. Jacob set up a pillar in the place where he spoke with him, a pillar of stone. He poured out a drink offering on it and poured oil on it. Jacob called the name of the place where God spoke with him Bethel." (Genesis 35:1-7, 10-15, NHEB)

First, the text reveals that the universe is God's house (Kingdom) and that we live in it, with all that that entails. Heaven and Earth are interconnected, and I will explore this systemic interconnectedness and wholeness in Step 4. Second, it sheds light on the nature of the relationship that the Lord wishes to have with every one of us. It is not just a God-people relationship, but a parent-child or Shepherd-flock one. The type of care that God revealed to Jacob at Bethel, and by extension, to all of us, is of a paternalistic nature; and, as such, both parties have rights and responsibilities.

It is this love and commitment to truth, righteousness and justice that led the Lord to promise Jacob to return him to his father's homeland and to reconcile him with his brother. Jacob had fled from his irate brother because he had offended Esau, even though, he was only doing what the Lord had wanted him to do. The Lord had chosen Jacob to receive His blessing because Esau had despised it, when he sold his birthright for a plate of food. Esau's disregard for God and His blessing cost him his firstborn right to God's blessing. Yet, Jacob had to reconcile with his brother despite all of this. This was not an easy task as Esau's anger was to the point of threatening Jacob's life. To bring Jacob back to the land, forgiveness and reconciliation had to happen between the brothers. God had waited 21 years to fulfill His promise to Jacob to reconcile him with his brother and return him to his homeland. God did not forget His promise but fulfilled it.

That is the essence of this paternalistic covenantal relationship. The Heavenly Father has rights and responsibilities and likewise, every person that enters this covenant with Him has rights and responsibilities as His children. Indeed, it is vitally important that every human being understands that they are born into this unchanging paternalistic reality. When you accept Jesus as your Lord and Savior, you are, in fact, through spiritual rebirth, restoring this paternalistic covenantal relationship, which was lost due to our rebellion. As God is eternal this covenant is also everlasting; thus, the relationship requires continuity, steadfastness and faithfulness for all eternity. This is an important paradigm shift in our understanding of our life journey, of the relationship with our God and Lord, and of the important roles we play in the ecosystem. So, let's look at Jacob's vision at Bethel in more detail because it not only reveals a lot about life, but also illumines the nature of our relationship with God.

Elisha's Reflections on His Journey to Bethel with Elijah

> *Elijah said to Elisha, "Stay here; the* L*ORD has sent me to Bethel." But Elisha said, "As surely as the* L*ORD lives and as you live, I will not leave you." So they went down to Bethel." (*2 Kings 2:2)

No one said a word as we walked briskly towards Bethel. I was walking on the clouds. I was full of the Lord's peace and joy; at times prophesying in song, and at times singing in Aramaic to the Lord. I was confident that the Lord was doing something wonderful in me and with me and, for this reason, I was so thankful.

I thought about Bethel and what it signified. God had revealed Himself there to my ancestors, Abraham, Isaac and Jacob, at very distressful and uncertain times in their lives. Abram was a stranger in the land the same as Jacob. It was at Bethel that God appeared to Abram after he had left his father's house and land and where he had made the covenant with God. It was where God had blessed him saying that He would multiply his heirs and give him the land, and He had then changed his name to Abraham. It was at the same location that God had appeared to Jacob when he was in distress after running away from his father's house and from his brother, Esau, who had threatened to kill him for usurping the firstborn's blessing. Again, it was there that God had renewed the covenant with Jacob changing his name to Israel.

In a vision, he had seen God in His house; God was at the top of the stairs and the angels were going up and down. God was the Head of the entire universe and of the armies of angels. I knew God would send the angels to watch over us, to send messages and do other errands. They were also warrior angels. Elijah would always tell me not to be afraid when the king would send a detachment of soldiers to get him because the angels that were with him were far stronger than all the kings' armies put together.

I understood too from the vision that His house (Kingdom) was comprised of both the heavens and the earth and we lived in it -- as servants or children, I wondered? As children, of course, because He had called Jacob, "*His son*". The promises He had made to Jacob, and hence to me and all those who covenant with Him, tell us that He desires a Father–Child relationship with us: "*I will make you multiply*"; "*I will bless you*"; "*all the families of the earth will be blessed through you and your descendants*"; "*I am with you*"; "*I will watch over you wherever you go*"; "*I will not leave you until I have done what I have promised you*"; and, "*I will bring you back to this land*". (Genesis 12:3; cf. 28:12-19)

As I meditated on these things, I again felt power come over me and I prophesied. I heard the Lord telling me, *"Elisha, I am taking Elijah away from you today but do not be afraid for I will be with you always, even as I have been and still am with Elijah. I will watch over you wherever you go and will never leave you. All the families of the earth will be blessed through you."* I praised and thanked the Lord for His goodness and loving-kindness towards me. What a wonderful feeling to know that the Lord, God of Israel, is with me always! Everyone needs to take advantage of this wonderful covenant and experience this amazing peace that comes from the knowledge of His eternal tender loving care and power!

I understood that God has rights -- the right to be worshipped truly, to be loved and adored and to be Lord of Lords and King of Kings. He is my Lord, King, God and Leader. He is who He is and deserves nothing less than to be treated as who He is. He is the Only True God; there is no one besides Him; there never was and there never shall be. He was with me not only as the One and Only True God, but as my Heavenly Father.

Like a flood, verses pertaining to God's Fatherhood came to mind:

'His arms were strengthened by...El your Father.' (Genesis 49:25)

> *"Then you will tell him, 'This is what the LORD says: Israel is my firstborn son. I commanded you, "Let my son go, so he can worship me." But since you have refused, I will now kill your firstborn son!'" (*Exodus 4:22-23)

> *"Surely you are still our Father! Even if Abraham and Jacob would disown us, Lord, you would still be our Father. You are our Redeemer from ages past."* (Isaiah.63:16)

> *"And he will call out to me, 'You are my Father, my God, and the Rock of my salvation.'"* (Palms 89:26)
>
> *"I will be his father, and he will be my son. If he sins, I will correct and discipline him with the rod, like any father would do."* (2 Samuel 7:14).

Many Jewish names also acknowledge God's fatherhood: Abiel, means: *'My father is El';* Eliab means *'My God is Father'*; Abiyah or Abijah, means *My Father is Yah; Abiad, means 'My Father is Eternal or My Father Eternal.*

I knew He was a Father towards Elijah as sometimes he would address Him as Father. I have never done so. I must begin to do so. Do I understand what it means to be God's son? I'm afraid I am not sure. As God is Father, what are His rights and responsibilities? *"Lord, help me to fully know what it means to be your son with all its rights and responsibilities and to fully understand what your rights and responsibilities are. Amen!"* As I am His son, the Father will bless me and make me a blessing, not only to Israel, but to the entire world. This was hard to understand since Yahweh was the God of Israel, but I quickly realized that He, as Creator of heaven and earth, would also be the God of the whole world. If I am a prophet of God, I will also be His messenger to the whole world. I understood then that God had intended Israel, as His first-born, to be the propagator of His message to the entire human race. I was amazed at these thoughts as they passed through my head. It all made sense.

God's faithfulness is without question. The Lord was faithful towards Abraham in giving his descendants the land of Canaan, now called Israel. He was also faithful towards Jacob in bringing him back to his family and land after his fleeing from Esau his brother. Jacob's greatest fear was that Esau would never forgive nor reconcile with him. It would take a miracle. At the right time, Jacob returned with great fear, and found Esau waiting to complete the process of forgiveness and reconciliation. Praise be to our Lord! Upon hearing the stories of the Exodus and the peoples' unfaithfulness, their constant complaining and their acts of rebellion, I am amazed at His perseverance in bringing Israel into the Promised Land. Yes, almost an entire generation never made it to the Promised Land, but their children did. Not even Moses and Aaron made it. God is truly faithful in carrying out His responsibilities. I must be too. Praise be to you Father for your faithfulness, goodness and loving-kindness!

I must not be afraid of what the people can do to me for He will watch over me constantly. I will be careful and remember to calm myself when fear tries to overwhelm me, for the Lord is my Father who is always with me. *I trust in you, my Lord and my Father.*

I was so wrapped up in my thoughts that I did not realize that we were practically in Bethel. The other disciples met us there on the outskirts of the city and discretely asked me, *"Did you know that the LORD is going to take your master away from you today?" "Of course, I know," I said. "But be quiet about it". Then Elijah said to him, "Stay here, Elisha; the LORD has sent me to Jericho."* (2 Kings 2:3)

Experiencing My Heavenly Father's Care – My Story Continued

As I reflect over my life, I can see God's fatherly care for me. I was 14 when I accepted Jesus as my Lord and Savior, and six months later, I moved to Brazil with my family. My parents were not believers at the time and my Dad gave me a hard time as he did not understand my new-found faith and relationship with the Lord. He thought I had got involved in some cult and was acting weird. He would often mock me and once even threatened to burn my Bible as he was afraid that I would become a fanatic. So many nights, I would cry myself to sleep. There was no one to run to or to call whenever I had questions or when I wanted to unload my burdens. There was no one to comfort me except the Lord. When I left Georgetown, Guyana, I had not brought with me the phone number of my pastor. I did not know Portuguese sufficiently well and had not found a local church yet.

Thus, I cried out to the Lord often. One night, He answered me. He told me to trust in Him; that my parents would soon become believers like me and would then understand. I felt the huge burden leave me. I was no longer anxious. I became happy. The Lord was with me. He was my Father and He loved me dearly. He would take care of me as a Father does His son. I no longer felt alone as I was part of His family. He would save my family members, even my dad. I can leave that in His capable care as I knew He was trustworthy. He never lied. I believed and knew that, eventually, they would turn to Him. It was only a matter of time. I began to wonder who would be the first, Mom or Dad. Mom happened to be the first. Dad was the last of the whole family. I recall when he finally decided to give his life to the Lord. He came to me one night, crying, and asked for forgiveness for all the hard times he had given me. We both cried for quite a while. I offered to buy him a Bible. He said no; he would get himself one. I went to sleep that night a very happy young man. I felt like jumping for joy. Finally, the war was over. My dad was saved thanks to my Heavenly Father's faithfulness.

Over the years, I came to expect God's great blessings, as I had been born again into His family and tender loving care. I was no longer a spiritual orphan, but God's son, with all its rights and responsibilities. I knew that everything would be okay. My God was El-Shaddai who multiplies blessings upon those who place their trust in Him. Later, when I found my dream wife, I said to myself – *"I am glad for He has done great things for me."* The people will say, "*The Lord has done great things for him."* (Psalm 126: 2-3) *"Surely your goodness and unfailing love will pursue me all the days of my life, and I will live in the house of the LORD forever." (*Psalm.23:6)

I expected His teaching, so I determined to be an excellent student, which is not always easy. One time, I realized that I had to grow up and apply the principles I had been taught. I was in Medical School at the time. My Dad had lost his job and being the only bread winner, he needed to find another job. I prayed and prayed to no avail, it seemed. After 10 months and no job, I felt anger -- anger that the Lord was not answering my prayers and cries, and anger because I felt useless. One Sunday morning, I felt so angry that I decided not to attend church that day. I did tune in, however, to a Christian program that I loved to watch -- the Rex Humbard Family Show.

That morning, a newly crowned Miss Universe was giving her testimony. She recalled that when she was seven, she had been involved in a car crash, which resulted in a short leg due to multiple fractures. She walked with a modified shoe to make up for the 7cm or so difference and hid it by using long dresses as she was ashamed of her handicap. One Sunday morning, when she was sixteen, she heard a message that challenged her to believe and apply God's truth found in His Word. The text was (Mark 11:22-25, GWT):

> *"Have faith in God! I can guarantee this truth: This is what will be done for someone who doesn't doubt but believes what he says will happen: He can say to this mountain, 'Be uprooted and thrown into the sea,' and it will be done for him. That's why I tell you to have faith that you have already received whatever you pray for, and it will be yours. Whenever you pray, forgive anything you have against anyone. Then your Father in heaven will forgive your failures."*

She was thus challenged to command her short leg to grow and become equal to the other leg. She quickly realized that she did not have that sort of faith, so she purposed to spend more time in devotions to get to that point. After three months, she felt her faith was strong enough to make that sort of resurrection or mountain moving prayer. After revealing her handicap to her friends at school, she went home, went to her bedroom and prayed.

"I command my short leg to grow and be equal in length with my other leg. In the NAME of Jesus. Amen!"

Within seconds, her leg grew until both legs were equal in length.

I cried as I listened to her testimony because I realized that my anger was unjustified. I had never realized that I had that right as His child. I never thought that I could make such a prayer. I had never prayed a mountain moving prayer before. I realized that the Lord wanted to teach me to use my authority as His son and pray in that way because the situation required it. I felt I had the faith and I had no unforgiveness towards others to deal with, except towards the Lord, so I prayed after asking His forgiveness.

"In the Name of Jesus, I command this mountain of unemployment in my home to go away. Be cast into the sea, in the Name of Jesus. Amen!" Thank you, Lord!

As I sat there thinking about how I had just prayed, I felt an inner urge to tell someone about it as an act of faith. I reluctantly told my parents, who were still new believers at that point. They just listened, not saying a word. Later, my friend, Lucia Helena, came to visit me wondering why I hadn't been to church. I told her as well. I felt I had done all that was required. Now it was just a matter of waiting.

That Tuesday of the same week, a friend called and told my dad to apply to a recently opened position. He applied, and he was called for an interview that Thursday. When he came home afterwards, he told us the great news -- he had the job. We were all overjoyed, especially me. I had just been taught a lesson. I felt like a son who did not know he had the right to use one of God's kingdom keys to unlock and solve a vexing problem. I had not only learned my lesson but had experienced firsthand the power of resurrection/ mountain moving prayer. I had, especially, learned that I had rights -- the rights of God's children. I had the right to ask and the authority to bind and to loosen. *Thank you, my dear Heavenly Father!* I realized that there was much to learn on this life journey with the Lord. What would be my next lesson, I wondered? Whatever it was, I was determined to never again distrust my Lord. *I will always trust in you, dear Father! Forgive me for ever distrusting you.*

In my 20's, I was an ardent student, not only in Medicine, but in ministry. I trained in evangelism, did short term mission stints with OM (Operation Mobilization) and became active with IVCF (Inter Varsity Christian Fellowship) at UFRJ (Universidade Federal do Rio de Janeiro - Federal University of Rio de Janeiro), where I studied. I learned how to engage in spiritual warfare, divine healing and lead. Throughout that decade, I grew in maturity and grace. I did not realize it at the time, but later I understood that one's 20's is our decade of learning. Every priest was called into training on turning 20, before assuming the priesthood at age 30. Even Jesus began his ministry at around this age.

Later, I was involved in grooming leaders to assume ministry leadership positions. On one occasion, I was about to reject a person for a leadership assignment, when the Lord told me: *"You are called to help, not to judge. I am the Judge."* I realized immediately that it was part of my purpose in life to help whenever the opportunity arose and never to judge.

I expected God's ongoing guidance, so I told myself to be quick and careful at following Him. I recall the first time that I decided to trust in the Lord to guide me. I was a newly converted teenager sent on an errand by my parents. After leaving on my bike, I realized I had forgotten the note with the address written on it. As I did not want to go back home, I decided to pray and ask the Lord to guide me to my destination. As I went, I would hear a little voice saying turn here or there. I finally arrived at a street and the same voice said, "*There is the house.*" It was the right place, so I completed my errand and returned home overjoyed.

When the time came to decide on a career, I looked to Him for guidance. I knew that He would bless me richly if I followed Him carefully. I felt nudged towards Medicine, which was confirmed when I obtained a full scholarship at one of the best universities in Rio de Janeiro and Brazil. This had not been easy as I had had to compete for a place with thousands of prospective students from across Brazil in the Vestibular (a sort of SAT or ACT) -- having only been in the country less than five years. When I obtained the scholarship, I said to myself, "*Wow! It's great to have God as my Heavenly Father!*"

Later, when I needed help, He moved the hearts of the brethren from the church, relatives and family friends to provide, as gifts, all my textbooks and medical equipment throughout the years of medical school. I felt blessed and secure. I felt special. I looked forward to my future as I felt that the Almighty God was taking care of me as a Father takes care of his son. *Life in the Kingdom of God was truly great! What a blessed life!*

The same year that I was to start Medical School, the MV Doulos arrived in Rio. This was one of the OM ships that went around the world taking the Good News of salvation. I was 19 years old and I was excited at the prospect of possibly joining the ship and going into the mission field. Again, I consulted my

Lord, but I was scared that He would tell me to go and give up the scholarship and Medicine. I couldn't imagine the hassle I would get from my parents who were so proud of me for being in Medical School. Anyway, I was committed to God being my Lord and Father and would do whatever He told me. As I prayed, I felt the Lord's peace and conviction that I was to complete Medical School and leave the mission field for afterwards. I did go together with my wife the year I completed the post-graduate resident program in Cardiology, which was ten years later.

YOUR JOURNEY --THE LIFE LESSONS—

THE KINGDOM OF GOD

Bethel, the Hebrew word that means 'God's house', was the place of encounter first between God and Abram and now between God and Jacob. "*Then God said to Jacob, "Go up to Bethel and settle there, and build an altar there to God, who appeared to you when you were fleeing from your brother Esau."* (Genesis 35:1) God's call to Jacob to live there affirmed the truth that, as we are residing in God's Kingdom, which encompasses both heaven and earth, we are called to abide by its rules, foremost of which is to be in submission to the King of the Kingdom. *"The LORD has established his throne in heaven, and his* Kingdom *rules over all." (*Psalm 103:19; cf. Psalm 83:18) *"Heaven is my throne, and the earth is my footstool."* (Isaiah 66:1)

The staircase connecting heaven and earth is the Biblical representation of what occurs in nature, for Heaven and Earth are interconnected in one giant, organized universal ecosystem that works together in synergy and is self-regulating. This is an important truth about our world, which will be explored in greater detail in Step Four. So, whether you dwell on Earth, God's footstool, or Heaven, where His throne is, you dwell in God's Kingdom. Yahweh is God of Heaven and Earth now. It is not a future reign, but was from the beginning, is now and will be forever.

Make a Name Change, if Necessary

To emphasize further the paradigm shift for Jacob from orphan to sonship in God's Kingdom, it was at Bethel that God said to him, *"Your name shall not be Jacob any more (means 'cheater'), but your name will be Israel",* which means 'God's prince'. So, some might be moved by the Holy Spirit to change their name to reflect their new identity, especially, if their names reflected old allegiances to other false gods. Others may have been given names to reflect some attribute that they were to live out. Simon, for example, was given the name Peter which means 'rock'; so, he had to become an unflinching rock-solid leader of the church. Abram's name was changed to Abraham to reflect better his God-given destiny to become the father of many nations. Saul changed his name to Paul (means, little or small) probably to demonstrate humility and to better represent himself to the Gentiles to whom he was called. Saul had been a purely Jewish name.

So, it was not just a physical relocation to Jacob and his clan, but a mental shift from a careless disregard or rebellion against the King of the Kingdom, to coming around to finally acknowledging and submitting to Him. It was a matter of filling a void and re-integrating into the wholeness that is the kingdom of God. In this 21st Century, we are witnessing a resurgence of adult children returning to their parents' homes for different reasons and once again subjecting themselves to parental oversight. To further illustrate the concept of a Fatherhood and Son relationship, let's look at the story of the Prodigal Son which Jesus taught.

The Story of the Prodigal Son

To illustrate the point further, Jesus told them this story:

"A man had two sons. The younger son told his father, 'I want my share of your estate now before you die.' So his father agreed to divide his wealth between his sons. "A few days later this younger son packed all his belongings and moved to a distant land, and there he wasted all his money in wild living. About the time his money ran out, a great famine swept over the land, and he began to starve. He persuaded a local farmer to hire him, and the man sent him into his fields to feed the pigs. The young man became so hungry that even the pods he was feeding the pigs looked good to him for no one gave him anything.

"When he finally came to his senses, he said to himself, 'At home even the hired servants have food enough to spare, and here I am dying of hunger! I will go home to my father .... And while he was still a long way off, his father saw him coming. Filled with love and compassion, he ran to his son, embraced him, and kissed him. His son said to him, 'Father, I have sinned against both heaven and you, and I am no longer worthy of being called your son.' "But his father said to the servants, 'Quick! Bring the finest robe in the house and put it on him. Get a ring for his finger and sandals for his feet. And kill the calf we have been fattening. We must celebrate with a feast, for this son of mine was dead and has now returned to life.....' So the party began. "Meanwhile, the older son was in the fields working. When he returned home, he heard music and dancing in the house, and he asked one of the servants what was going on. 'Your brother is back,' he was told, 'and your father has killed the fattened calf. We are celebrating because of his safe return.' "The older brother was angry and wouldn't go in. His father came out and begged him, but he replied,

'All these years I've slaved for you and never once refused to do a single thing you told me to. And in all that time you never gave me even one young goat for a feast with my friends. Yet when this son of yours comes back after squandering your money on prostitutes, you celebrate by killing the fattened calf!' "His father said to him, 'Look, dear son, you have always stayed by me, and everything I have is yours. We had to celebrate this happy day. For your brother was dead and has come back to life! He was lost, but now he is found!'" (Luke 15:11-32)

This story is acting as an analogy of first, the younger son's rejection of the Kingdom of God and of the older son's lack of understanding of his rights and responsibilities within the Kingdom. The purpose of this story is to illustrate …

1. The Father's heart to fix what is broken – a life and a relationship
2. The Father's joy when the broken is fixed, the lost is found and wholeness is restored.
3. The essential need that everyone has for the Heavenly Father.
4. That the Kingdom of God is the union which everyone must integrate.

The story also reveals:

1. The essential need to live in the Kingdom of God consistently
2. The rights of God's children
3. The responsibilities of God's children

First, we see the son's totally rejecting the Kingdom of God as he said, *"Give me my share of the estate"*. He **then abandoned the Kingdom of God**, His Father, and in so doing, **rejected the Father's Heart** -- he left the family circle and

rejected his Father's care and leadership. He also **rejected his rights as his father's / God's child and his responsibilities towards the Heavenly Father and the common good.** All things in life considered, the most important relationship in life is the one you must have with your Heavenly Father. We are to:

- Love the Lord with all your heart and soul and strength
- Praise and thank Him for His goodness and loving kindness towards you forever
- Learn from, obey, be guided by, and be in communion with the Father,
- Demonstrate the Father Heart

Look what happened when he abandoned the Way of Life -- The Result was an upset apple cart. *"He squandered his wealth with **loose** living.* "How are we supposed to live? We are supposed to: *"Keep the charge of the LORD your God, to walk in His **ways**, to keep His **statutes**, His **commandments**, His **ordinances**, and His testimonies, according to what is written in the Law of Moses, that you may **succeed** in all that you do and wherever you turn."* (1 Kings 2:3, NASB) Everything goes wrong when we transgress from the way of an abundant and quality life provided to us by the Father and we enter the '*broad way'* of adversity that leads to death. Removing ourselves from the Divine Whole (Order) only leads to disorder and confusion.

"For my people have done two evil things: They have abandoned me--the fountain of living water and they have dug for themselves cracked cisterns that can hold no water at all!" (Jeremiah 2:13).

The Humble and Long Return to the Father's House (The Kingdom of God)

No restoration happens without reconciliation with the ones we have offended. We must be prepared to place ourselves back into the Divine Whole. *"Repent, then, and turn to God, so that your sins may be wiped out, that times of refreshing may come from the Lord."* (Acts 3:19) As we re-submit to our Heavenly Father's leadership, return to right behaviors and correct mistakes, we will find our life getting better as balance is gradually restored. The return is not easy. It is rather painstakingly uncomfortable and riddled with guilt. However, we must persevere to the end – until balance is restored and comfort (shalom) regained.

This is a story of two varied reactions. First, the Father's (Righteous and Kingdom of God) Reaction -- *"In the same way, there is more joy in heaven over one lost sinner who repents and returns to God than over ninety-nine others who are righteous and haven't strayed away!"* (Luke 15:7). The father of the Prodigal Son and our Heavenly Father experience great joy because no restoration can happen without reconciliation with the ones we have offended, foremost being the one with our Heavenly Father; and, because:

- A soul repents
- A soul is saved and
- A community (whole) is restored

Second is the orphan or slave/servant reaction -- Our Identity Crisis: Son or Servant?

When you have become disjointed from the whole, which is the Kingdom of God, confusion and frustration enter from your being apart from your Heavenly Father. "*The sovereign master says, "These people say they are loyal to me; they say wonderful things about me, but they are not really loyal to me. Their worship consists of nothing but man-made ritual."* (Isaiah 29:13) It is not only important that you have a proper understanding of the role of God, our Heavenly Father, but it is equally important that we fully understand, acknowledge and live out our roles as sons and daughters residing in God's house, His kingdom. The older son's complaints demonstrated a lack of understanding of his rights and responsibilities as a son, which caused him to reject the Father's reasoning, which is based on love, truth, knowledge, understanding and wisdom.

Let's see how it manifests itself... *'All these years I've* ***slaved for you*** *and never once refused to do a single thing you told me to."*

Problem #1 – A Slave or Servant Mentality – The son was wrong for misunderstanding the context of his labor -- He obviously didn't believe in his rights as a son or as God's child because he utilized the word '*slaved*' to describe his work for the Father. Slaves are owned by their masters and have no claim to their master's assets. Servants work for their employers, get a salary and have no other claim to their employers' assets. Children, though, see the assets of their father as their inheritance. They are working and building a fortune for the common good of the family and for themselves.

Father's Response - *'Look, dear son, you have always stayed by me'*

The Father confirms the son's rights and loyalty, thereby upholding his right as heir to his inheritance.

> *"And in all that time you never gave me even one young goat for a feast with my friends"*

Problem #2 – He was angry, wrongfully blaming his Father for being irresponsible, while he himself did not believe or take advantage of his own rights as a child of God.

Father's Response - "*all that is mine is yours*"

What a revelation! As heirs and co-heirs with Christ we have access to all of heaven's resources. We must believe in our rights as His children to **ask**, (Matthew 6:22-7:11; cf. Philippians 4:6) **take** (Mark 11:22-24), **bind** and **loose,** as we also have the "*keys of the kingdom of Heaven*". (Matthew 16:19)

> *"Yet when this son of yours comes back after squandering your money on prostitutes, you celebrate by killing the fattened calf!"*

Problem #3 – Unwillingness or refusal to forgive and reconcile

Principle: The Kingdom reaction is to forgive, forget and reconcile

This is an important principle in our interconnected and synergistic kingdom and the older brother was demonstrating his immaturity by not understanding it. He had decided not to give his younger brother anything as he was undeserving because of his past actions. However, he failed to realize that for the sake of his own happiness and of the common good, one must always be willing to reconcile and restore relations with a repentant person.

Problem #4 – Unwilling to fulfill his responsibilities regarding restorative justice.

Father's Response - "*We have to celebrate this happy day. For your brother was dead and has come back to life! He was lost, but now he is found!'*"

Principle: Restorative justice is an important aspect of nature's and God's Kingdom economy because it restores balance and maintains synergy

Principle: The Kingdom reaction is to welcome every repentant soul back into the fold

Principle: Our purpose in life is to restore what is lost and broken.

Principle: God's Child must resemble Him, i.e. be compassionate.

When you can love, and be compassionate like God is, then you will have joy. Love maintains and restores relationships when they are broken; avoids pathological fear; prevents a host of debilitating problems, such as, bitterness, depression, hatred, and other mental and physical illnesses; and, builds a solid foundation of wholesome living and happiness. When you take full responsibility for your actions as your Father's child and faithfully do your part, you will find yourself doing the same things and having the same attitude as your Heavenly Father; you will find yourself in the center of His Will.

The Father's heart is to have compassion for the lost: "*He doesn't want to destroy anyone but wants all people to have an opportunity to turn to him and change the way they think and act."(*2 Peter 3:9, GWT; cf. Matthew 28:18-20; Isaiah 42:6-7) The Lord once told me: *"You are called to help, not to judge. I am the Judge."* Our happiness is tied to how best we demonstrate the Father's heart of love, which is a river of running water rather than the Dead Sea. Life and love are to flow in and life and love are to flow out. The Dead Sea is dead and does not produce life because nothing flows out of it. It is useless. What makes you fruitful to others as well as an effective member of God's Kingdom and the community is that you share what God gives you. God pours life into you; and this life you share. You are then a peacemaker and restorer.

Throughout the rest of this book, you will come to understand that wholeness can only be achieved when you and the things around you become whole; it is towards this end that we and our Heavenly Father are constantly working. Similarly, you and I are returning to our Heavenly Father's house and to His rule. When you accept Jesus as your Lord and Savior you are also acknowledging and accepting the rights and responsibilities which come with life in His Kingdom. It is indeed essential that you make this paradigm shift from a life of rebellion to a life of submission to the Head of the Kingdom for you to benefit from the re-integration, for God does rule the affairs of humanity. There are benefits when you acknowledge this reality and negative consequences when you don't, as you will see throughout this book.

WHAT ARE WE SUPPOSED TO DO?

Jesus carried the Fatherhood theme into the New Testament. In his famous Sermon on the Mount, He highlighted the Father heart of God by showing His compassionate nature: *"So if you sinful people know how to give good gifts to your children, how much more will your heavenly Father give good gifts to those who ask him."* (Matthew 7:11) He went even further, encouraging us to address God as *"'Our Father in heaven…"* (Matthew 6:9) while acknowledging our common sibling status: '*I am ascending to my Father and your Father, to my God and your God.*' (John 20:17)

We are all aware of what it means to be earthly parents and children so let's address some well-known facts. As God is our Heavenly Father, He has rights and responsibilities which correlate perfectly well with our own rights and responsibilities as His children. His rights correspond to our responsibilities and our rights parallel His responsibilities.

First, let's look at His rights.

1. Accept His Right to be God

First, we must acknowledge -- He is the One and Only God. *"I am Yahweh, and there is no other; apart from me there is no God. I will strengthen you, though you have not acknowledged me."* (Isaiah 45:5) *"Before me no god was formed, nor will there be one after me."*(Isaiah.43:10d) Then again, *"… there is but one God, the Father, from whom all* *things came and for whom we live; and there is but one Lord, Jesus Christ, through whom all things came and through whom we live."(*1 Corinthians 8:6) It is extremely interesting to note that we all benefit from God's paternalistic nature whether we acknowledge it or not, similar to how we all benefit from the life-giving resources of the sun, whether we acknowledge it or not. Of course, the more we acknowledge and align ourselves with God's will, the more we benefit. However, the opposite is true as well. The more we rebel and are out of alignment and disjointed, the more we lose. The fleeing Jacob needed to know that there was 'Someone Who was able and willing to take up his cause, and Someone who was bigger than his problems'. This 'Someone' was the Almighty God, the One at the top of the stairs, the One and Only God. Elisha and all of us can take comfort in the knowledge that there is no other god, and, as God, He has the right to be the Head of everything.

2.) Accept His Right to Rule

Principle: Yahweh is in control of Heaven and Earth

The image of God at the top of the stair reveals this most important principle of Bethel -- that Yahweh is in control. He rules heaven and the angels. He rules Elisha and the earth, including you and me. We, alongside Elisha, must have no doubt as to God's role -- He is Ruler. Heaven and Earth make up His Kingdom. He is "*the King of Kings and the Lord of Lords*". (Revelations 19:16) He emphasized this truth in a unique and powerful way to King Nebuchadnezzar, the King of Babylon, the greatest empire that ever existed: "*... your Kingdom will still be there for you* ***after you learn that it is heaven that runs things.****" (Daniel 4:26 MSG)* As was previously prophesied by Daniel, King Nebuchadnezzar suddenly developed a severe mental illness that side-lined him from his reign for seven long years, until he finally acknowledged that it was Yahweh, the God of Israel, who had sovereignty over the affairs of humanity. This mental illness began immediately after he ranted, exalting himself above the Almighty God. Read his interesting perspective of his God-orchestrated 'time out' in Daniel 4:34ff.

God's rule is expressed in and through nature. The sun's regulation of earth is a natural expression of the Lord's leadership. His jurisdiction over heaven and Earth is wonderfully exemplified by the sun's regulation of the affairs of earth. *"Do you know the laws of the heavens, or can you determine their rule over the earth?"* (Job 38:33) The sun's control over the earth can be observed in the beautiful changes of the four seasons that we have all come to appreciate -- summer, fall, winter and spring. Even our body system is intricately interconnected with the sun through circadian rhythms, which function like an internal clock, modulating the production of hormones, which, in turn, stimulate tissues in the body into action.

Early humans (and many today) were in such awe of the sun and moon that they worshipped them as gods, but the sun, moon, planets and stars are mere creations of God; the sun being a very good representation of His sovereignty over the earth and all its inhabitants. Even as the sun gives life and light to all living things on earth and regulates days, seasons and years, so does the Lord. Even as the sun is the central component in the Solar System with all the planets with their moons revolving around it, so must humans (and everything) as well, align with the existing divine order. To ignore or go against the solar order has repercussions the same as ignoring and going against the divine order of God.

Angels are an important part of God's reign. A lot of God's dealings with earth and humans are through His army of angels. The word *'angel'* also means '*messenger'* in the Hebrew language. One of their roles is to watch over all those who are in covenantal relationship with the Lord: *"Therefore, angels are only servants--spirits sent to care for people who will inherit salvation."* (Hebrews 1:14) *"For he will order his angels to protect you wherever you go."* (Psalm 91:11) They delivered messages (Psalm103:20), gave instructions on how to accomplish certain tasks, (Joshua 5:13-6:5) defended people, (Matthew 18:10) led them to safety, (Lot and his daughters) (Genesis 19:1-22) and generally assisted God's people at His command. (Hebrews 1:14) They will accompany Jesus on His return (Matthew 25:31) and will gather God's people who inherit salvation, and those destined for hell, at the end. (Matthew 13:39-42, 49)

I have not knowingly had a personal encounter with a heavenly being, but the testimonies of those who have, reveal just how subtle these encounters can be. One man, Salomão dos Santos, said that an angel accompanied him back to his body, which was lying in the morgue of the hospital where he had died on the operating table. A hospital worker who had accompanied his long hospital journey, and who was also from his mother's church, was in the morgue praying over the body. At one point, the angel whispered in the worker's ear to hug the body and command it to live. He refused, and instead, rebuked any spirit in the room, thinking that the thought was of demonic origin. Anyway, Salomão came back to life and stood up, to the utter amazement of the hospital worker. However, as he stood up, his abdominal contents spilled out when the surgical stitches burst open. He was rushed back to surgery, recovered and today he is a pastor in Brazil. You can contact him by email: bispo.salomão@ig.com.br or hear his testimony on YouTube in Portuguese: https://www.youtube.com/watch?v=JUK60Purfdk.

Angels know God's rights and are extremely careful at giving Him what is His due. When humans would worship them, out of ignorance, the angels would immediately stop them, deferring worship to the Only True God. (Judges 13:16; Colossians 2:18; Revelations 19:10 and 22:8, 9) However, rebellious angels have tried to usurp the worship due only to their Creator and God and are responsible for the false pagan worship practiced today by billions. Any angel who does not acknowledge that Christ has come in the flesh is anti-Christ. (1 John 4:2-3) A fascination with demons, with their power and deception, has led to the fall of many, including Israel. (Ezekiel 20:7-8; Exodus 20:3-5) They have led many naive humans astray causing their suffering, through psychological and psychiatric disorders, chaos, death and destruction. As these demons are actively working against God, anyone who listens to or follows them would be adversarial against His rule. So, one must have nothing to do with them.

As God, He not only has the right to reign but to set the rules of engagement.

3.) Accept His Right to Make the Rules of Engagement

As Creator, He created the rules of engagement that govern everything, including our behavior. As was mentioned above, these rules are expressed, taught by and built into nature. The Creator left us this Natural Order with universal and natural laws that cannot be ignored or disobeyed with impunity. God's divine justice is partly expressed through this Natural Order's restorative justice, which enables us to live as whole people. These rules dictate our responsibilities in God's Kingdom. Our responsibilities correspond with His rights and the common good. This way of righteousness and life will be explored further in Step Four.

Now, let's look at our responsibilities.

1.) Accept Your Responsibility to Worship Him

As the "*One and Only God*", He has the right to be worshipped in the manner He prescribes. The first three of the Ten Commandments spell out clearly some of these rules. *"I am the LORD your God, who brought you out of Egypt, out of the land of slavery. "You shall have no other gods before me."* (Deuteronomy 5: 6-11) There are no other gods. Therefore, don't listen to or worship any other entity that deceives you into false worship. Everything that exists, including angels, were created by Him. It continues:

> *"You shall not make for yourself an image in the form of anything in heaven above or on the earth beneath or in the waters below. You shall not bow down to them or worship them; for I, the LORD your God, am a jealous God, punishing the children for the sin of the parents to the third and fourth generation of those who hate me, but showing love to a thousand generations of those who love me and keep my commandments."* (Deuteronomy 5: 6-11)

Icons are a major feature of pagan worship. The prohibition of icons is clearly spelled out, so it's a pity that this rule, has and still, is being disobeyed by many, even within Christianity.

"You shall not misuse the name of the LORD your God, for the LORD will not hold anyone guiltless who misuses his name."

Yahweh or I am what I am, is a fundamental truth and must never be misused, misrepresented, disbelieved or distrusted. His names are holy and fully represent who He says He is. Do not use God's names in vain or in mockery; it is a grave mistake. For this purpose and to help you become a true worshipper, His Holy Spirit indwells you. The Holy Spirit will move you to develop intimacy with the Lord – to know you and to be known by you. To this end, He will move you to develop the spiritual disciplines.

> *"But the time is coming--indeed it's here now--when true worshipers will worship the Father in spirit and in truth. The Father is looking for those who will worship him that way."* (John 4:23, NLT)

Spending time in **Bible reading** is the time to listen to the Father. The Bible is God's Word compiled over millennia. It contains the words of God, Himself, and the experiences of Godly men and women that are very helpful and insightful. This reveals the way of right living and the acts of transgression. Altogether, these enrich our lives with knowledge, understanding and wisdom. Plan to use this time to complete the reading and study of all the Scriptures rather than just reading for pleasure, such as reading your favorite verses and books over and over. Take advantage of free software and online resources such as BibleHub.com and Scripturetext.com. There you can go beneath the surface of the text and explore the meaning of words and expressions in their original languages (Hebrew and Greek) and their historic-cultural contexts.

Plan also to make it a time of bonding with the Heavenly Father through His Holy Spirit. This style of reading (*lectio divina*) is slow and engaging with the Spirit as you seek discernment (full understanding) and feedback. This feedback comes in the form of visions, dreams and words of knowledge, understanding and wisdom, accompanied with or without speaking and singing in tongues, which is prophesying.

The Spirit will help you fully understand God's attributes in all His true glory. When there is a great dentist or a doctor or a coach, everyone glorifies the person for his or her abilities. We use these attributes, references and recommendations in making wise choices. We benefit from knowing the truth about that person's abilities. Similarly, knowing God's abilities helps us align our footsteps with them to our greater benefit. They will enrich our speech, our environment and us. The knowledge of each one of them gives us hope, as our Heavenly Father has all these abilities, which are available to our benefit and glory.

Thus, it is in your best interest to know God, so you can worship Him truly. Study the Scriptures well and utilize the

Holy Spirit's help in increasing this intimacy with God. Knowing God in the fullest sense – especially, when it results in the right behavior, a God-fearing attitude, and a firm trust -- all aspects of true worship -- will lead to abundant health. This intimacy will enrich you greatly, especially, your prayer language.

Prayer fosters intimacy with Him. Communication is the key in any relationship, especially, as it fosters Father-Child bonding. Children communicate their wishes, love and gratitude through prayer, song and intercession, which is the act of prayerfully and lovingly intervening on someone's behalf. Note that the Spirit will move you to pray for the needs of others before your own. Trust must be the key component of your prayers, and knowing God's attributes, will foster both trust and intimacy.

In the **Oxford Dictionary**, trust is the "*firm belief in the reliability, truth, or ability of someone or something*"; while, faith is a "*complete trust or confidence in someone or something*". Your speech expresses the true nature of the relationship you have with your Heavenly Father. Prayer is the verbal expression of your belief and trust in Him, or the lack thereof. In other words, the words you choose demonstrate maturity or immaturity in your relationship. It is impossible to have a healthy relationship without faith. The Author of Hebrews said, "*And without faith it is impossible to please Him, for he who comes to God must believe that He is and that He is a rewarder of those who seek Him.*" (Hebrews 11:6, NASB) Your speech (prayer, song) must truly express your security in the Heavenly Father's abilities and care for you. "*Never worry about anything. But in every situation let God know what you need in prayers and requests while giving thanks.*" (Philippians 4:6, GWT)

Jesus taught us to pray to our Heavenly Father with this complete trust and firm belief. "*Hallowed be your Name*" means

"*Your Name is holy*" and, therefore, trustworthy and entirely reliable. Prayer can be an expression of grumbling and reflect your anxiety rather than express the security in the Father's care for you. For example, Jacob at Bethel struggled with the Angel of the Lord to obtain a blessing that he had already received by promise. The disciples cried out to the sleeping Jesus in the boat on the Sea of Galilee, *"Teacher, don't you care that we're going to drown?"* (Mark 4:38*)* It would have been better if Jacob had returned to his father's home with praise and thanksgiving rather than in fear and anxiety. The disciples should have awakened the Lord to verbalize the security that his presence brought them rather than, in panic, expressing their distrust in his power and care. They should have expressed thanks for his presence in their time of trouble rather than criticize him for his perceived lack of care. *"Think of it--the LORD is ready to heal me! I will sing his praises with instruments every day of my life in the Temple of the LORD."* (Isaiah 38:20, NLT)

Spirit-empowered **Praise and Worship** is the highest form of worship, for the Spirit knows how and when to praise the Lord, in a manner becoming the truth of His Highness -- *"He will glorify me because it is from me that he will receive what he will make known to you."* (John 16:14) So, when the urge arises within you to praise, whether in your own language or in tongues, let it loose. Don't resist the urge. This Spirit-empowered praise is pleasing to the Lord. It is passionate and may even break forth in dance, as in "*Praise his name with dancing"* (Psalm 149:3a, NLT)***;*** and, lead to the composition of new songs, such as, ***"****Praise the LORD! Sing to the LORD a* ***new song****"*. (Psalm 149:1, NLT*)* Therefore, before you come with your requests unto your Heavenly Father, *"Enter his gates with thanksgiving and his courts with praise; give thanks to him and praise his name."* (Psalm 100:4) As you learn of all the things your Heavenly Father has done on your behalf, you should always come into His Presence with praise and thanksgiving. Praise and thank Him in every situation because you know *"that all things work together for the good of those who love God."*

(Romans 8:28, GWT) It is not easy to worship, praise and give thanks when you are amid crises, but it demonstrates faith in the One who has promised to be with you always. Paul, while in prison, said these words: *"Always be joyful in the Lord! I'll say it again: Be joyful!"* (Philippians 4:4, GWT) *"Praise your way out of your problems,"* said Juanita Bynum. Prison to Praise and Power in Praise by Merlin Carothers are excellent books about the power of praise. As recipients of the fullness of His love and grace, thank, praise and love Him with all our hearts, soul and strength, because He is more than deserving of all our passionate love, praise and thanksgiving. He deserves all and more.

Jesus was referring to this style of worship when he told the Samaritan woman that the place of worship was not important, but rather how one worshipped: "*Yet a time is coming and has now come when the true worshipers will worship the Father in the Spirit and in truth, for they are the kind of worshipers the Father seeks. God is spirit, and his worshipers must worship in the Spirit and in truth."* (John 4:23-24) As we have the right to His Holy Spirit, Whose Presence and purpose is to help us in this area, allowing Him to empower our worship has now become our responsibility. Resisting His help would not only go against our commitment to allow Him to be Lord of our lives and affairs but would be irreverent and ungodly. Paul referred to these people who resist the Spirit when he said, "*They will act religious, but they will reject the power that could make them godly."* (2 Timothy 3:5)

2.) Accept your Responsibility to Submit to Him

He is our Heavenly Father and the One in control, so we, as His children, have the responsibility to submit to Him. He has the right to be obeyed absolutely. As God and His reign are eternal, this relationship we have is obviously an eternal one that calls for continuity, steadfastness and faithfulness. As Creator, He made the rules of engagement and embedded them into nature, thus creating the way of righteousness and making our

Judeo-Christian values into natural ones. He expects and requires our total submission knowing that we benefit on both fronts -- pleasing Him as obedient children, on the one hand, and, on the other, reaping the benefits of a naturally-balanced lifestyle: peace, prosperity, health and security.

As we submit to and obey Him, we acquire more of His ways and character. His greatest desire is that we be people of integrity. A child resembles the parent not only physically, but also in character. What is cherished by our Heavenly Father should also be cherished by us. What is abominable to Him should also be abominable to us. The Devil is an evil and false father figure in that his 'children' adopt his ways.

> " *Jesus told them, "If God were your Father, you would love me, because I have come to you from God. I am not here on my own, but he sent me...For you are the children of your father the devil, and you love to do the evil things he does. He was a murderer from the beginning. He has always hated the truth, because there is no truth in him. When he lies, it is consistent with his character; for he is a liar and the father of lies."* (John 8:42, 44)

So, who do you resemble? In the beginning, you probably resembled more the Devil than the Lord, but more and more you are coming to resemble your Heavenly Father. Life is a journey in which you gradually learn and adopt your Heavenly Father's ways -- His love, joy, peace, patience, kindness, goodness, faithfulness, gentleness and self-control. He teaches, trains, guides and molds and purifies your character and behavior to conform to His foreordained standards of righteousness besides providing your food, shelter, clothing and protection. It is your responsibility, therefore, to submit to Him so that He can do all these things successfully rather than your being resistive and rebellious and losing out on the benefits. He showed this pleasure in Abraham, *"For I know him, that he will command his children and his household after him, and they shall keep the way of the LORD, to do righteousness and justice; that the LORD may bring upon Abraham that which he has spoken of him."* (Genesis18:19, WBT) The benefits are not only heavenly, but also earthly, and in Step Four, we will look at how nature's justice system works to benefit the obedient and 'guide' the disobedient.

Therefore, make the paradigm shift and relate to Him as your Heavenly Father and not just as your God. As He adopted you, adopt Him as your Heavenly Father and accept your new identity and role as His true son or daughter, not as a bastard or as a second-class citizen. Sons and daughters have a stronger and different emotional attachment than mere servants or slaves because of their rights and responsibilities. You have become a full-fledged heir. It is good, therefore, to celebrate your new child of God identity and relationship by reminding yourself daily by calling Him Father rather than God or Lord, when you communicate with Him. It took me a while to make the paradigm shift in my prayer language from that of "*Dear God*" or "*Dear Lord*" to "*Dear Heavenly Father*".

Jesus taught us to pray "*Our Father in Heaven, holy is your Name*", (Matthew 6:9) for this very reason. He wanted us to know that God is who He says He is. If He says He is "Our Father in Heaven" then He is truly our Father in Heaven, with all the connotations and implications, rights and responsibilities that go with it. He has a reputation to keep and cannot lie. Solid trust in Him is, therefore, essential to your making the successful transition from Spiritual orphans to Spiritual sons and daughters, from being dead to being alive to the Father's Spirit. Faithfully embracing your rights and carrying out every responsibility will result in security, peace and hope, healthier and more stable emotional states, quality lives and bright futures.

3.) Accept your Responsibility to Love and Walk in Unity with His Other Children

Love is the language spoken in God's House. As Yahweh is 'our' Heavenly Father, He is not just 'my', but 'Our' Father. It is important to align with this basic truth and have the proper respect and love for the rest of the family. *"... All of you are equal as brothers and sisters",* (Matthew 23:8b, NLT*)* but diverse in your level of maturity, understanding, knowledge, language, ethnicity, tan and gender. Does the Gentile (Non-Jewish) Christian have the same rights as the Jewish people in the eyes of God? YES!!! There is no more separation between Jew and Gentile.

> *"Don't let foreigners who commit themselves to the LORD say, 'The LORD will never let me be part of his people.' "I will also bless the foreigners who commit themselves to the LORD, who serve him and love his name, who worship him and do not desecrate the Sabbath day of rest, and who hold fast to my covenant. I will bring them to my holy mountain of Jerusalem and will fill them with joy in my house of prayer. I will accept their burnt offerings and sacrifices, because* ***my Temple will be called a house of prayer for all nations****. For the Sovereign LORD, who brings back the outcasts of Israel, says:* ***I will bring others, too, besides my people Israel****."*
> (Isaiah 56:3a, 6-8)

Why does the Church continue to divide into multiple denominations seeing that all are brethren? Denominations are created when well-meaning leaders interpret things differently and wrongly desire to be separate and have their own identities. Some have separated based on doctrinal preferences, most notably about differences regarding the Holy Spirit. Others have separated based on color and others over language and ethnicity.

Sometimes churches have been forcibly segregated. One big divider is between Charismatics and Pentecostals on one side and the non-charismatic on the other. Another is between the Calvinists and the Arminians. These differences became enshrined in constitutions, thus creating denominations. We must never forget, though, that we all have the same Father. This diversity must never be a reason to disassociate or segregate, persecute, harass, discriminate, put in jail and even kill those who are different. We must rather gloss over trivial differences, celebrate the strengths and enjoy the diversity of the mosaic, which is God's family.

We must not separate and try to 'make a name for ourselves', whether as an individual or as a group, as Nimrod did, when he built Babel saying, *"Come, let's build a great city for ourselves with a tower that reaches into the sky. This will make us famous and keep us from being scattered all over the world."* (Genesis 11:4) This is very displeasing to our Heavenly Father. We must be careful to maintain the unity of the Body of Christ. Churches must thus examine their constitutions and make sure they celebrate the diversity of the Body, while ensuring its unity. Jesus was so concerned with this unity issue that just before he was crucified, he asked His Father to keep us all united:

> *"I'm not praying only for them. I'm also praying for those who will believe in me through their message. I pray that these people continue to have unity in the way that you, Father, are in me and I am in you. I pray that they may be united with us so that the world will believe that you have sent me."* (John 17: 20-21, GWT)

So, not only must we remain united with the Godhead, but we must also maintain unity with one another, for we are **one body** with Christ as our Head. This is of crucial importance as we must all work together with our Heavenly Father in Kingdom business and for the common good.

4.) Accept Your Responsibility to Engage with Our Heavenly Father in Kingdom Business

Every father and mother groom their children to be able to fulfill their responsibilities and purposes in life successfully. As well, an important part of God's Kingdom, is that He trains His children to work with Him in His garden -- the world, so they can clear the soil of weeds and rocks, plant, and harvest bountifully. We are groomed to *"preach the Gospel to the uttermost parts of the earth"* (Acts 1:6) and *'bring salvation to those who sit in darkness'* (Luke 1:79), be peace-makers, curse-enders, breach repairers and problem solvers in a disjointed world full of broken people and shattered hopes. This is the Church's ongoing Great Commission.

We are anointed to be compassionate and not sit by, while the world is falling apart, and people are being oppressed, harassed and enslaved. We are expected to answer the cries for help even as our Heavenly Father does. As God's children, we are called to be big brothers and sisters who 'father', 'mother' and 'pastor' the peoples, cities and nations. Our responsibility is to seek their welfare and restoration to the Way of Life. Our own welfare and happiness are tied to restorative justice, which will be explored further in the following steps.

Believe in Our Heavenly Father's Responsibilities --Believe in our Rights

Principle: God is Heavenly Father to all who covenant with Him

God's compassionate nature is portrayed in the Scriptures and in nature -- *"For you are our Father, though Abraham does not know us and Israel does not recognize us. You, LORD, are our Father; you have been called our Protector from ancient times."* (Isaiah 63:16, NET) The Hebrew word for 'compassionate' originates from the word meaning 'womb'. As the womb gives life to the developing child, caring for, tending to its every need, protecting and advocating for its welfare, so is God to all those who live in His Kingdom. Even as the placenta and amniotic membranes produce life-giving water (amniotic fluid) in the uterus, the indwelling Holy Spirit produces the River of God that flows out of God's Temple (House) bringing life-giving resources to all the inhabitants of the land; in it and by it, life thrived and multiplied (Ezekiel 47). *"Whoever believes in me, as Scripture has said, rivers of living water will flow from within them. By this he meant the Spirit, whom those who believed in him were later to receive."* (John 7:38-39a*)*

There is a beautiful illustration of the Father's compassionate and loving care in the allegorical story of Jerusalem as an abandoned new born baby on whom the Lord had compassion, adopted and cared for; who grew up to become like a queen (Ezekiel 16:1-14). God presented Himself to Jacob (and to Elisha) as this compassionate paternal figure, who would take care of him; even though, Jacob didn't fully acknowledge, nor understand, God's, and his own, rights and responsibilities. As our Heavenly Father, God has responsibilities towards us, His children, which directly match our rights. He takes each responsibility so seriously that He incorporates each one into His Names. So, let's look at them.

God as Our Heavenly Father, Yahweh Abba --The Right to be God's Children

Before, we were Spiritual orphans, because we failed to acknowledge God's right to be our Heavenly Father; but now, we are no longer orphans. *"Yet to all who did receive him, to those who believed in his name, he gave the right to become children of God."* (John 1:12) We are His true children, not second-class or bastards. Orphans tend to have difficulty believing in their rights as children. They have a hard time accepting and living in their newly-acquired status as heirs and co-heirs. Orphans must fend for themselves, so are very independent, rather than family, team-oriented or interdependent children, as is required in our systemic world. They do not have the habit of going to a father when in need or when in crisis, so they may not acknowledge or respect a father or fatherhood. In fact, they have a hard time fully understanding the whole idea of fatherhood as they may have never experienced it. We must, therefore, make the mental shift to this new status and get rid of our orphan mentality.

As children, you have the right to be …

Heirs and co-heirs with Jesus -- *"And since we are his children, we are his heirs. In fact, together with Christ we are heirs of God's glory"* (Romans 8:17a.) The glory of heaven awaits us. Jesus ascended to heaven and so shall we if we remain faithful.

Like Jesus, we are…

Members of His family and kingdom and, as such, we must *"seek first his kingdom and his righteousness"*. That is, we must acknowledge that we are full members of His family and kingdom, which encompasses Heaven and Earth, and therefore subject to:

His leadership – Our Heavenly Father is the King of the Kingdom; and,

Its righteous standards – As you will see later, these righteous standards are also the same as our ecosystem, thus making our Judeo-Christian values into natural ones

As children, you have the right to …

Ask -- Why be anxious when we have a powerful, compassionate, good and loving Heavenly Father to whom you can boldly come and ask -- *"Never worry about anything. But in*

every situation let God know what you need in prayers and requests while giving thanks." (Philemon 4:6; cf. Matthew 6:22 – 7:11; Hebrews 4:16). And, to…

The Keys of the Kingdom, i.e. Take, Bind and Release -- "*To you I shall give the keys of the Kingdom of Heaven; everything that you will bind in the earth will have been bound in Heaven, and anything that you will release in the earth will have been released in Heaven.*" (Matthew 16:19; cf. Mark 11:22-24) As the former Miss Universe and I discovered, our Heavenly Father expects us to demonstrate maturity in believing in, and taking advantage of, our rights as His children to 'move the mountains' in our lives and for the common good. Children have the authority to use heaven's resources to build the Kingdom, release the captives, heal the sick, rebuke the devourer and the oppressor, cast out evil spirits, raise the dead, teach and give guidance, understanding and wisdom to the needy. Jesus gave us the authority, (Matthew 10:1-8) commanded us to teach exactly what He taught His first disciples (Matthew 28:18-20; Mark 16:15-18) and reminded us not to be afraid, but to be confident, strong and courageous, because "*I am with you always even to the end of the age.*" (Matthew 28:20)

You can use the same words and attitude that Jesus exemplified for us, in the application of this authority:

- "*Be clean*" (Matthew 8:1-4),
- "*Go! Let it be done just as you believed it would.*" (Matthew 8:5-13)
- "*... he drove out the spirits with a word and healed all the sick*" (Matthew 8: 14-17; 9:32-33)
- "*... he got up and rebuked the winds and the waves*" (Matthew 8:23-27),
- *The demons begged Jesus, "If you drive us out, send us into the herd of pigs." He said to them, "Go!"* (Matthew 8:28-34)
- "*Get up, take your mat and go home.*" (Matthew 9:1-2)

- *Then he touched their eyes and said, "According to your faith let it be done to you"* (Matthew 9: 27-31)

Furthermore, look at this text from Isaiah:

"But this is a people robbed and spoiled; they are all of them snared in holes, and they are hid in prison houses: they are for a prey, and none delivers; for a spoil, and none said, Restore." (Isaiah 42:22, AKJV)

It is obvious that we must develop from children, who only know to ask, to the more mature, who can take, bind and release. The older brother in the Prodigal Son story lost out because he was not mature enough to enjoy the privileges of sonship but instead grumbled about his lot as a slave. Believe in your rights and privileges as God's children; and utilize your strengths, gifts and talents, with confidence, to your own benefit and enjoyment, and for the common good of the kingdom!

Our Father as Nurturer

- *He is Yahweh Racham,* the Compassionate One
- *He is Yahweh Roi,* my Shepherd who watches over me
- *He is Yahweh Rophi,* my Healer

Your Right to His Nurturing Care

It is important for you to know that God is with you. He watches over you in much the same way that He watched over Abraham, Isaac, Jacob, Israel, Esther, Mordecai and so many others, both in the Bible, as well as in post-biblical times. *"Remember, I am with you and I will watch over you wherever you go"* (Genesis 28:15a, b; GWT*);* and again, *"For I know what I have planned for you,' says the LORD. 'I have plans to prosper you, not to harm you. I have plans to give you a future filled with hope."* (Jeremiah 29:11, NET) As any normal human being, we are always in need of a father and the Lord has placed

Himself in this position to be our Heavenly Father. Thank you, Father!

> *"Sing to God, sing in praise of his name, extol him who rides on the clouds; rejoice before him —his name is Yahweh, a Father to the fatherless, a Defender of widows, is God in his holy dwelling. God sets the lonely in families, he leads out the prisoners with singing; but the rebellious live in a sun-scorched land."* (Psalm 68:4-6, ISV)

He, especially, cares for orphans, widows and the otherwise deprived of family-life and places them in families. An orphan (or widow) is lonely, feels rejected and abandoned, with no one to care for them, when in need. I, myself, am fortunate to have both my parents, but I have seen the tears and despondency of true and functional orphans, who do not have a father and/or mother. So, whether you have a father and mother or not, you still need your Heavenly Father, as He fills that important Heavenly-Father-sized void that every human has. *"As a mother comforts her child, so will I comfort you; and you will be comforted over Jerusalem."* (Isaiah 66:13)

Like the sun, He provides an essential life-giving and -sustaining service. Situations arise in life that only He can handle; no human being, either alone or banded together, can handle those. Thus, God's role becomes vital to our survival in a corrupted environment. God's Holy Spirit tends to us in a motherly fashion. It's good that God's care is complete, encompassing both fatherhood and motherhood. The Lord nurtures you to be a blessing: *"... and make you and your descendants a blessing to all the peoples of the earth."* (Genesis 12:7; 13:15, 17; 15:18; 26:3, 24; Isaiah.42:6-7)

Principle: Your purpose in life is to be a blessing to ALL peoples of the earth.

We are created in God's image, to be like Him -- compassionate, good and kind, oozing with and giving life to everyone and everything around us. Jesus envisioned the Holy Spirit filling us, so that, out of us would flow '*streams of life-giving water*' (John 7:38). We are to '*make disciples of all the nations (and peoples)*', '*teaching*' them the Good News of salvation (Matthew 28:18-20). This will be further developed in the next Step.

Our Father as Guide and Teacher

- He is *Yahweh Tsidkenu*, Our Righteousness, who loves, and guides us, to do what is right.
- He is *Yahweh Shalom*, God of Peace and Complete Wellness (wholeness), who guides us there for our benefit and everyone's welfare.

Your Right to be Taught and Guided

He gave us His Spirit to indwell us, the Scriptures with the Ten Commandments, as well as, nature to teach us the way, in which we should walk. *"But he, The Redeemer of the accursed, The Spirit of Holiness, whom my Father sends in my name, he will teach you all things and he will remind you of everything whatsoever I have told you."* (John 14:26, ABPE) The life principles our Father teaches us are not only beneficial for here on earth, but also in Heaven, for they are eternal.

One of the ways that our Heavenly Father guides us is through correction or discipline. *"My child, don't reject the LORD's discipline, and don't be upset when he corrects you."* (Proverbs 3:1) *"Think about it: Just as a parent disciplines a child, the LORD your God disciplines you for your own good."* (Deuteronomy 8:5) Accepting criticism is crucial to facilitating your Father's guidance; and the opposite is true, when you have difficulty accepting criticism. The fourth Step will outline how our Father utilizes nature to discipline and guide us.

He is with us wherever and on whatever mission He sends us. Jesus repeats this promise to his disciples and us, "Lo, *I am with you always, even to the end of the age."* (Matthew 28:20) The Lord is with you by His Holy Spirit, who indwells us and moves, leads, overshadows and empowers all of us. Psalms 23 and 91 portray Yahweh as the Shepherd who watches over and tends to His sheep. *"You will hear a voice behind you saying, "This is the way. Follow it, whether it turns to the right or to the left."* (Isaiah 30:21, GWT)

Our Father as Provider

- He is *Yahweh Jireh*, our Provider. He sees our needs beforehand and provides for them.
- He is *El Shaddai*, the All-Sufficient or All-Bountiful God.

Our Rights to the Riches of God's Kingdom

He will bless you as the All-Bountiful God. God, as did His Son, loves to use parables, that is, analogies found in nature, to describe some aspect of Himself. *"As El Shaddai I will bless you."* (Genesis 12:7; 13:15, 17; 15:18; 26:3, 24) The Hebrew word, *shaddim*, meaning breasts, implies that God, like breasts, is the source or fountain of bountiful, life-giving and sustaining resources. It implies abundance and not scarcity. His plan is to be gracious to us making us look like kings and queens (Ezekiel 16).

The Holy Spirit is there to strengthen us when in time of need. *"The eyes of the LORD search the whole earth in order to strengthen those whose hearts are fully committed to him."* (2 Chronicles.16:9) As we allow the Holy Spirit to empower us, we will see He gives us an abundance of joy, peace, love, kindness, goodness, faith, gentleness, patience and self-control. These are for our own benefit. God requires these of us, but He also provides these to help us carry out our responsibilities, so we do what is expected of us.

We also have a right to the rich resources of earth -- our home. We are born with this innate right, but with it comes the responsibility to use it wisely, because abusing it will be detrimental to everyone, not just us. This too will be explored further in Step Four.

Our Father as Protector

- He is *Yahweh Sebaoth*, God of the Hosts of all the Heavenly Armies
- He is *Yahweh Nissi,* my Banner. He is an Ensign to all around me, both to my friends and to my enemies.
- He is *Yeshua*, Savior
- He is *El Gibbor*, the Warrior God, who fights on my behalf
- He is *Yahweh Abir*, the Mighty One

We have a **right to safety --** *"Do not fear, Abram, I am a shield to you."* (Genesis 15:1, NASB)

> *"Those who live in the shelter of the Most High will find rest in the shadow of the Almighty. This I declare about the LORD: He alone is my refuge, my place of safety; he is my God, and I trust him. He will cover you with his feathers. He will shelter you with his wings. His faithful promises are your armor and protection."* (Psalm 91:1-2, 4)

Aldo Nascimento, in his testimony, told a story about when he targeted a young 15-year-old teenager to be a sacrifice, but didn't realize that she was a believer in Christ. When he kidnapped her and was about to kill her, she rebuked him and the evil spirit that was empowering him. He suddenly grew weak, fell to the ground and released his hold on her allowing her to flee. None of his subsequent spells on her worked as the spirits told him that she was untouchable.

Our Father as a Zealous Advocate

- He is *Yahweh El Qanna*, the Zealous God
- *He is Yahweh Ezeri*, my Helper
- *He is Yahweh Mepalti*, my Deliverer
- He is *Yahweh Haqadosh*, the Holy One, who is pure in His intentions; a God of Integrity
- He is *Yahweh Emeth*, God of Truth, who is faithful, steadfast; loves and teaches us life truths
- He is *Yahweh Tsur*, the Rock of Stability and Reliability
- He is *Yahweh Shammah*, The Lord is there; He is always there when you need Him.

Your Right to Reliable Help

He is our Anchor for life's stormy seas, an Immoveable Rock, instead of shifting sands. Look at all His great promises to us: "*For I hold you by your right hand-- I, the LORD your God. And I say to you, 'Don't be afraid. I am here to help you"* (Isaiah 41:13); *and again, "And my God will supply your every need according to his glorious riches in Christ Jesus."* (Philippians 4:19, NET*)* We also read, *"I will bring you back to this land"* (Genesis 28:15c); and, ***"****I will not leave you until I have done what I have promised you.****"*** (Genesis 28:15d)

Principle: Your faith and hope are founded on God's faithful reputation or trustworthiness

Our Heavenly Father, through His Holy Spirit, is our Great Encourager (Comforter). He knows His own power and ability to provide everything, so we too must believe and trust in His reputation and ability to do so. We are told to honor God by obeying, trusting, believing and resting in His Father's heart. God's holiness does not allow Him to lie. He does what He says. *"God is not a man, so he does not lie. He is not human, so he does not change his mind. Has he ever spoken and failed to act? Has he ever promised and not carried it through?"* (Numbers 23:19) He is not like the Devil, who will do things to harm us and lead us to disaster. In other words, as God has committed to be our Heavenly Father, we can trust in His Fathering abilities and, especially, in His love, compassion and trustworthiness -- *"Give thanks to Yahweh, for he is good; for his loving kindness endures forever."* (Psalm 136:1)

CONCLUSION

The Kingdom of God incorporates a paternalistic covenant with rights and responsibilities. God is the Shepherd, who watches over His flock -- us, His children, molding and perfecting us, providing for us, blessing and protecting us, guiding, leading, inspiring, motivating, and nurturing us, advocating for us and planning for our future and teaching us the values that are dear to Him and essential for our health and success in the world He created.

God's rights and responsibilities, as our Father, match our own rights and responsibilities toward Him and towards others. His rights conform to our responsibilities and similarly, His responsibilities coincide with our rights. We must faithfully dispense our responsibilities regarding God's rights and towards the common good and have a rock-solid trust in His faithfulness to dispense His responsibilities towards us. Our Lord's covenant with us, to be our Heavenly Father, has its benefits. He is our Father, with all the privileges and duties thereof, which make us His children, with all the privileges and duties thereof. He has given us His Holy Spirit to help us in these very areas. By His Spirit, He promises to be with us always and to bless us; and, in so doing, He makes us a blessing to Himself and to all the families of the earth. What comfort to know that our Heavenly Father takes into consideration the fact that we are weak!

God says that we are His children and no longer slaves or orphans. Unfortunately, it is not easy for those of us who have lived so many years (or decades) as such and must now make the paradigm shift from the mindset of a slave or orphan to that of a son or daughter. However, you must persevere in making the shift, because the benefits are out of this world. In due time, the child-of-God mindset will be matched by an impassioned heart and will be revealed in your serene demeanor and healthier lifestyle. You must look out for the pitfalls of the orphan or slave mindset and intentionally try to avoid them, by reminding yourself that you are now God's child, with all its privileges and duties. No longer will you be called second-class, a bastard child, a Gentile or disabled; too white or too dark, with a lot of protective melanin -- no longer will you be treated as the down trodden. It doesn't matter what others feel or think, but you will be living what is true -- you are a child of the Most High God.

Remember, never look back at the former years, but contemplate rather on what is current -- your new identity, your experiences with your Heavenly Father and the extent of His heavenly promises and assets. Begin to look forward, with confidence and hope, to a bright and prosperous future. Remember, you now represent your Heavenly Father, so don't behave like the devil is your Father. Your most important duties are only to honor and love Him and your fellow siblings; follow His commands, teachings and ways carefully; and, all together, be responsible members of His family and of His Kingdom of righteousness. You are now one of His children, so do not hurt the integrity of His House or His Name, by not demonstrating the Father's heart in all your doings. By doing so, you work for the common good, as the Father's will is for you to love and not to hate. His house (and Kingdom) is built in such a way as to incorporate love into its infrastructure, that is, into the ecosystem, as you will see in Step Four.

As God's children, we automatically embark upon a journey to, not only experience the Father's Heart, but also to develop and demonstrate it. Any earthly parent will teach their children everything they know, so that they can develop from immature children into mature fathers and mothers. It is precisely in this area that the Holy Spirit helps us. Like a mother, He will help, lead, and motivate you, in all ways. Look out for when He will add new responsibilities to move you to higher maturity levels. Of course, for Him to be successful, you must collaborate fully with Him, so don't '*resist*', '*quench*' or '*put out his fire*'. (1 Thessalonians 5:19) Only then will you attain the glory of being children of the Most High God and experience the full extent of His grace, with its inherent joys. As He blesses you, you in turn will share them and become blessings to all the families of the earth. *"Surely goodness and lovingkindness will follow me all the days of my life, And I will dwell in the house of the LORD forever."* (Psalm 23:6, NASB1977)

Remember, He is "Our Heavenly Father", not just yours. He has many children, of all colors, ethnicities and languages. So, we are not to discriminate against each other as that is highly displeasing to Him. Rather, we are to celebrate one another's strengths and victories and gloss over one another's weaknesses. He wants us all to be united with one another and especially with Him.

Heavenly Father,
Thank you for being a loving Father to us;
Thank you for watching over us and taking care of us;
Thank you for blessing us and making us a blessing;
Thank you for being a true and faithful Father;
We love you!

Now that you have been revealed the Savior at Gilgal and the Heavenly Father at Bethel, let's proceed to Jericho and learn to work with the third Person of the Trinity, the Holy Spirit, your Helper.

“Then Elijah said to him, "Stay here, Elisha; the LORD has sent me to Jericho." And he replied, "As surely as the LORD lives and as you live, I will not leave you." So they went to Jericho.” (2 Kings 2:4*)*

STEP THREE

JERICHO:
TO TRANSFORM OUR WORLD TOGETHER

Now that balance has been restored within at Gilgal and you have re-connected with the Heavenly Father at Bethel, God's next focus is to integrate you into the team of those willing to fulfill their community and citizenship duty that will bring about restoring equilibrium in the world, which is necessary for wholeness. As a newly healed 'born again' person, with a strong and stable relationship with the Lord, He will now show you how to fulfill your purpose in life and how to become a healer and a peacemaker at Jericho. Here, you will learn the art of successful peacemaking -- how to conquer and restore an unrighteous, corrupted and hurting land and people to a Kingdom-wellspring of life, health and joy. You will learn to work with the third person of the Trinity, the Holy Spirit, the Initiator and Enabler of every mission, to achieve this.

When God created humans, delegated them with the task of taking care of the land and ruling the other created beings, He was very happy at what He had accomplished. As time went by, though, He sadly had to witness the resultant disastrous consequences of humanity's continuously making bad choices, when they had better options. God lamented their unrepentant, irresponsible and unfaithful behavior, to the point of even regretting having created them, for there could be no restoration without repentance.

He always sought faithful and responsible sons and daughters, who would work with Him at restoring the people and the land. However, first He had to find people, who were willing to be fathered by Him and willing to change. As Father, He had to first bless before He could make the people and the land blessings to the nations and to Himself. How could He bless us if we were not willing to collaborate with Him? How could He teach us if we are unwilling to humble ourselves and learn new things? It's like trying to reform a homeless person, who is stubborn and 'stuck' in their ways.

God is constantly at work seeking to restore the land, nations and people to a perfect balance. In nature, He embedded sensors that unleash powerful homeostatic mechanisms with the sole purpose of restoring the errant component back into the synergistic and harmonious fold. The efforts of justice within society act very much in the same way to restore the trouble-making prodigals back into a peacemaking mold. We will learn from the lessons of the fall of Jericho how the Lord partners with us to transform the land, a city and a village, at a time. It is about learning how to solve problems, accomplish tasks, fulfill purposes, reach our destiny, attain vision and fulfill the Great Commission, together and in partnership with the Holy Spirit, rather than in our limited and divided humanness.

Many occasions in life and in ministry will occur, in which you can apply the spiritual principles you will learn in this Step, in order for you to become a successful peacemaker. There will be real people, situations and problems that transpire -- some small, some huge, some simple, some complex, some in which there seems to be hope while others seem hopeless and impossible, like Jericho might have appeared to be. However, all these issues need to be solved. Our Heavenly Father is the ultimate Problem Solver; '*all things are possible with Him*' (Matthew 19:26); nothing is impossible for Him. He desires to solve all of them with your help.

Let's first look at the text:

> *"When Joshua was near the town of Jericho, he looked up and saw a man standing in front of him with sword in hand. Joshua went up to him and demanded, "Are you friend or foe?" "Neither one," he replied. "I am the commander of the LORD's army." At this, Joshua fell with his face to the ground in reverence. "I am at your command," Joshua said. "What do you want your servant to do?" The commander of the LORD's army replied, "Take off your sandals, for the place where you are standing is holy." And Joshua did as he was told. Now the gates of Jericho were tightly shut because the people were afraid of the Israelites. No one was allowed to go out or in. But the LORD said to Joshua, "I have given you Jericho, its king, and all its strong warriors. You and your fighting men should march around the town once a day for six days. Seven priests will walk ahead of the Ark, each carrying a ram's horn. On the seventh day you are to march around the town seven times, with the priests blowing the horns. When you hear the priests give one long blast on the rams' horns, have all the people shout as loud as they can. Then the walls of the town will collapse, and the people can charge straight into the town."* (Joshua 5:13 - 6:21, NASB)

So, Joshua did what he had been told and walked around the city walls for six days.

"On the seventh day...they went around the town seven times... When the people heard the sound of the rams' horns, they shouted as loud as they could. Suddenly, the walls of Jericho collapsed, and the Israelites charged straight into the town and captured it. They completely destroyed everything in it with their swords—men and women, young and old, cattle, sheep, goats, and donkeys." (Joshua 5:13 - 6:21, NASB)

Jericho represents the gate of destructive forces working against God, the land and the people. We are told that "*the gates of hell shall not prevail against us*" (Matthew 16:18), which means that the opposing, adversarial forces of chaos shall not prevail against us. How to wage warfare effectively? Paul describes this spiritual warfare that leads to restoration like this:

"We are human, but we don't wage war as humans do. We use God's mighty weapons, not worldly weapons, to knock down the strongholds of human reasoning and to destroy false arguments. We destroy every proud obstacle that keeps people from knowing God. We capture their rebellious thoughts and teach them to obey Christ. And after you have become fully obedient, we will punish everyone who remains disobedient." (2 Corinthians 10:3-6, NLT)

So, in order to restore the land, we must first bind, and then overcome the operating forces of darkness in the land. We must wage spiritual warfare.

Elisha reminisces on his Journey to Jericho with Elijah

Elijah continued to walk briskly as if he was on an urgent errand. He never said a word, which suited me, as I was too engrossed in my own thoughts, speaking and singing in the power of the Holy Spirit. I was living an amazing moment and I was not going to waste this wonderful opportunity. Each place we had visited so far, Gilgal and Bethel, told me a lot about God's wonderful plan for me and humankind. I realize now that Israel is not the sole beneficiary of God's vision and blessings, but Israel was His first project and centerpiece. He was blessing Israel so that, in turn, the entire world would be blessed through Israel. What a fantastic plan! Our Heavenly Father is truly awesome! Father, teach me and tell me things I do not know. Amen!

My thoughts drifted to Jericho as we approached the city. It's hard to imagine that this was the same city that had been miraculously penetrated and completely wiped out by the Israelites under Joshua's leadership, over 500 years ago. Joshua's steps had been chosen and ordained by God. He was truly a man of God, for he had waited patiently for the Lord to tell him what to do, and when that moment had arrived, he treated His Messenger with the utmost respect. He had demonstrated the warrior attitude that is one of the characteristics of the anointing. As well, as he had rightly discerned that the Angel had been sent by the Lord, he proceeded to demonstrate the fear of the Lord before the Lord's representative. He then humbled himself, attentively listening to and carefully following every one of the instructions he was given.

If, and when, I have such an opportunity, I trust that I too will engage the Lord's Messenger respectfully and be fearless and reliable in carrying out my ordained duties. I understand the awesome responsibility of representing the Lord. I must be a true and faithful servant -- careful to discern messages from the Lord. I must never voice what is from my own heart as if it was from the Lord. I have seen and heard too many false prophets to know how troubling they are to the Lord and to the people they are supposed to be helping, guiding and teaching. Elijah has been a good example, teacher and guide. I am glad that the Lord chose me to be his apprentice. I have had many rich experiences walking with him. He has trained me well. I am not afraid to be God's prophet to His people and, even if He sends me to the nations, I will obey and go, for I know that He goes with me. Thank you, Heavenly Father, for placing your trust in me. I will be your true and reliable son. Amen!

As soon as I finished praying, *"the company of the prophets at Jericho"* came up to me and asked, *"Do you know that the LORD is going to take your master from you today?" "Yes, I know,"* I replied, *"so be quiet." Then Elijah said to me, "Stay here; the LORD has sent me to the Jordan."* (2 Kings 2:5-6)

MY STORY – CONTINUED ONCE MORE

In my own life, I recall my own growing concern with the situation around me and my equally growing realization that I was too fearful, immature and ill-prepared to do anything about it. As I look back on my life, I must acknowledge that the Lord was following His usual pattern of developing His children into successful peacemakers. He had called me when I was 12 years old and I said yes at 14. He immediately began working on my emotional health getting rid of my *baggage*. I began training with OM in the year I turned 20; that same year, I also began medical training, which lasted an entire decade. Throughout that decade, I did ministry training in my church, and experienced, many times, the moving of the Holy Spirit in my life, mostly in pastoral leadership, teaching, evangelism and altar ministry. I was 28, when I was called and ordained as a Pastor, at Igreja de Nova Vida de Tijuca (New Life Church) in Rio de Janeiro, Brazil. In my 30th year, I accepted the call, together with my beautiful wife, Rosane, to go on our first intercontinental transformational assignment with OM, as the (newly minted) Medical Officer, onboard the MV Doulos.

I boarded the ship in Hobart, Tasmania, Australia in 1989, and together with about 300 young men, women, some seniors and children, began my transformational assignment. Aside from the routine work of looking after this floating community on a loud (you can probably hear the generators from across the city), aging (just-as-old-as-the-Titanic) ship, the Douloids, as we were called, cried out to God in intercession, waged spiritual warfare, praised and thanked God daily, organized conferences, presented dramas, showed the Jesus movie and other videos, and proclaimed the Good News, both onboard (the main room could hold over 500 people) and on shore -- in churches, conference halls and open stadiums -- on a daily basis, to hundreds of thousands of people, over the course of the 17 months that we were onboard. We witnessed miracles, both in nature and in the thousands of those, who accepted Jesus as their own personal Savior and Lord, in response to the hundreds of altar calls.

In one instance, one of our outdoor meetings, attended by tens of thousands of people, in the Solomon Islands, was in danger of being washed out by a thunderstorm; so, one of our Korean brothers went up to the microphone and made a powerful plea for the rain to stop inside the stadium. It had stopped, even before he had finished praying, but it remained strong in the rest of the city. I was onboard the ship at the same time as the ship's captain was battling the strong winds and waves to dock the ship at the port. It had been anchored away from the dock awaiting permission to dock and had only received permission, just as the storm burst upon the city. That meeting continued and hundreds answered the call to consecrate their lives to the Lord. Such were the examples of working alongside the Holy Spirit to transform the land and the people.

Life flowed from the MV Doulos as it passed through Australia, Papua New Guinea, the Solomon Islands, Vanuatu, Fiji, Tonga, the Philippines, Indonesia, Malaysia, Thailand and Singapore. Christians were encouraged to stay faithful on their journey and hundreds went on to become missionaries within their own nations and elsewhere; many also joined the OM ships, Doulos and Logos 2. One of my fellow douloids, Kini Kila, from Papua New Guinea, later became the OM Director in that island nation. However, we were not pioneering in these places. Missionaries had been there before us and, together with the Lord, they had redeemed many of those island nations for the Kingdom of God. It was pleasant to see that almost the entire populations of some of those Pacific island nations were either Methodists or Presbyterians. The King of Tonga and the entire Kingdom of Tonga were practicing Christians.

Here are the lessons which God wanted Elisha and us to remember and learn from the conquest of Jericho.

YOUR JOURNEY --THE LIFE LESSONS –

Principles of Successful Peacemaking and Spiritual Leadership

You became a child of God when you were anointed by His Holy Spirit; and, it then became your responsibility to follow His lead, *"for those who are led by the Spirit of God are the children of God."* (Romans 8:14) Now that you are a leader, you must continue to be led by the Holy Spirit, for that is the hallmark of Spiritual leadership. In other words, your entire lifestyle and everything you do, in His service, must be Spirit-led, whether you are evangelizing, leading, pastoring, worshipping, prayer-walking, -driving, or praying for healing or deliverance. Throughout the rest of this book, we will explore how to implement and assure His leadership, whether you are an individual or a corporate body. First, though, the Lord wants you to divinely catch the vision of the land and its needs, so that, together, we can restore the land and the people.

Catch the Vision of the Land and Its People

The land had been corrupted by uncaring inhabitants and has been 'groaning' for relief and restoration. The victims among the people were crying out: *"Who will save us?" "Is there anyone who cares?"* Children were being sacrificed to demons and even thrown alive into fiery furnaces. God Himself was crying out, *"And I sought for a man among them who should build up the wall and stand in the breach before me for the land, that I should not destroy it, but I found none."* (Ezekiel 22:30, ESV)

Jesus was born into a world very much like the wretched state upon which came the Israelites. Israel had been occupied first by the Babylonians, then by the Medo-Persians, then by the Greeks and now by the Romans who practiced the same sort of pagan witchcraft and immorality that had corrupted the land and its people. For these reasons, the land and the people 'groaned' for their promised Savior, who not only fulfilled His peacemaking purpose, but also called, trained, empowered and commissioned His disciples to do the same: *"Therefore go and make disciples of all nations, baptizing them in the name of the Father and of the Son and of the Holy Spirit, and teaching them to obey everything I have commanded you. And surely I am with you always, to the very end of the age."* (Matthew 28:18-20)

This commission has come down to us today. It is everyone's duty to care for the land, beginning with their own neighborhood and city, in order to restore wholeness. Jesus, aware of our weaknesses, fears and gross indifference, on the one hand, and the need to align with God's headship, on the other, told his disciples to "*wait for the gift my Father promised"* (Acts 1:4) -- the Spirit's empowerment -- for just such an undertaking: *"But you will receive power when the Holy Spirit comes upon you. And you will be my witnesses, telling people about me everywhere—in Jerusalem, throughout Judea, in Samaria, and to the ends of the earth."* (Acts 1:8)

Now that you have caught the vision of the land and of the peoples' needs, you must prepare yourself for the Divine visitation as you wait on the moving of the Holy Spirit…

Prepare for the Divine Visitation While You Wait on the Holy Spirit

The Israelites were always told to clean up and **be ready for the Lord's visitation**: "*Then he said to them, "Listen to me, O Levites. Consecrate yourselves now, and consecrate the house of the LORD, the God of your fathers, and carry the uncleanness out from the holy place."* (2 Chronicles 29:5, NASB) They bathed themselves, put on clean clothes, repented of their sins, and removed any idols, or things that should be set apart for the Lord, such as, tithes. Jesus reminds us also to first forgive and reconcile, before He will act powerfully on our behalf. (Mark 11:22-25; cf. Matthew 5:23-24) Joshua's sandals were dirty as they had been in contact with the unclean environment, hence the command to remove them -- *"Take off your sandals, for the place where you are standing is holy."* This is symbolic of the removal of any uncleanness we may be harboring, including stopping whatever we are doing and giving our undivided attention to the Lord.

As the disciples awaited their Spiritual commissioning or ordination, they would have readied themselves for their anointing. Peter, of course, would have sought the Lord's forgiveness for his cowardice in denying the Lord before the people. Fifty days after Passover, at the right time and, without warning, they were filled with power -- "*All of them were filled with the Holy Spirit and began to speak in other tongues as the Spirit enabled them.*" (Acts 2:4) The disciples would have felt comforted, confident and full of Holy Spirit power and passion for service. What happened subsequently is described in Acts Chapter 2, when the Church was born, and with what power!

We must all learn to wait patiently for our divine ordination without grumbling or losing hope -- *"It is not for you to know the times or dates the Father has set by his own authority. But you will receive power when the Holy Spirit comes on you; and you will be my witnesses in Jerusalem, and in all Judea and Samaria, and to the ends of the earth."* (Acts 1:7-8) I recall my growing impatience at my own lack of anointing. I was aware that I needed to wait on the Lord's timing, but that was so difficult. I finally did decide to wait and not worry about it. Sometime later, at Church, I was filled with the Holy Spirit, speaking in tongues. I was ecstatic. I had finally experienced my own Pentecost. I was ordained for service in my Father's kingdom.

Subsequently, I have had similar ecstatic experiences. One of those occurred, one day, while I was watching TV. I suddenly began to pray in tongues. I immediately recognized the Lord's visitation, turned off the TV and focused on what was happening. I prayed for a few minutes and, as suddenly as it had started, it stopped. I just sat there wondering what had just happened. I asked for clarification and discerned that I had just prayed for the country of Indonesia. I was humbled by the whole experience and thanked the Lord for this wonderful opportunity to be of service. Later, that week there was an earthquake in that country.

Wait on the Spirit's Lead

Principle: God must lead, therefore, always wait on the moving of the Holy Spirit

Now that we have been ordained and empowered for service, we must be careful to await His moving, before we embark on any project. The Holy Spirit is our major partner in every project and we are the junior. As God is the initiator of every project, wait on Him to take the lead. Knowing the right moment to act is the key and a matter of spiritual discernment. Saul was told to wait upon Samuel before he attacked and was severely reprimanded for not doing so. As a result, he lost the battle, the Kingdom and the anointing. (1 Samuel 13:7-14) You cannot force the timing of God's visitation; it is His prerogative. Are you seeking and awaiting God's visitation and blessing? Are you about to engage with the Holy Spirit in some project? Then, consecrate yourself by heeding the Holy Spirit as He seeks to make you holy and successful at making true shalom (peace).

Now that the proper foundation is in place, you can proceed to build under His leadership. Key, from here on in, is that you learn to ...

Recognize the Time of God's Visitation and the Messenger's Divine Anointing

"I tell you the truth, anyone who welcomes my messenger is welcoming me, and anyone who welcomes me is welcoming the Father who sent me." (John 13:20, NLT)

"It is not for you to know the times or dates the Father has set by his own authority," (Acts 1:7) but it is essential that you recognize when it does happen. Joshua recognized the time of God's visitation by the angel. The Holy Spirit gives us the ability to know who is with us and who is against us. In this case, Joshua quickly discerned the angel as being sent by the Lord. How could one tell? *"This is how we know if they have the Spirit of God: If a person claiming to be a prophet acknowledges that Jesus Christ came in a real body, that person has the Spirit of God."* (1 John 4:2, NLT; cf. 2 John1:7; 1 Corinthians 12:3) Jeremiah stated that God's true spokesperson is one who enters into His presence, (Jeremiah 23:18,22) does not utter words of his or her own heart (Ezekiel 13:17-23) or by demonic inspiration (1 Kings 18:29), but utters words or acts on behalf of

the Lord (Isaiah 6:8; Jeremiah 1:7); upholds and teaches fidelity to the covenant with the Lord; (Deuteronomy 13:1-5; 18:19-20) and declares words or actions before they actually occur (Deuteronomy 18:21-22; Isaiah 46:1). The Lord Himself legitimizes them by accompanying signs and wonders. (Exodus 3:12; 4:5, 8, 17, 21, 28, 30; Isaiah 7:10-14; Psalm 74:9) The ecstatic manifestations (speaking in tongues, prophesying) accredited that the Messenger was inspired by the Holy Spirit, but these, by themselves, were not enough, as pagan worshippers also could demonstrate similar manifestations -- sometimes even accompanied by miraculous signs. (Exodus 7:11-12, 22; 8:7; cf. Deuteronomy 18:20-22; Jeremiah 14:14)

It is important to accurately discern the anointing by God's Spirit as mistakes can be considered blasphemy. When the Pharisees declared that Jesus was casting out demons by Beelzebub, he rebuked them,

> *"So I tell you, every sin and blasphemy can be forgiven -- except blasphemy against the Holy Spirit, which will never be forgiven. Anyone who speaks against the Son of Man can be forgiven, but anyone who speaks against the Holy Spirit will never be forgiven, either in this world or in the world to come."* (Matthew 12:31-32, NLT)

So, be careful before you write off God's true messengers and be even more careful before you wrongly categorize one of them as being a messenger from Satan.

Are all of God's representatives fully mature and perfect, making no mistakes in all their doings? No! When the Lord called the disciples (apprentices, trainees, students) and sent them out, Jesus knew they would be criticized for their immaturity, hence all the encouraging statements that He gave them. (John 13:20) These statements, directed at the disciples, are also meant for all recipients of divine actions and messages right down to today, in order that they would treat, what is sacred, with the necessary respect.

Even though, it is often tempting to criticize the ministers of God due to their weaknesses and imperfections, (whether they are true or not), I have learned to refrain from doing so. I see my own imperfections and am aware of my own weaknesses. I am sure others are also aware of their own, so it would be very discouraging to always be criticized. We are all God's projects. The Holy Spirit is constantly working to perfect us so that we become blameless representatives and so that we continuously grow into the fullness of God's image – Christ-likeness with the Father's heart. In the end, He will judge us righteously. The Lord taught me once that it is not my job to JUDGE, but only to HELP. I have tried ever since to refrain from criticizing and to help, wherever and whenever possible.

Quite often, we meet and hear of those who, are not only errant with regards to the way of righteousness, but also teach others that it is okay to practice unrighteousness. Notice that Jesus did not reject them, but simply called them 'the least in the Kingdom of heaven':

> *"Therefore anyone who sets aside one of the least of these commands and teaches others accordingly will be called least in the Kingdom of heaven, but whoever practices and teaches these commands will be called great in the Kingdom of heaven."* (Matthew 5:19)

As you develop in knowledge, understanding and maturity, Paul's words will, without a doubt, refer to you as well, as they did to me:

> *"Now we see things imperfectly, like puzzling reflections in a mirror, but then we will see everything with perfect clarity. All that I know now is partial and incomplete, but then I will know everything completely, just as God now knows me completely."* (1 Corinthians 13:12, NLT)

So, let's not be overly critical seeing that we too make the same mistakes, but let's be patient with one another, all the while, encouraging and helping one another, whenever we have the opportunity. We must learn from the geese travelling in their famous V-formation. They take turns leading and are always heard honking encouragement to the leader. When the Lord chooses someone for a specific task, who are we to criticize? He does not wait until we are perfect before He uses us but sends out students and trainees – '*even the least of these*'. Jesus' encouraging, but warning, words to his disciples (Matthew 10; John 13:20), as He sent them out, should leave no doubt that everyone should refrain from criticizing those He sends.

Also, we are not to criticize the women that the Lord ordains for service. Prophetesses, such as Deborah, Miriam and Huldah, represented God's leadership in the Old Covenant period. Jeremiah and Joel spoke of the future New Covenant (Jeremiah 31:31,33) when the universality of God's anointing would be independent of ethnicity, age, gender or social class:

> *"And afterward, I will pour out my Spirit on all people. Your sons and daughters will prophesy, your old men will dream dreams, your young men will see visions. Even on my servants, both men and women, I will pour out my Spirit in those days."* (Joel 2:28-29)

This anointing of the Spirit empowers and commissions every recipient to serve and lead, even women. Paul, himself, had been brought up in a patriarchal society, but acknowledged this anointing and learned to value one of these anointed women that he came across. Priscilla, the wife of Aquila, was mentioned first on several occasions as is customary when one supersedes the other in importance and leadership (Romans 16:3; 2 Tim.4:19), as opposed to the beginning of their acquaintance, when she is mentioned second. (Acts 18:2; 1 Corinthians 16:19) Luke also makes the shift from "*Aquila and Priscilla*" (Acts 18:2) to "*Priscilla and Aquila*". (Acts 18:18, 19)

What about the Lord's stipulation that "*your desire will be for your husband, and he will rule over you"?* (Genesis 3:16b) The rule certainly refers to the chain of command inside the home, so the question is: Should we extend that curse outside the home seeing that the Lord did not do so? Women certainly do have important responsibilities inside the home to care for the children, which is the practical reason why so many women are stay-at-home-moms. The children are better off when their mothers stay home rather than their being cared for by sitters. It is for this same reason that not many mothers are ordained to full-time ministry but are mightily used on a part-time basis. Some might argue that men are better equipped to lead, but the Lord said that *"it is not by power or by strength, but by my Spirit",* so it really doesn't matter. The Holy Spirit is both the means and the end to successful peace making. So, let's receive the women whom He will send because, in doing so, we are receiving the One who sent them. (John 13:20) Otherwise, you are '*scattering*' and being adversarial to what the Lord is doing: *"Anyone who isn't with me opposes me, and anyone who isn't working with me is actually working against me.*" (Matthew 12:30, NLT)

In this same regard, beware of moles. It's wise to know who is pulling with us and who is working against us. Our enemies are not just evil spirits, but also 'moles', who are inadvertently accepted into church membership and sit on church boards. They profess to be Christians but are not led by God's Spirit. They could have made insincere commitments and believe that they could deceive others into believing that they were Christians and entitled to leadership positions. They could have fallen away from their initial commitment, as I did at the beginning, and are no longer being led by the Holy Spirit. These are '*false prophets*', '*springs without water*', (2 Peter 2) '*hidden reefs in your love feasts*', '*clouds without water*', (Jude 1) and false 'Christians' or *'false prophets'* -- *"having a form of godliness but denying its power."* (2 Timothy 3:5) Freemasons and others involved in secret and occult societies, have been known to naively (or maliciously) infiltrate churches and their leadership boards, thinking that they could utilize their secular leadership skills. Moles will work against the Holy Spirit and you as they do not discern the will of God. They willfully usurp the leadership role of the Holy Spirit. They build Satan's Kingdom right in the middle of the church, when they are let in.

Strategic Planning: Goals, Objectives and Action Plans

The Messenger delivered the message that their first objective towards reaching the overall vision -- the capture of Jericho -- was '*fait accompli*' in heaven. Joshua could visualize the victory over Jericho even before it happened: "*I have delivered Jericho into your hands...*" (Joshua 6:2-5) This was not human visualization, but God-inspired; this was not positive thinking, but Spiritual envisioning. God enables us to see, through our Spiritual eyes, what is not visible to human sight. Victory was first achieved in heaven, before it was made-on-earth. So, we must always wait until the objective is secured in heaven, before we embark on it on earth.

Waiting on the Lord is the most difficult thing to do. I can understand King Saul's difficulty when he was told by Samuel to wait. I remember once during my days at Medical School when our Christian Fellowship group was considering whether to organize an event taking advantage of the visiting MV Doulos, with its team of about 300 people from all over the world. I went home that day determined to wait on the Lord for an answer. I knelt and told myself I would not arise, until I heard from the Lord what His wishes were. I was afraid though. What if God did not answer? What if He delayed? Could I stay on my knees for so long? I sincerely hoped that the Lord would answer me quickly. Fortunately, He did. I heard His voice telling us to go ahead and organize an event in which a ministry team from the ship would come and minister at the University. The next day, I met with Rubecy and the rest of the group to relay what I had heard. Everyone was fired up. We organized the event. The team came and ministered to the students. It was a great success, especially for me, as I had learned that waiting on the Lord was worthwhile!!! He did not let me down and I had obeyed an important principle – that every project must be Spirit-led, -initiated and -inspired. AMEN!

He also gave Joshua specific instructions on how to accomplish the task. When the Lord finished creating the world He said, "*It is very good.*" His entire creation was synergistic and in perfect balance. It was a 'well-oiled machine'. This synergism and balance must be maintained, thus the need for us to fit into God's strategic plan, not Him into ours. God`s instructions, on how to conduct ourselves, are the best way possible. No human expert can do any better. In fact, any changes to God`s plan will result in failure or loss of quality, that is, they will fall short of the glorious outcome that God intended. (Romans 3:23) Even minor changes will have the same disastrous outcome.

Jesus admonished his disciples to "*Be perfect (complete) therefore as your Heavenly Father is perfect*" (Matthew 5:48), so we can all enjoy the intended glorious outcome; for whatever is done, must be aligned with the Divine order, as well as, with the natural order. Therefore, we are not to subtract or add anything, for any reason. Many go their own way as they or others are not comfortable with some aspect of God's plan. They may even feel they have to implement human changes to make it more politically correct. Jesus called these '*human rules*' and quoted the prophet Isaiah in warning us that any changes dishonor God. (Matthew 18:7-9; cf. Isaiah 29:13) Self-righteousness is when one believes that one's plan is better than God`s or they implement a plan or rule that is different from His.

So, to obtain success, we must carefully record and carry out all His instructions, paying careful attention to every detail. Jesus was very careful to obey all His Father said -- "*So, whatever I say is just what the Father has told me to say*" (John 12:49-50); *"I do exactly what my Father has commanded me to do."*

(John.14:31) It should leave no doubt in our minds the importance of diligently recording every one of the Lord's instructions for a mistake can nullify a glorious outcome. I often receive instructions for sermons, etc. during my early morning devotions. I have learned not to rely on my memory, but to immediately get a notepad, which I keep handy at my bedside, and write down everything. Today, I use the notepad on my cell phone.

Prayer walking (driving, riding), 24-hour and all-night prayer vigils, Houses of Prayer, etc. are all ways of seeking insights and leadership from the Lord. *'Spiritual Mapping'*, a term coined by George Otis in the '90s and described in more detail in his book 'The Last of the Giants' (1990), Tom White's 'Breaking Strongholds' (1993), Hawthorne and Kendrick's 'Prayer Walking: Praying On Site with Insight' (1993) and Peter Wagner's 'Breaking Strongholds in Your City' (1997) – all seek to make area-specific assessments regarding strengths, weaknesses, opportunities and threats and to discern peace making strategies, goals, objectives and action plans from the Holy Spirit.

I was fortunate to be part of the North Toronto Pastors and Leaders gathering under the leadership of Alvin Koh that is currently organizing 24-hour prayer vigils across Toronto. These churches volunteer to provide worship leadership for two-hour slots over a 24-hour period once a month. These 24-hour prayer vigils will certainly have a lasting impact on Toronto and the GTA. Houses of Prayer are popping up in cities around the world. Men and women are tirelessly standing in the gap for their cities and regions for which the Church must be extremely grateful. Here, in Mississauga, Bill Koene at The Dwelling, and others, stand in the gap. If we, the church, do not stand in the gap for the cities who will? Hillel, the Elder said it best, *"If not you, then who? If not now, then when"*. "May there be Houses of Prayer in every city of the world. In Jesus' Name, Amen!"

Let's examine the Ark of the Covenant and what it symbolized to Israel and to us, today.

Principles of Corporate Worship

It is interesting to note the Trinitarian symbolism of the Ark of the Covenant. The Almighty God sat on the throne above the cherubim. In the Ark, were the tablets of the Ten Commandments that symbolized Jesus Christ, the Word of God, as well as, the symbols of Israel's experiential dealings with God's Holy Spirit -- Aaron's budding rod and the bowl of 'manna'. We are to:

1. Submit to Yahweh's (God's) Leadership
2. Live and Minister by His Righteous Standards
3. Cherish the Father's Heart Experiences

SUBMIT TO YAHWEH'S (GOD'S) LEADERSHIP

"Take up the Ark of the LORD's Covenant and assign seven priests to walk in front of it, each carrying a ram's horn... the priests continually blowing the horns."

God instructed Joshua to have the priests take up the Ark of the Covenant. The Ark was more than just a symbolic depiction of God sitting on His throne and carried by the Holy Cherubim. (Exodus 25:1-22; cf. Ezekiel 1:22-28; 10:1, 18-19) It was a true depiction of what was transpiring -- the Almighty God sat on the throne and was leading His people into battle, hence "*whenever the Ark set out, Moses would shout, "Arise, O LORD, and let your enemies be scattered! Let them flee before you!"* (Numbers 10:35, NLT; cf. Psalm 68:1-2). Thus, it occupied a central place in the procession around the walls of Jericho. The priests went before it, blasting away on the shofars (rams' horns/trumpets) and proclaiming His Magnificent Presence. The warriors went in front and behind and the people followed. This whole imagery perfectly symbolizes the central position that the Kingdom of God must occupy in our corporate life and affairs, like how the Sun, as the head, occupies a central place, with the planets and moons revolving around it. God is

Ruler of Heaven and Earth, therefore, true worship places the entire corporate body and structure in submission. In contrast, rebellion is adversarial, akin to the '*sin of witchcraft*'. As in everything in life, there is a proper way to walk with the Lord, to ensure that He occupies His proper position as God, King of Kings and Lord of Lords.

In the next Step, we will look at the instructions that God gave Israel, through Moses, to ensure that the corporate leadership structure allows God to occupy His central position in everything that we do. Successful peacemaking cannot occur unless we proclaim and assure God's leadership over us, the project, the people and the land. He is King of the Kingdom of heaven and earth and therefore the Initiator and Finisher of every project. He lays out the overall vision and mission, the goals and objectives, and the action plans that we are to carefully implement.

Create an Atmosphere of Praise and Worship

Principle: Creating an Atmosphere of Praise and Worship proclaims God's leadership and unleashes the Heavenly Armies

Every time Israel went to war, the Levites carried the Ark of the Covenant, played musical instruments and sang songs or psalms of praise, adoration and thanksgiving to the Lord. This act of proclamation, enacted by the priests blowing the shofars, created an ambience of worship that was fitting, for He and His Army of Angels were engaging in spiritual warfare on their behalf; besides being a very pleasing act to Him. He leads us into every battle and thus deserves the glory for every victory. The armies of heaven fought on behalf of the Lord and His people and overcame their enemies, both evil spirits and people. Its power to dispel the adversaries was displayed when David played the harp for King Saul, when he was oppressed by an evil spirit. Saul literally found relief from the demonic oppression. (1 Samuel 16:23).

First Bind the Strong One Before You Steal His Property

Should you intentionally engage in spiritual warfare? Yes, because problems are not just man-made; they are also devil-made. Unfortunately, our adversaries are not just human; they are unseen spiritual forces of darkness that are constantly at work against us and the common good. The latter must be dealt with first, before we can deal with our human adversaries. Jesus taught: *"No one can go into a strong man's house and steal his property. First he must tie up the strong man. Then he can go through the strong man's house and steal his property."* (Mark 3:27, GWT) So, we must be proactive and prevent problems by standing in the gap, both for ourselves and for others -- binding, rebuking and casting out, and asking Yahweh Sebaoth to rebuke and cast out, as well. While some evil spirits might not respond to our rebuke, they will certainly respond when they see our two-pronged defense/assault.

Principle: Victory is first achieved in the spirit world before it is achieved in the physical.

Exercising our God-given authority with confidence grows over time. Take the first step, as I did, with mountain-moving prayer. I recall the first time I had to engage in spiritual warfare by myself. On my way to the OM base, I saw a family friend, who I was in the process of evangelizing, drunk outside a bar; so, I took her home. Upon arriving at home, she fell to the ground and a strange sounding voice began talking about her in the third person. I immediately discerned that she was possessed by an evil spirit or by multiple spirits. It was certainly nerve-wracking, but I knew, without a shadow of a doubt, that I had His authority to cast out evil spirits (Matthew 10:1-8). The situation demanded that I act and not abandon the friend. I immediately asked her two teenage daughters, who were home, to sing worship songs and create a worship environment. Then, I proceeded to rebuke the evil spirits. I hardly had any experience and must have demonstrated a lack of authority in my voice, because the evil spirits began to mock me saying that they had left. This went on for about an hour and after seeking the Lord's help, I angrily commanded the evil spirits to leave and requested that the Lord cast them out into the Abyss. Finally, she 'awoke' from her stupor and I knew that the battle was won. We all gave thanks to the Lord and I left to retake my journey to the OM base, where we were meeting for discipleship training.

One church, in Brazil, The Universal Church of the Kingdom of God, was especially effective in spiritual warfare. They called out and cast out the spiritual forces of darkness that were actively engaged in oppressing Cariocas (the people of Rio). They challenged the notion that you shouldn't call out evil spirits, but instead did what the prophet Elijah did in 1 Kings 18:19. They freely distributed Christian literature that taught Brazilians about the dangers of Santeria-style witchcraft, which was prevalent in the nation. Yes, they endured a lot of persecution from the media, politicians and even from segments of the Church, but they were right, and the Lord was with them.

Principle: An atmosphere of worship releases the 'river of life-giving water'

Praise and worship not only please the Lord but release the transformational and life-giving power of the River of God. Keith Duncan in his book, 'The Throne Zone: A Worship Revolution', speaks at length about the awesomeness of entering God's Throne Room through uplifting adoration. He emphasizes that the lyrics that please the Lord are not those directed at us (teaching, calling, and evangelizing), but rather the ones that offer praise, thanksgiving and adoration to an awesome God sitting on His throne. As people worship in the Throne Zone, the angels join in and the river of healing, deliverance, transformation, salvation and revival is released in awesome power and grace. An eruption of freedom takes place as people are saved, delivered, healed and revived.

I recall, in those years, there was an urge to gather and pray throughout the night. Many times, together with other youth, we would gather for all-night prayer and worship *vigilias* (vigils). The atmosphere of praise and worship, it created in Rio, paved the way for the revival, which I will call the Rio Blessing, similar to the Toronto Blessing that emanated from the Airport Church (now called Catch the Fire). The transformations observed in society were astounding. It became 'cool' to be an *evangélico (*a Christian believer*).* Professional athletes, the social elite from the entertainment industry, Catholics, *macumbeiros* and *candomblistas* (Santeria-style witches and wizards) were all converting in droves. The world-renowned Rio Carnival Samba schools began to complain because they were losing their dancers, singers and musicians to the Evangelical churches. Many were called into politics, and today, there is a strong evangelical bloc of influential politicians, in the various Government bodies.

True Worshippers allow the Holy Spirit to Inspire Worship

When Jesus told the Samaritan woman:

> *"Yet a time is coming and has now come when the true worshipers will worship the Father in the Spirit and in truth, for they are the kind of worshipers the Father seeks. God is spirit, and his worshipers must worship in the Spirit and in truth."* (John 4:23-24)

He was referring to the style of worship that was aided and empowered by the Holy Spirit. The Holy Spirit, our Helper, should be the Distinguished Guest at every gathering. He helps us to worship the Lord in a manner that is befitting His glory. He knows how and when to praise the Lord, in a way that is becoming the truth of His Highness, as He *"will glorify Me because it is from Me that he will receive what he will make known to you."* (John16:14) As the Spirit knows when something is done in the heavenlies, He appropriately moves us to worship the Lord, at times when we least expect. He helps us worship with words that truly represent the occasion -- words that truly extol the Lord for His actions and character. (Psalm 29:2; 96) We offer praise, thanksgiving and adoration to the Lord for what He has done, is doing and will do. Spirit-empowered praise is the highest form of worship and is manifest as speech or singing in tongues or in one's own language: "*All of them were filled with the Holy Spirit and began to speak in other tongues as the Spirit enabled them...How is it...(for) we hear them declaring the wonders of God in our own tongues!*" (Acts 2:4, 11)

So, it is unfortunate that some churches have even enacted policies that prohibit any ecstatic manifestation, for these reasons:

The teaching that the spiritual gifts ceased upon the death of the last apostle and hence any such manifestation is fake. Jesus commanded his disciples to teach "*everything I have commanded you*" (Matthew 28:20a), which would include the command to wait "*until you have been clothed with power from on high.*" (Luke 24:49b) The apostles did not leave out, nor deny, this essential work of the Holy Spirit in the life of the church. Speaking or singing in tongues or prophesying, as it was referred to in the Old Testament (1Samuel 10:5, 10; 19:20; Ephesians 5:19; 1 Corinthians 14:15), was a normal component of every minor and major revival in the history of the Church and should never be discouraged. This is highly disrespectful to the Head of the Church, besides being an act of rebellion. I cannot be more forceful in exposing the danger of blasphemy here for "*anyone who speaks a word against the Son of Man will be forgiven, but anyone who speaks against the Holy Spirit will not be forgiven, either in this age or in the age to come.*" (Matthew 12:32)

The fear that it could be demon-inspired or of human origin. When these do occur, you must deal appropriately with each -- cast out the demon and free the oppressed person, in the former scenario, and, in the latter, teach that it is deceptive to mimic Spirit-inspired prophetic speech, even if you have had previous genuine experiences.

Some argue that it is disorderly. While this can be considered so from a human stand point, it is not true from a Spiritual one. The Spirit, as the Head, has the right to intervene at any time. While this might disrupt the Minister's plans or increase the duration of the service, the Spirit's intervention should always be welcomed, and contingency plans made beforehand. Churches, where the Spirit is free to act, have contingency plans in place for these special occasions and wisely know when to stop and when to carry on while the Spirit is edifying. The Spiritual gift is the individual's strength. It gives the person credibility that the Holy Spirit is involved. Therefore, we should never discriminate against the 'perpetrator', but rather celebrate the person's strengths, as this brings a Spiritual dimension to the service that can only benefit and edify the entire body.

It disrupts the unity of the Church or organization. The Body of Christ is composed of people of all levels of maturity and, therefore, everyone, especially those expressing Spiritual gifts, must be valued for what they have to offer. The habit of reverse discriminating against those with Spiritual gifts does disrupt the unity of the Body. In discriminating against the anointing, you are also rejecting the Anointer. Therefore, do not resist the Holy Spirit or limit Him in any way, but allow His Spirit-empowered praise in all its ecstatic glory. Encourage those who are moved by the Spirit and hope that it will spread like wildfire, releasing streams of life-giving water into the church and community.

Passionate Spirituality

As we allow the Holy Spirit to empower and enrich the church, we will observe a passionate Spirituality developing in the congregation. Spontaneous raising of the arms in reverence, clapping and other bodily expressions should not be considered irreverent, but rather highly pleasing to the Lord.

New Compositions are a result of this passionate Spirituality. *"Praise the LORD! Sing to the LORD a* ***new song****."* (Psalm 149:1, NLT; cf. Revelation 4:3) The Lord greatly enjoys the praises of His people. New songs, when Holy Spirit-inspired, are expressions of renewal by the Holy Spirit and, therefore, right and acceptable. It is not right to discard the new because "*the old is better*" or vice versa, as some feel. If they are acceptable to the Lord, then we should receive them as such. Songs are for the Lord not for people. The Psalms were ancient songs – Spirit breathed to David and others. They were acceptable to the Lord as they originated from God's faithful children as they were moved by the Holy Spirit. Therefore, avoid man-made traditions -- singing only hymns and not allowing choruses or contemporary songs -- for they are displeasing to the Lord. *"You have let go of the commands of God and are holding on to traditions of men."* (Mark 7:8) Don't despise what the Holy Spirit is doing or count it as garbage as that is blasphemous. Keep the old but encourage the new.

Dance… *"Praise his name with dancing."* (Psalm 149:3a, NLT; cf. 2 Samuel 6:12-15, 20-23) Here again, the Lord shows pleasure in His children who dance as part of their passionate and worshipful praise offering to Him. Dance was always a part of traditional Jewish worship (and still is), yet it was ostracized in the Church for many centuries, as it was considered too emotional and therefore irreverent. When Michal, David's wife, criticized his emotional worship as irreverent, she was reprimanded. Fortunately, it is slowly returning and should be a staple aspect of worship for it is a display of passionate worship that is highly pleasing to the Lord.

Musical Instruments... and with all sorts of musical instruments. "*Praise him with a blast of the ram's horn; praise him with the lyre and harp! Praise him with the tambourine and dancing; praise him with strings and flutes! Praise him with a clash of cymbals; praise him with loud clanging cymbals.*" (Psalm 150:3-5, NLT; cf. Psalm 149:3) The Lord rejoices in the use of all musical instruments. While those were the traditional ones of those days, any of our current musical instruments can be utilized to offer praise and worship. They are the tools with which one worships. I don't see any church utilizing the old instruments today; organs and pianos are not original: the organ was said to have been invented in the 200's BC, while the piano only appeared in the 17th century AD. So, again, keep the old without despising the new. Even my father plays the Congo drums in the service – to the glory of God!

Yahweh is the Head and the One who sits on the throne. This is the cornerstone of the foundation on which the Church is built. The second symbol of the Ark of the Covenant is the Word of God.

LIVE AND MINISTER BY HIS RIGHTEOUS STANDARDS

"Similarly, anyone who competes as an athlete does not receive the victor's crown except by competing according to the rules." (2 Timothy 2:5)

Principle: Successful peace making happens when you act according to the rules.

The second person of the Trinity, "*the Word of God, became flesh and dwelt among us*" (John 1:14). Jesus Christ was the embodiment of righteousness displayed in both the living and the written Logos as well as the spoken Rhema. The Ark of the Covenant contained the Ten Commandments, the Law, which codified behavior that transgressed the way of righteousness -- the first three revealed transgressions against God and the last seven, sins against self and others. As these were built into the fabric of nature when God created the heavens and the earth, all have repercussions on the land. The rules of engagement of the way of righteousness differentiate love from hate and right from wrong. They protect the natural balance and synergy in the systemic, interconnected Kingdom of God. I will explore this further in the next Step. Therefore, everything, including successful peace making and true worship are to be done '*according to the rules.*' Hudson Taylor declared, *"God's work done in God`s way will never lack God`s support."*

The third symbol of the Ark of the Covenant…

CHERISH THE FATHER'S HEART EXPERIENCES

The Third Person of the Trinity, the Holy Spirit, engaging with us daily, like a mother, results in Divine experiences. The Ark of the Covenant contained symbols of the Israelites' experiences: Aaron's budding rod and a bowl of manna.

Principle: Successful peace making happens when you incorporate the lessons learned from past Divine experiences, whether yours or of others.

Aaron's budding rod reminded the Israelites (and us) to listen to those whom the Lord sends and places over us because "*whoever listens to you listens to me, and whoever rejects you, rejects me, and whoever rejects me, rejects The One who sent me."* (Luke 10:16)

The Pot of Manna was a sign of the Spirit's watchful care and provision. It was a reminder to rest in God's compassionate

Fatherly care. We are told in Psalm 46, "*Calm yourself and know that I am God*". (Psalm 46:10) We are not to be anxious about the necessities of life. God will provide even before you have need of them. Whenever you are aware of the need, ask with thanksgiving and praise and expect in '*quietness and confidence*', for He cares for you and is faithful.

Furthermore, obey His instructions and…

Stay Away from Things that are Consecrated to the Lord

Principle: Stay away from things that work against you.

As you engage in ministry, you will undoubtedly be at risk of being contaminated by the sins of the people to whom you are ministering. The people of Jericho were steeped in pagan idolatry, which was called abominable by the Lord and prohibited, because of its dangers.

> *"When you come to the land that the LORD your God is giving you, never learn the disgusting practices of those nations. You must never sacrifice your sons or daughters by burning them alive, practice black magic, be a fortune teller, witch, or sorcerer, cast spells, ask ghosts or spirits for help, or consult the dead. Whoever does these things is disgusting to the LORD. The LORD your God is forcing these nations out of your way because of their disgusting practices. You must have integrity [in dealing] with the LORD your God. These nations you are forcing out listen to fortune tellers and to those who practice black magic. But the LORD your God won't let you do anything like that." (*Deuteronomy 18:9-14, GWT)

When an item is associated with idol worship it becomes a point-of-contact with the evil spirit world, a breach in your wall of defense, through which evil spirits can come into your life, home or organization, to oppress and harass you. It is, therefore, no wonder that the Lord told the Israelites to destroy everything. When Achan did not follow God's instructions and kept back some items for himself, he brought a curse upon the whole nation. He, and all his family, became accursed and lost their lives. (Joshua 7) Israel lost the subsequent battle and the partnership with God that could not be regained, except through repentance:

> *"Get up! Command the people to purify themselves in preparation for tomorrow. For this is what the LORD, the God of Israel, says: Hidden among you, O Israel, are things set apart for the LORD. You will never defeat your enemies until you remove these things from among you."* (Joshua 7:13, NLT)

Metallic objects, which could be purified by fire, were to be given to the priests, who had the divine power and authority to decontaminate them. *"Everything made from silver, gold, bronze, or iron is sacred to the LORD and must be brought into his treasury."* (Joshua 6:19) Items that could not be purified by fire were to be destroyed. Every Israelite king was encouraged to destroy all items of idolatry if they wanted to have Yahweh as their Savior and God. Gideon was told to first *"Tear down your father's altar dedicated to the god Baal and cut down the pole dedicated to the goddess Asherah that is next to it. Then, in the proper way, build an altar to the LORD your God on top of this fortified place."* (Judges 6:25-26) The *candomblistas* and *macumbeiros,* who were heavily engaged in witchcraft, in Brazil, renounced the same destroying all articles of witchcraft before they could experience the fullness of the healing and transforming power of God's Holy Spirit. When the people of Ephesus saw the destructive power of witchcraft, *"many who became believers confessed their sinful practices. A number of them who had been practicing sorcery brought their incantation books and burned them at a public bonfire. The value of the books was several million dollars."* (Acts 19:18-19, NLT)

As I mentioned, I was oppressed by nightmares as a child and teenager. I had been warned by the Lord about these points-of-contact and prohibited from watching films, reading books, playing video games or any games associated with witchcraft. However, once, I inadvertently watched a movie that I had thought was an innocent documentary about a youth oppressed by evil spirits. I couldn't sleep that night as I was attacked by an evil spirit. I rebuked and cast it out, to no avail. When I asked the Lord why this was happening, He chastised me for my disobedience. At once, I repented and asked for His forgiveness. I immediately felt relief and peace, thanked the Lord and fell fast asleep. Today, I am extra cautious and obedient to the Holy Spirit.

Today there is a fascination with the occult -- from items of idolatry brought back while on vacation to Santeria-endemic Cuba; to video games with villain role playing; to films, such as, The Exorcist; to games, such as, the Ouija Board, Dungeons and Dragons; and, to books, such as, the popular Harry Potter series. It's wise to stay away from everything that pertains to the occult or witchcraft as they open the door of opportunity for evil spirits to invade your life and harass or oppress you. They are the main reason for the psychotic features in many psychiatric (DSM-V) disorders. The Lord warns us today not to follow in the sins of past congregations, Pergamum and Thyatira, whose leadership tolerated the abominable sins of witchcraft and sexual immorality, or else "*I... will fight against them with the sword of my mouth*" and "*I will strike her children dead*". (Revelation 2:16,23)

Principle: Do not take what belongs to the Lord.

"Will a man rob God? Yet you are robbing Me! But you say, 'How have we robbed You?' In tithes and offerings." (Malachi 3:8, NASB)

Taking what belongs to the Lord is foolish and will result in a curse (Joshua 7; cf. Malachi 3:9) rather than in the promised abundant blessings. The giving of tithes and offerings is an opportunity to share voluntarily in the community (ecosystem), which also cares for you and shares its resources with you. It is a natural responsibility and a spiritual act of obedience -- an act of love towards those who dedicate their time to work for the Lord. Do you want to restore your broken relationship with your Heavenly Father? Then first, you must repent by paying the tithes that you have withheld.

> *"Bring the whole tithe into the storehouse, that there may be food in my house. Test me in this," says the LORD Almighty, "and see if I will not throw open the floodgates of heaven and pour out so much blessing that there will not be room enough to store it. I will prevent pests from devouring your crops, and the vines in your fields will not drop their fruit before it is ripe," says the LORD Almighty. "Then all the nations will call you blessed, for yours will be a delightful land," says the LORD Almighty."* (Malachi 3:10-12)

Moreover, we are expected to offer the **first fruits** of our labor to Him, even as Abel and the Israelites did. This is pleasing to the Lord and will bring enormous benefits.

If you wish to see the Lord work powerfully on your behalf, then cleanse yourselves, and continuously repent and take advantage of the blood of the Lamb. Forgive, forget and reconcile, stay away from accursed things, and do not withhold your tithe, but release it and your first fruits to the Lord, in a timely manner. (See also Mark 11:20-26) In this way, you will be holy and pure, ready to engage God's Holy Spirit, and witness His awesome transformational power at work, in and through your life.

The Bible is full of these divine teaching opportunities, so by reading and meditating on them, you can learn valuable lessons for every situation. It is vitally important to study each one of these lessons and meditate on them continually, day and night. Then, integrate each lesson into your (corporate) lifestyle. They will make you wise, a valuable teacher in the land and a blessing to all the families of the earth.

These experiences or epiphanies are proof that God was/is with you. These personal and corporate experiences with God are yours: seen with your own eyes or heard by your own ears; they are not the experiences of others, only yours. They cannot be taken away, but they can be forgotten; so, you should write them down and meditate on them constantly to keep them fresh in your memory. They will go far to enhance your current experience with the Holy Spirit, your Helper. You must regularly remind the people of these valuable lessons in order to preserve your corporate health. As you proclaim God as your Head and obey His every instruction, …

Walk in Unity

"All the men of war" and "All the people shout as loud as they can."

Two considerations must be explored in successful peace making:

1. Synergy is key
2. A role for everyone

Synergy is Key

Synergy is a key aspect of our ecosystem and of the Kingdom of God because it maintains wholeness (unity). Whatever your role is, synergy is expected -- with the Holy Spirit, as well as, among individuals and between institutions.

Whenever, in unity, the Israelites engaged their enemies, they were successful; but when they were divided, they failed. When they all shouted as one, at Joshua's command, the walls of Jericho fell flat and they all could go forward, in one accord, to conquer the city -- *"Do not shout; do not even talk," Joshua commanded. "Not a single word from any of you until I tell you to shout. Then shout!"* (Joshua 6:10, NLT) When most of the leaders rebelled against God and Moses by refusing to enter the Promised Land because of their fear and gross indifference, God respected their collective decision. They remained in the desert for 40 years, instead of only one year. Later, when the two and a half tribes had already received their inheritance, they were reminded of the need for unity and synergy as they had to assure that all the other tribes would first possess their inheritance before they returned to their own families and inheritance. (Numbers 32:20-23; Deuteronomy 3:20)

Just as the Israelites often divided themselves along tribal lines, so does the Church today along denominational, ethnic and language lines. Notwithstanding, the Great Commission is our God-given and Holy Spirit-led responsibility, so the Church must come together as one to restore God's Kingdom -- territory by territory. Alistair Petrie summed up this need nicely when he said: *"There is a greater need today for territorial rather than denominational alignments."* Again, this issue will be explored further in the next Step.

A Role for Everyone

Principle: Success comes when all the valiant peacemakers engage in the project and stems from **T.E.A.M**. (**T**ogether **E**veryone **A**ccomplishes **M**ore)

"Anyone who isn't with me opposes me, and anyone who isn't working with me is actually working against me." (Matthew 12:30, NLT)

There is a role for the valiant peacemakers (frontline workers) and for the rest of the people. While the valiant warriors (pastors, evangelists, marketplace ministers, and missionaries, of today) marched with the Ark and the priests every day, the rest of the people only came into the picture on the last day, when they were commanded to shout at the sounding of the long shofar blast. God defeated the Midianites through Gideon's much down-sized army of 300 fearless and valiant warriors, while the rest completed the victory. (Judges 7)

Our role is to go forth and possess the land, not just the land of Israel, but the entire earth, and restore its rebellious people and corrupted land to His righteous ways, to wholeness and to its rightful King and Owner, the Almighty God. In the kingdom of God (and in the ecosystem, as you will see in the next Step) by-standing is not appropriate. You either work for the whole or you work against it. There is no such thing as sitting on the fence. Those who do so are working against God and the common good. If you do not respond favorably then you are a troublemaker.

You cannot be a bystander unconcerned with the needs of the community and of your Father's Kingdom -- meaning you cannot be more concerned with your own entertainment and business ventures or building your own empire. You should not care how you look or what university degrees you have or don't have. Rather, you must care about what you do with them -- all your resources and strengths – and with the Holy Spirit to pacify your household, your extended family, the community and the environment. Whether you are a valiant front worker or not, you have an important part to play in Kingdom of God service. We are all called to be peacemakers. That's what it means to be a peacemaker, repairer of the breach, salt of the earth and lamp of the world.

Bystanders have no place in God's Kingdom nor in the ecosystem. God, through Deborah, criticized all those who "*did not come to help the LORD -- to help the LORD against the mighty warriors.'* (Judges 5:23) Many did not help due to fear. If God is with you, then do not fear your enemies. Place your entire trust in the Almighty God, your Heavenly Father, and you will experience His mighty support. In everything, you must stand firm in your trust in Him, if you are to be supported, for He is more than able. (2 Chronicles 20:20; Isaiah 7:9) Many did not help the Lord due to plain indifference. They did not care. They were more concerned with their own affairs or business than with helping God or the common good or the community.

Jesus blamed this same indifference in the Parable of the Dinner (Luke 14:16-24) as the reason why people lost their opportunity to spend eternity with Him. You are gifted with the Holy Spirit for the purpose of engaging with Him in Kingdom business and work for the common good. He is there to help you with every responsibility you have so you are without excuse.

CONCLUSION

The image of the Ark of the Covenant's occupying a central position in the social infrastructure is like that portrayed by the Sun in our Solar System, wherein the planets, with its respective moons, revolve around it. Jacob's vision at Bethel confirmed this portrait of God presiding over a systemically interconnected Kingdom of Heaven and Earth – the whole. He rules in Heaven and Earth just as He placed the Sun to rule over the planets. The order replicated here is the exact same order that we must acknowledge and place ourselves in, wholeheartedly, both individually and corporately, if we are to succeed at anything in life or in ministry. Whether it is life, evangelism, ministry or leadership, it must be Spirit-led to be truly effective. This is the essence of life in God's Kingdom.

God sent the Israelites to the Promised Land at one of its worst times, when it needed and longed for redemption and renewal. Jesus, our Savior, came to the same land when it was suffering under the violent occupation of the pagan Roman Empire. Similarly, we too live in a broken and fallen world. Together, we must work to restore our broken and fallen world to wholeness and to the way of righteousness. Your purpose in life is to work with God and those He places around you to be a blessing to all the families of the earth. As we live in an interconnected world, we cannot achieve wholeness without restoring our habitat. This is restorative justice. All of us has the responsibility, whether as an individual or as a corporate body, to effect justice in the world under the Spirit's leadership. Doing it well by respecting the order is, therefore, of prime importance; for lives depend on it.

In the Parable of the Ten Minas, Jesus tells us to bear fruit, that is, to engage in Kingdom business, until His return. Therefore, let's fulfill our responsibilities in life utilizing the gifts provided, that is, our strengths, and following His principles, so we can enjoy the fruit of our labor. Catch His vision and carefully walk in tandem with His Holy Spirit and you will become a successful peacemaker and a blessing to the nations. It is your duty, not only to yourself, as you will see, but to your family, to the community (common good) and to the entire Kingdom of God.

Now, that you have been healed at Gilgal and learned and understood His and your rights and responsibilities within the framework of His paternalistic covenant at Bethel, you can now return to carrying out all those responsibilities in life. At Jericho, you came to learn and understand how to do so successfully. Our Heavenly Father is the Chief Peacemaker and you and all His children are His helpers. He anointed you with His Holy Spirit, so you can work synergistically with Him and with all His other children for the common good of all. Now, we will proceed to the Jordan River where you will understand the principles that will allow you to thrive in the land.

STEP FOUR

THE JORDAN RIVER: TO THRIVE IN OUR SYSTEMIC WORLD – UNDERSTANDING NATURAL LAW

I hope you have caught God's vision as it has been laid out so far. I pray you have understood the essence of the lessons taught at Gilgal, Bethel and Jericho and laid hold of each one. They each fulfill an important purpose in your restorative journey -- you have benefitted from the restorative work of the Savior at Gilgal; experienced the Father's heart and reinforced your new identity as God's sons and daughters at Bethel; and, learned to engage with the Holy Spirit and the community in fulfilling your peacemaking purpose in life at Jericho. Now, you will catch the rest of the vision of life and learn to thrive, both as an individual and as a corporate body, at the Jordan River.

River basins are typically where communities thrive, as a river is the source of life-giving water. This Step will complete the vision the Lord is revealing to us all and show you how to thrive in the land and in His Kingdom. It will shed light on many of life's truths and clarify many spiritual principles. Understanding these will allow you to engage life more intelligently and make the wise choices that are before us all. If you are in a leadership position in society, this will only result in a greater benefit for the common good. I wish all leaders would understand the principles here revealed and explained. It was important for Elisha, groomed to be an important leader in his time, to understand, as he would not only have to teach life's truths, but care for, guide and motivate the people, with the same confidence and power that Elijah had demonstrated in life.

> *"Now fifty men of the sons of the prophets went and stood opposite them at a distance, while the two of them stood by the Jordan. Elijah took his mantle and folded it together and struck the waters, and they were divided here and there, so that the two of them crossed over on dry ground. (Then) Elijah said to Elisha, "Ask what I shall do for you before I am taken from you." And Elisha said, "Please, let a double portion of your spirit be upon me." He said, "You have asked a hard thing. Nevertheless, if you see me when I am taken from you, it shall be so for you; but if not, it shall not be so." As they were going along and talking, behold, there appeared a chariot of fire and horses of fire which separated the two of them. And Elijah went up by a whirlwind to heaven. Elisha saw it and cried out, "My father, my father, the chariots of Israel and its horsemen!" And he saw Elijah no more. Then he took hold of his own clothes and tore them in two pieces. He also took up the mantle of Elijah that fell from him and returned and stood by the bank of the Jordan. He took the mantle of Elijah that fell from him and struck the waters and said, "Where is the LORD, the God of Elijah?" And when he also had struck the waters, they were divided here and there; and Elisha crossed over."* (2 Kings 2:7-14)

The Lord, like any father would be, was worried that the people had not learned the lessons and principles taught them, throughout their life journey, and were now entering the Promised Land, unprepared to meet life's challenges. They would not only fail to fulfill their purpose to alleviate the suffering of a land groaning for relief from the destructive behavior of its current landowners, but they would also repeat their own life story and suffer the same consequences as the previous inhabitants. *"You must keep all my decrees and regulations by putting them into practice; otherwise the land to which I am bringing you as your new home will vomit you out."* (Leviticus 20:22)

Many had thought that they needed to acknowledge and appease the gods of the land before they could succeed, but the Lord was telling them that they instead needed to integrate into the whole by knowing Him -- the God of the entire Heaven and Earth -- and the laws of the land, that is, nature's laws, to succeed. Why? *"My people are destroyed for lack of knowledge."* (Hosea 4:6a, NASB) We must know life's requirements or else we will not be able to enjoy the benefits of living. The entire Book of Deuteronomy narrates these instructions on how to live, succeed and thrive, with confidence. It reveals the life course every living being must walk. The land of Israel was no different from any other land on the face of the planet. It, and everyone who lived in it, was subject to the very same laws of nature existent everywhere, throughout the earth. There is a divine order which is expressed in the natural order, with its natural laws, that we must know and obey.

Elisha was taken back across the Jordan River to contemplate what had happened there, over 500 years before, when the people of Israel were preparing to cross over into the Promised Land. It must have been exciting to stand on the eastern side of the Jordan River. It was the Gateway into the Promised Land -- a new life to be lived as life was supposed to be lived – secure, confident, healthy, joyful and prosperous. This represented the end of a 440-year-long saga of pain and suffering: from slavery in Egypt to a prolonged desert experience. **What must it have felt like? Perhaps, like:**

- Awaking after spending years in a coma.
- Ending a prolonged jail sentence or captivity and returning to society.
- Coming to the end of a period of rehabilitation from some form of addiction and preparing to return to society and life.
- Being lonely, widowed or divorced and planning to remarry.
- Being released from some form of enslavement and preparing to begin a new life in freedom.
- A tree about to bear fruit after years or even decades of unfruitfulness.
- Finally, being able to, not only see the light at the end of the tunnel, but also being at its end, at last.

The questions that faced Israel, and should be on the top of our own list, are:

- ✓ Am I ready… to go back into society?
- ✓ Have I learned from all my past successes and failures and made the adjustments needed to succeed in the future?
- ✓ Am I ready to put my past with all its heartaches, grudges, resentments, bitterness, anger, hatred, shame and guilt behind me?
- ✓ After living for so long in a fallen state, do I know how to 'stand'?
- ✓ How can I now succeed in life?
- ✓ Do I know life's requirements?
- ✓ Or, am I going to repeat the same old lifestyle with all its pain and suffering?

You will not. You must not! There must be change!

As they crossed into the Promised Land, God's and Moses' first preoccupation was to ensure that the proper leadership structure was in place. In a land that has rules and regulations, we must know them and make up our minds to obey them. I am not just speaking of society's laws, but of God's and nature's laws, which many today ignore, to our collective detriment. Therefore, whether you are an individual or a corporate entity, we must be led by reason and logic and fueled by passion, not by emotions. We must be led by our heads and not by our hearts. We must HONOR those who have the right and the integrity to lead, ENSURE that right, and then AGREE and DO exactly as we are told.

YOUR JOURNEY
--THE LIFE LESSONS –

ALIGN WITH THE H.E.A.D.

= Honor, Ensure, Agree and Do

HONOR THE HEAD

Look around you. You can learn a lot from observing the **structure of our physical world, including our human body. Our head is our natural leader.** It was created and built to lead. It is the logical seat of decision-making because it is the only organ capable of properly analyzing the input from all sources and outputting the right and wise choices. This leadership is carried out through hormones and nervous attachments to every organ and tissue, which then acts on those instructions of what needs to be done. The individual is part of, and has an important role in, a greater ecosystem; thus, coordination and maintaining harmony within the ecosystem are essential. The head plays an important role receiving input from the five human senses -- touch, smell, taste, hearing and sight -- helping the individual interact with the rest of the ecosystem; the soul/ spirit has the purpose of interacting with the Creator. The head follows the course laid down in our DNA, which is part of every cell in the body. The DNA, in its perfect and unaltered state, is the physical representation of the Word of God, functioning like software carrying out action plans, in coordination with the head of the ecosystem. It is thus setup to follow the way of righteousness to maintain wholeness as laid down by the Creator.

In a healthy and normal living being, nothing happens without the head's leadership. Each member of the body naturally acknowledges and submits to the head's leadership and coordinating capabilities. Failure to do so, as in the case of certain diseases, would result in loss of quality of life, not only for that member, but for the entire body. Case in point is paralysis of an arm. If the arm, for whatever reason, cannot communicate with the head, then it is dead to the head and useless to the body. Imagine life without your right or left arm. Now imagine if you were the arm in the Body of Christ and you were unresponsive or dead to the head, which is the Lord.

In our Solar system, everything revolves around the sun, the head of the ecosystem. The sun is the head of the earth, consequently, our brain and the entire human body sub-system is setup, in such a way, to interact with it naturally. Our body has circadian rhythms, which function like an internal clock regulated by sunlight. These modulate the production of hormones, which, in turn, stimulate tissues in the body into action. The sun's control over the earth can be observed in the beautiful changes of the four seasons that many of us have all come to appreciate -- summer, fall, winter and spring. It is wise, therefore, to be awake and go outdoors during the day, to maximize the sun's benefits; and, foolish to sleep during the day and work during the night for we lose its life-giving resources. Those of us who have had the misfortune of working night shifts for a considerable amount of time should realize the adversities that stem from insufficient exposure to sunlight -- low Vitamin D, lowered immunity, which result in higher incidence of infections, loss of bone mass, cancers and immune diseases. So, it doesn't make sense to ignore the God-given sun's leadership. Align with it, be submissive to its great role, and take full advantage of its free life-sustaining resources.

In the family unit, the father's role is similar to the sun's leadership and the mother's, to that of the moon, which revolves around the planets (the children). Altogether, God created the planets and the moon to revolve around the sun, which, together, are symbolic of the family unit, with man and God as head over all. To the woman he said, *"... Your desire will be for your husband, and he will rule over you."* (Genesis 3:16) While the husband is head of the wife, both are to be submissive to God and to righteousness. The husband's rule is therefore limited to the way of righteousness, meaning that he cannot demand submission if first he does not submit to God nor is righteous. It is important to seek and maintain this order as the entire family benefits.

It is right and wise for children to honor their parents as they are the head of the family unit. *"Honor your father and mother. Then you will live a long, full life in the land the LORD your God is giving you."* (Exodus 20:12, NLT) Their responsibility is to guide, protect, teach, advocate for and nurture their children towards wholeness. When parents carry out their responsibilities, children benefit from their loving, wise and knowledgeable care. Governments would be wise to honor parents in their leadership in the home rather than dishonor, hinder and take over child rearing duties, which they are incapable of, as they do not have the resources or the time to do so. The exception is when a child's life is in danger.

Our Heavenly Father, in His wisdom, chided Job, *"Do you know the laws (fixed order) of the heavens, or can you determine their rule over the earth?"* (Job 38:33) God here reveals two things: not only that He has placed the sun as a physical representative of Heaven's rule over the earth, but also that He has placed Himself as the Absolute Ruler over the earth and everything in it. He emphasized this fundamental truth to King Nebuchadnezzar, the reigning king of Babylon, the superpower at the time, by afflicting him with a severe mental illness, *"until you acknowledge that the Most High is sovereign over all Kingdoms on earth."* (Daniel 4:25)

Both the Old and the New Testaments reveal the substance of what is necessary to honor Yahweh, as our God and Heavenly Father, and Jesus Christ, as our Lord and Savior. They reveal the foundation on which is built our relationship with the Lord. We have no effective relationship without it. In fact, it's the foundation of life itself. As was mentioned in Step One, the core of this foundation is honoring Yahweh as our God and Heavenly Father, His Son, Jesus Christ, as Lord, and the Holy Spirit, as His indwelling Presence.

It makes absolute sense, therefore, to let the head rule, whether it is your own head over your body; the sun, taking full advantage of its life-giving attributes; or, our Heavenly Father, acknowledging and honoring Him, as the true Head over you and over every affair of the earth. It is wise, and to do otherwise, would be extremely foolish, as common sense teaches that one cannot live effectively without one's head. So, *"worship the LORD your God, fear him, obey his commands, listen to what he says, serve him, and be loyal to him."* (Deuteronomy 13:4, GWT*)*

It is not only wise to honor the head as head, but we must also ensure the integrity of its leadership.

ENSURE THE INTEGRITY OF THE HEAD'S LEADERSHIP

We are all aware of the importance of protecting the head by wearing a helmet when riding a bicycle or motorcycle or when snowboarding or engaging in extreme sports. Damaging your brain only leads to a shortened life span and a drastically reduced quality of life. You must ensure the integrity of the head rather than endanger it and invalidate the benefits of its leadership.

Similarly, it is essential that parents be validated as heads of their family unit because the survival of their children is dependent upon it. (I am referring to those parents who choose to lovingly and carefully carry out their responsibilities -- not to those who are flagrantly disobedient as to how they look after God-given children and corrupt due to their lack of integrity.) Parents are their children's strongest and most passionate advocates simply because they love them unconditionally.

One of their responsibilities is to guide and steer a child away from danger, by utilizing their God-led teaching, rewards, time out, a loss of privilege, and their compassionate and controlled spanking. Pain has always been a powerful and effective deterrent that is prevalent in nature. Our skin is loaded with nerves, so when it is endangered, for example, by fire, these nerves transmit pain stimuli, which cause a reflex retraction from the source of danger. In the same way, it is foolish to undermine the parents' authority and make their already gargantuan task even more difficult to accomplish, if not impossible, by implementing zero spanking laws. This appears to be the desire of certain segments of society with the encouragement of UNESCO and the UN. Yes, it should not be the only disciplinary tool but, as in nature, it should be a part of the set of tools required at certain times. It should not be discarded. Imagine, if you had the misfortune of being born with a hereditary error that prevented you from feeling pain. While you may be tempted to think of the benefits of a pain-free life, imagine the scenario that I used previously. If you inadvertently placed your hand on a hot burner and did not pull it away because you were unaware due to the lack of pain, you would be in grave danger of sustaining third degree burns. The fear of pain is a healthy deterrent, and without it, children would be highly susceptible to danger, harm and delinquency.

The Creator was wise to institute traditional marriage between a man and a woman to create proper heads of the family unit. These must be equally committed to the head, which is God, the Father, and to the way of righteousness. If there is failure of proper parenting, whether from neglect, a 'laissez faire' (let it be) attitude, or a lack of skills, the following statistics substantiate the costs to society, at every level:

- *63% of teen suicides come from fatherless homes. That's 5 times the national average (***US Dept. Of Health/Census)***; 90% of all runaways and homeless children are from fatherless homes. That's 32 times the national average; 80% of rapists with anger problems come from fatherless homes. 14 times the national average (***Justice & Behaviour, Vol 14, p. 403-26***);*
- *85% of children with behavioral problems come from fatherless homes. 20 times the national average* (Centre for Disease Control);
- *85% of all youths in prison come from fatherless homes. 20 times the national average (*Fulton Co. Georgia, Texas Dept. of Correction);
- *Daughters of single parents without a Father involved are 53% more likely to marry as teenagers; 711% more likely to have children as teenagers, 164% more likely to have a pre-marital birth and 92% more likely to get*

divorced themselves (National Household Education Survey)

- *Adolescent girls raised in a 2-parent home with involved Fathers are significantly less likely to be sexually active than girls raised without involved Fathers* (Journal of Marriage and Family, 1994).
- *Children with Fathers who are involved are 40% less likely to repeat a grade in school;* (National Household Education Survey)
- *Researchers of* Columbia University *found that children living in two-parent households with a poor relationship with their father are 68% more likely to smoke, drink or use drugs compared to all teens in two-parent households. Moreover, teens in single-mother households fared much worse. 98 % were likely to be involved in negative behavior.*
- *Even in high crime neighborhoods, 90% of children from stable 2 parent homes where the Father is involved do not become delinquents; Children with Fathers who are involved are more likely to get A's in school; Children with Fathers who are involved are more likely to enjoy school and engage in extracurricular activities* (Development and Psychopathology 1993)

It is common sense to uphold the parents, and especially, the leadership of fathers in the homes.

> *"Without two parents, working together as a team, the child has more difficulty learning the combination of empathy, reciprocity, fairness and self-command that people ordinarily take for granted. If the child does not learn this at home, society will have to manage his behavior in some other way. He may have to be rehabilitated, incarcerated, or otherwise restrained. In this case, prisons will substitute for parents."* (Morse, Jennifer Roback. "Parents or Prisons." Policy Review, 2003)

Government, the Church and the rest of the community must do their part to step in to assure children's rights to responsible parenting and assist parents in their leadership duties in the home. The Church should strategically target fathers and make them 'promise keepers' and keepers of the Word. Statistics prove that the father's influence over the future of their children is significantly higher than the mother's.

- *When a child is the first person in the family to come to faith, the rest of the family will follow 31% of the time. When a mother/woman is the first person in the family to come to faith, the rest of the family will follow 17% of the time. When a man/father is the first person in the family to come to faith, the rest of the family will follow 93% of the time* Bob Horner, Ron Ralston, & David Sunday, Promise Keepers at Work (Colorado Springs: Focus on the Family, 1996)
- *If both a father and mother attend church regularly, 33 percent of the children will be regular churchgoers, 41 percent will end up attending irregularly – almost 75 percent. Only 25 percent, one-in-four, will end up not attending church as adults* (Barna);

Everyone must *"take up their cross daily and follow me*". (Luke 9:23) Just as Jesus carried His cross to the very end, we must all commit to taking up our cross of His covenant with all its rights and responsibilities. We must rest solidly in the former and carry out the latter carefully to its completion and follow Him. In so doing, we ensure that His will is done in our lives daily and that the Head of the entire universe is our **H**ead. It is, therefore, wise and beneficial to make sure that all our interactions, both individual and corporate, are aligned with this pre-existing divine order. Paul tells us to "*put on the helmet of salvation.*" (Ephesians 6:17) Just as you should put on a helmet to protect your head, you should protect God's headship over you by first covenanting to make Him your head and Jesus your

Lord by totally surrendering to His leadership. This is not an "*idle commitment for it is your life.*" (Deuteronomy 32:47)

Moses reaffirmed the covenant between God and those who had not yet done so: *"You are standing here today to enter into the covenant with the LORD your God."* (Deuteronomy 29:12) The ritual act of circumcision, including the constant sight of the circumcised penis, was a daily reminder of their covenantal rights and responsibilities, which helped them ensure their acquiescence and take full advantage of their covenantal benefits. He came to them all in their time of need and offered them a way out, a second chance, and an opportunity to thrive in a land that would be theirs by inheritance.

Similarly, as individuals, we ensure the integrity of God's sovereign rule over us by being baptized in water and participating in Holy Communion. These both serve as a constant reminder of our covenantal rights and responsibilities. The covenantal benefits are extraordinary. God promises to be a Father to all those who commit to being obedient children. This covenantal relationship is one of daily submission to Jesus as our Lord and to our Heavenly Father -- rather than our constant insubordination, stiffening of the neck and hardening of our hearts. It is a daily looking for any sinful ways that have not yet been put to death and, upon finding any, choosing to leave them off. It is daily choosing this new way of life and obedience, rather than going down the broad path of death and rebellion, where there is no love or relationship to be found. Every day, you must ensure that it is His will that is done in your life. Jesus taught us to pray "Our Father in Heaven" to remind us to ensure that that is the case. I certainly never ignore Him. I remind myself constantly and make sure that I stay consistent with my commitment to Him as my Head, Lord and Heavenly Father.

Corporate Spiritual Leadership

At the Corporate Level

Moses reminded the people of the importance of Spiritual leadership and taught them how to set it up. A Spiritual leader, or in other words, a Spirit-led leader, is one who faithfully represents the Lord God before the people. It is a servant leadership because he/she is God's servant to the people. Put another way, that Spiritual leader is God's ambassador who represents His wishes and, like the Angels, listens for His voice and does His bidding faithfully.

Principle: Yahweh alone is God. Therefore, we are to set up a leadership structure that ensures His leadership over us.

Corporately, the leadership structure you set up must assure and enliven, not endanger, God's day-to-day, situation-to-situation leadership over the group. For this to happen, we look again at Deuteronomy, where the Lord told the people, through Moses, to choose *"wise and discerning and knowledgeable men from your tribes, and I will appoint them as your heads.'* (Deuteronomy 1:13, NASB) Jesus himself echoed this when he said: *"I am sending you prophets and wise men and teachers."* (Matthew 23:34)

Wise, according to the Oxford Dictionary, means: *"Having or showing experience, knowledge, and good judgement; sensible or prudent; having knowledge in a specified subject; aware of, especially so as to know how to act.* Wisdom is the main requirement for leadership. It becomes complete when the wisdom of the Holy Spirit is accessed through the anointing. The result is the wise decisions we make on His behalf. This wise, Spirit-led leadership is a sign of God's ordination and empowerment for our leadership, which gives us credibility as His representatives and children. In Acts, we read, "*Brothers and sisters, choose seven men from among you who are known to be full of the Spirit and wisdom. We will turn this responsibility over to them.*" (Acts 6:3; cf. 1 Timothy 3:1-13)

Discerning (understanding), again from the Oxford Dictionary, *means "Having or showing good judgment."* This discernment is evidence that we are filled with understanding given to us by the Holy Spirit. Discerning goes beyond human understanding, as it utilizes more than the input of the five human senses, relying instead on the Holy Spirit. This may mean ignoring the input of the human senses, as these can be misleading:

"...by his God-fearing attitude, he will not judge by what his eyes see nor make a decision by what His ears hear but with righteousness He will judge the poor and decide with fairness for the afflicted of the earth..." (Isaiah 11:2-3) (my own translation underlined).

The Hebrew word Bin (transliteration) translated here as '*discerning*' means '*understanding*', but because it implies a divine, truth-based relationship with God's Holy Spirit, which prophets have, Jesus' word choice is appropriate -- *"I am sending you ...prophets..."* (Matthew 23:34) He helps us discern the truth in every case that He moves us in, as well as, the solutions, objectives and action plans to take. Discernment, especially, helps us navigate the treacherous waters of heresy and apostasy. There are many wrong teachings and dangerous philosophies that are propagated, either intentionally, maliciously or ingenuously. Whatever the case, the Spirit of truth helps us discern them and guides us in how to deal with them.

Knowledgeable or the Hebrew word '*Yada*' means "*intimate knowledge, fullness of knowledge*". We become Spirit-filled and knowledgeable of God, of all His commandments, statutes and ordinances, and His situational Will. We become sufficiently knowledgeable to teach, which is our true God-given role (1Timothy 3:2; Acts 6:3). Hence, Jesus' statement, *"I am sending you ...teachers."* (Matthew 23:34)

Principle: We must be led by the Holy Spirit as evidenced by the spiritual gifts before we can be a Spiritual leader.

The apostles sought men who "*were known to be filled by the Holy Spirit and of wisdom*" (Acts 6:3), when they looked for men to assist them in the ministry to the widows at Jerusalem. Thus, you are a Spirit-led or Spiritual leader when you are 'filled', 'moved', 'carried along', 'enabled' or 'led' by the Holy Spirit. You 'live' by and 'keep in step' with the Spirit. You become 'filled' with wisdom, knowledge, understanding, power, counsel, strength, and the fear of the Lord and with the Spirit of Yahweh, your Heavenly Father. You are 'filled up' with love, peace, joy, faith, kindness, goodness, patience, gentleness and self-control by the same Spirit. You speak in tongues and prophesy when 'moved' by His Holy Spirit. This 'filling' is thus a sign of the Holy Spirit's leading and of your willingness to be movable.

Thus, *'prophesying'* or '*speaking in tongues*' is a sign of spiritual maturity (Mark 16:17). It was the sign of true 'prophet hood' or 'acting like a prophet' and was evidence of the willingness of the individual to let the Spirit literally 'take over', not only his or her speech, but also his or her entire being. You see, for the Holy Spirit to speak through a person, he or she must overcome the brain's normal opposition to uttering speech that it perceives as incoherent. The Spirit doesn't take over the brain, only the speech; hence, the individual always maintains control of his or her mental faculties. This contrasts with an epileptic convulsion or demonic possession in which the person loses control. I look for this sign when I need confirmation that the instruction I have received is from the Lord and not just 'gut feelings'. I would be skeptical of the latter. Many have made the mistake of relying on gut feelings, which has led them to make false prophecies. We should only look for discernment in its full force, that is, accompanied by tongues and peace and/or joy. Otherwise, we must be skeptical. Tongues or prophesying is also a sign of divine ordination.

Divine Ordination is the Spiritual or Divine commissioning of an individual as evidenced by spiritual gifts: *"... and I will appoint them as your heads.'* (Deuteronomy 1:13, NASB) This is a sign of one's appointment by God to represent Him on earth. While we are to choose wisely, it is God who confirms the choice by the demonstration of the spiritual gifts. In the New Testament, the spiritual gift of tongues was expressed every time people were chosen for any leadership capacity. When the 70 elders were appointed by the Lord, they all spoke in tongues, even though only once. (Numbers 11:16-17, 25-29). When Saul was ordained, he also prophesied (1 Samuel 10:9-13) and Jesus' disciples broke out in ecstatic speech when the Spirit came powerfully upon them on the day of Pentecost (Acts 2:1-13).

It must be said, though, that demonstrating the sign of 'tongues' does not guarantee that the person will let the Spirit lead situationally. King Saul was an example of a person ordained by the very Holy Spirit to whom he was to be in submission, but failed miserably and so, was unceremoniously 'dumped' by the Lord (1 Samuel 15:22-23, HCS). Jesus told his disciples to be careful, because their faithful submission to the divine order was tied to their salvation:

> *"not everyone who says to me, 'Lord, Lord,' will enter the Kingdom of heaven, but only the one who does the will of my Father who is in heaven. Many will say to me on that day, 'Lord, Lord, did we not prophesy in your name and in your name drive out demons and in your name perform many miracles?' Then I will tell them*

plainly, 'I never knew you. Away from me, you evildoers!'" (Matthew 7:21-23)

A Spiritual leader is to faithfully represent or follow our Lord as He is the Head. Manifesting the sign of tongues is not absolute, as the person could also be speaking in tongues under false pretenses, such as, when a person twists his tongue intentionally to deceive or is under the power of a demonic, deceiving spirit. It is for this reason we are to "*Test every spirit*". (1 John 4:1-3) Both deceptive forms are observable, but the latter is uncommon. Jeremiah warned us of this danger: "*The prophets prophesy falsely, the priests rule by their own authority, and my people love it this way. But what will you do in the end?"* (Jeremiah 5:31, ISV)

Sadly, for the very reasons just mentioned, many have chosen to 'subtract' tongues and other Spiritual gifts from the requirements of church leadership, thus endangering the integrity of the Head and of the Spirit's leadership over the church. Some teach that tongues ceased with the death of the last apostle and others have even banned it from their services, establishing this heresy in their constitutions. At his departure from this earth, Jesus reminded his disciples to teach everyone "*to obey everything I have commanded you."* (Matthew 28:18-20) Everything means everything, and nothing is to be subtracted; otherwise, He would have said so. Therefore, waiting on the Spirit's empowerment for service is not an empty command. It was put in place to ensure our submission to the Spirit's leadership. If we cannot wait on the Spirit how will He lead? Therefore, do not 'subtract or add' from anything that the Lord has commanded us, or we will hurt the integrity of the Head of the Church. This is a mistake and a heresy for it builds on a different foundation than what was laid down "*by the apostles and prophets*" of which "*Christ is the chief cornerstone.*" (Ephesians 2:20) Thus, the purposes of the anointing of the Holy Spirit are to: ensure the Lord's leadership, to empower us for service, to enrich us to be in His image as well as to foment intimacy with Him.

First Purpose of the Anointing is to Let the Holy Spirit Lead

We are anointed by the Holy Spirit so that the Lord would lead through us. Irrespective of what we are called, whether layperson, deacon or elder; marketplace minister; pastor, evangelist, teacher, prophet or apostle, the Spirit comes upon us powerfully so that we will be "*My witnesses*", says the Lord. This is a crucial leadership principle. The success of any venture and the survival of any group (church, organization, denomination) depend on the consistent application of this principle. Failure will result in ineffective, Spiritually dead and Spirit-opposing churches.

A collegial leadership style assures that Yahweh remains leader over His people and process. As the purpose of the anointing is so that God would lead, the leadership style must be in such a way so as not to usurp His leadership. It takes wisdom to lead, as the true servant of God must be sure that he or she is in submission to God and not vice versa. This is the era of the apostolic/prophetic government, that is, situational or day-to-day Spirit-led leadership through one or more wholly obedient and faithful servants.

While a capital-H hierarchical style is needed in the case of one apostle (comes from the Greek word, *apostolous*, meaning sent), a small-h hierarchy with a fluid team leadership style is more appropriate when there are multiple apostles, as was the case seen at the Jerusalem Council session reported in Acts 15. No one person had the pre-eminence, but the counsel, deemed as from the Lord had, and that counsel was acknowledged by Peter, the leader of the apostles, and by James, the chief elder. It was this process that made them conclude that their decision was one that *"seemed good to the Holy Spirit and to us."* (Acts 15:28) It is interesting to observe this same leadership style among the geese as they fly in the V-formation. Those geese willing and able to lead take turns at doing so, while the others honk their encouragement and appreciation of their willingness and hard work.

The Holy Spirit is the true leader of the people and the One who makes the final decision, so it is incumbent upon us to discover what that is, no matter through whom it comes. It is for this reason that Virginia Satir, a pioneer in systems theory, "*sees the leader more as the leader of the process rather than the leader of the people*". (The Equipping Pastor: A System's Approach to Congregational Leadership). The pastor, then, is more like a coordinator or a manager, rather than a leader, and must delegate appropriately. It is interesting to note that Jesus used the term '*manager*' often in his parables.

King Saul, the first king of Israel, learned that as God rules us, we cannot disobey or rebel against Him with impunity. *"Then the LORD said to Samuel, "I am sorry that I ever made Saul king, for he has not been loyal to me and has refused to obey my command."* (1 Samuel 15:10-11) Jesus understood the principle of Spiritual leadership well, when he stated, *"I will do what the Father requires of me, so that the world will know that I love the Father"* (John 14:31); and then again, *"I don't speak on my own authority. The Father who sent me has commanded me what to say and how to say it. And I know his commands lead to eternal life; so I say whatever the Father tells me to say."* (John 12:49-50) Thus, any leader of the people must first be the Lord's follower in order to be an effective leader. We must be God's "*true and faithful servants*" as God is the *de facto* leader and CEO, while we are his managers and administrators, carrying out His instructions.

Take every opportunity to honor the Lord as the One whose power accomplishes things as failure to do so is dishonest and deceitful and will hurt your relationship with your Lord. *"Moses did as the LORD commanded him."* (Numbers 17:11)

Yet, he could not enter the Promised Land -- *"Listen, you rebels!" he shouted. "Must we bring you water from this rock?"* (Numbers 20:10b) It wasn't Moses and Aaron who were responsible for obtaining water, but their God. They were simply God's servants doing His bidding and exercising power on His behalf. *"Because you didn't trust me, didn't treat me with holy reverence in front of the People of Israel, you two aren't going to lead this company into the land that I am giving them."* (Numbers 20:12; MSG) Moses learned just how important this recommendation was as he had made the mistake of dishonoring the Lord before the people by not stating the obvious fact that it was the Lord who did everything through him.

A Good Manager has a Fatherly or Pastoral Heart

As God's leadership style goes beyond the Lord-slave or servant variety and, instead, is of the Father-child type, our leadership style must also reflect this. We are to be fatherly/motherly or pastoral in nature and otherwise, fraternal. Both you, as a leader, and the people you are seeking to help are God's children. Therefore, we are not to fall into the sibling rivalry trap trying to get the upper hand, but we must relate to our siblings as equals. The Father and all of us on earth must seek to bring His prodigal children home to join the rest of His children in His Kingdom; and, we are to care for all.

Principle: The shepherd's or father's heart is an essential attribute of every minister, whether you are an apostle, prophet, teacher, priest, marketplace minister, missionary, lay leader, deacon, elder, bishop, pastor or any other ecclesiastical leader.

God's representative is to father (and mother) the people 'from the Father's infinite love' even as our Heavenly Father does. We are created in God's image and, therefore, with His same capacity and responsibility to love. The Spirit is there to enrich our love when our love is lacking, as is quite common.

The Lord grooms us to have the same heart towards others as He has towards us.

We cannot be the Lord's representative and not demonstrate the shepherd's or father's (mother's) heart towards the people. I have often heard leaders say that they do not have the patience, love or compassion to be a pastor. This is unfortunate and based on a misunderstanding that only some are called to demonstrate the shepherd's heart (Ephesians 4:11). While you may never experience all the expressions of the Spiritual gifts, everyone is called to express all the Spiritual fruit. We are all called to pass around patience, love and compassion. These, and the other fruit, are evidence of the Spirit's infilling you. They are evidence that you rely on the Spirit's help to father or mother and pastor. Some cannot be called to be merciful, loving, patient and compassionate while other are not. It is for every one of us. For this very reason Jesus came -- that everyone would demonstrate loving kindness towards one another, so that everyone would know that we are *"My disciples."* (John 15:8-17; 17:26; Micah 6:8). Do you have insufficient love or patience or compassion or wisdom? Ask, for He is the El Shaddai and will give you abundantly what you lack.

A Good Manager Does Not Exalt Self nor Try to Be First

The leader must not try to be first but walk humbly with our Lord (3 John 9; Micah 6:8).

> *"You know that the rulers of the Gentiles lord it over them, and their high officials exercise authority over them. Not so with you. Instead, whoever wants to become great among you must be your servant, and whoever wants to be first must be your slave—just as the Son of Man did not come to be served, but to serve, and to give his life as a ransom for many" (*Matthew 20:25-28).

He taught his disciples never to cross the line:

"I tell you the truth; slaves are not greater than their master. Nor is the messenger more important than the one who sends the message. Now that you know these things, God will bless you for doing them." (John 13:16-17)

He railed at the Pharisees and doctors of the Law for getting caught up in titles and power over and above the responsibilities of the roles:

> *"And they love to sit at the head table at banquets and in the seats of honor in the synagogues. They love to receive respectful greetings as they walk in the marketplaces, and to be called 'Rabbi.' "Don't let anyone call you 'Rabbi,' for you have only one teacher, and all of you are equal as brothers and sisters. And don't address anyone here on earth as 'Father,' for only God in heaven is your spiritual Father. And don't let anyone call you 'Teacher,' for you have only one teacher, the Messiah. The greatest among you must be a servant. But those who exalt themselves will be humbled, and those who humble themselves will be exalted."* (Matthew 23:6-12, NLT)

Principle: A Spiritual leader does not try to be first; even though, he or she might be first among equals.

Those who champion the argument that titles are necessary often cite the fear of losing authority or the need to impose authority as the primary reasons to retain titles. However, Jesus Himself assured His disciples that the onus of accepting those who are sent rests solely on the receiver. The human giver/s of the message comes with the authority of the Sender and this must be tested and assumed. In other words, you give the message or act under the authority of the Sender. It is a borrowed authority. You are under the authority umbrella of the Lord Himself. You don't need a crutch such as titles, to be effective. Don't worry about effectiveness. Leave that to the Holy Spirit. *"It is not by force nor by strength, but by my Spirit, says the LORD of Heaven's Armies."* (Zechariah 4:6, NLT) It is always good to remember that you are the junior partner in the mission.

Pastors are only sheep with a father's (mother's) or pastor's heart. Therefore, accept the pastor's role, but reject the title. In this pastoral analogy, you do not transform from sheep to shepherd, but as sheep you develop and demonstrate the shepherd-like heart. In every flock, there are those sheep that have the shepherd heart. They know the shepherd's will and so demonstrate leadership over the other sheep. They lead the way and otherwise make the work of the Shepherd easier. Using this analogy, it is a mistake to assume a Pastor title as this takes away from the Lord's honor. Be a pastor without taking the title. In this way, you walk humbly with the Shepherd of us all. For this same reason, you should not say, 'my flock', 'my sheep', or 'my church'. It doesn't make sense since we are all sheep and members of His church and His Kingdom – not our own.

While you are to take 'ownership' of the role, you are not to take away God's glory and assume ownership of His position and title. I believe this was the essence of Jesus' warning to his disciples in Matthew 23 as it was common for prophets to be called 'fathers' (Elisha called Elijah "*my father*" 2 Kings 2:12) and teachers, '*rabbis*'. This command was certainly new to everyone as nowhere in the Old Testament was anyone discouraged from calling the prophets, '*fathers*'. So, we are to accept the role wholeheartedly, but reject the title. Today, many ministers of the Gospel are yet to heed our Lord's command as they still strive for, hold on dearly to titles, and demand respect as 'lords' over their siblings. We are still all sheep. "*You are all brothers.*" (Matthew 23:8b) The flock is still and will always belong to the Lord -- our Shepherd. Like the sent prophets and apostles of the Old and New Testaments, you must be careful to honor and hallow the real Leader and King and give Him His due. *"Hallelujah! For our Lord God Almighty reigns. Let us rejoice and be glad and give him glory!"* (Revelation 19: 6b–7a)

A Good Manager Fathers (Mothers) or Pastors the People with Equity and Justice

Unfortunately, partiality and discriminatory attitudes are observed once too many among Christians. This should be expected, as the Church is made up of people in all stages of development, from new-born to adulthood. We are, though, to be *"perfectly fair in your decisions and impartial in your judgments. Hear the cases of those who are poor as well as those who are rich. Don't be afraid of anyone's anger, for the decision you make is God's decision."* (Deuteronomy 1:16-17.)

To illustrate this and to exhort congregations to be impartial in their judgments of people, one Brazilian singer/evangelist would go around the churches dressed as a homeless bum and beg for an opportunity to sing. This act was usually done with the prior knowledge and cooperation of the Pastor. While many of the congregants were kind, some were mean and would even try to expel her. Eventually, she would get the microphone and sing with such a beautiful voice that the entire congregation would burst out in applause and worship. She would then proceed to preach about the test that had just occurred -- showing that while many had passed, many had failed.

Many instances in leadership occur where the temptation to speak untruths arise out of the fear of hurting somebody's feelings or of going against an accepted tradition of political correctness, even if it falls short of God's and nature's standards. Today, some denominations and leaders have bowed to the political correctness watchdogs and turned their backs on God and on the truth by tolerating homosexuality and same-sex marriage as an acceptable choice. Their fear of society is greater than their fear of God and their deliberate ignoring of knowledge, understanding and wisdom disqualifies them from leadership in God's Kingdom and in the Church. They are liable to be rejected by the coming King -- *'I don't know you or where you come from. Away from me, all you evildoers!'* (Luke 13:27)

Second Purpose of the Anointing is Spiritual Empowerment to Carry Out Tasks Appointed by the Lord

As you are working with/for the Lord, He does not expect you to be His witnesses in your own strength and with your limited skills, but *"by my Spirit, says the Lord Almighty."* (Zechariah 4:6) *"Please, let a double portion of your Spirit be upon me."* (2 Kings 2:9) *"But you will receive power when the Holy Spirit comes upon you. And you will be my witnesses, telling people about me everywhere -- in Jerusalem, throughout Judea, in Samaria, and to the ends of the earth."* (Acts 1:8; cf. Zechariah 4:6-7; Deuteronomy 1:29-31) So, allow the Lord to empower you with spiritual gifts as these are evidence of the Spirit's partnership with you. They also give you the credibility to be in His service. The seven Spirits of God (Revelation 4:5; Isaiah 11:2): The Spirit of **Yahweh**, the Spirit of **Wisdom**, the Spirit of **Understanding**, the Spirit of **Counsel**, the Spirit of **Might,** the Spirit of **Knowledge** and the Spirit of the **Fear of the Lord** enrich and empower you for service *"for the common good."* (1 Corinthians 12:7) These manifest in us through the Spiritual gifts (prophecy, tongues, interpretation of tongues, miraculous powers, healing, counsel that reveals wisdom, knowledge and understanding, etc.). (1 Corinthians 12:8-11)

The expectation of a team effort with the Holy Spirit and with our other Spirit-led siblings will help us go about our work with confidence and without fear. We are not alone nor helpless; although, this is easier said than firmly believed. In following and obeying all the rules of engagement, we can go about the Kingdom's business with power and confidence. Elisha, after having received the mantle of leadership, still lacked confidence. His first miracle, dividing the waters of the Jordan River, demonstrated this lack of confidence: *"Where is the*

LORD, the God of Elijah?" (2 Kings 2:14) You can see that his trust in God was not yet rock-solid: The Lord was more the God of Elijah than of Elisha. I am sure that he knew the Lord was also his God, but he was not yet confident enough to firmly believe that God would do the same for him as He had done for Elijah. So often, you might wonder, "Does God love me as much as He loved any of the great men and women of faith? Would He do the same works through me as He did through others?" Jesus tried to assuage the fears of his disciples by telling them that they "*will do even greater things than these, because I am going to the Father.*" (John14:12)

Some have even avoided greater responsibility in ministry, resisting the Holy Spirit in the process, out of fear of 'acting like a prophet'. The fear of speaking in tongues or of expressing some other aspect of the fullness in the Spirit has resulted in ineffectiveness and shallowness, not only in their own lives, but in the lives of those they are helping. Jackie Pullinger, in her amazing book, Chasing the Dragon, (Regal), talked about this same mediocrity and powerlessness before she too realized that she was lacking the infilling of the Spirit. She then wholeheartedly sought the full experience with God and finally spoke and sang in tongues, a little at first and then profusely. She, immediately, experienced a revolution in her ministry among prostitutes, drug addicts and dealers, and Triad gang members in the Forbidden City in Hong Kong. Today, Jackie is a well-respected speaker and author.

You may say – "I have God's Spirit already. Why do I need to be filled again with His Spirit?" It is true that you are anointed with the Holy Spirit when you are born again. It is the same Spirit that accompany you throughout your developmental stages: New-born – Toddler (2-3) – Memory Retention (5-7) – Puberty (11-14) – Young Adult (20+) – Adulthood (25+). Scriptures mention the various phases: 1 month to 5 years old; 5 – 20; 20 – 60; and 60+. (Leviticus 27:3-7) At each stage, the Spirit engages with you differently:

- When a child "*knows enough to reject evil and choose good*" (Isaiah 7:15-16);
- The age of love and commitment (Puberty, 11-14) (Ezekiel 16:8): this is when major hormonal changes occur in your body that move you from childhood to adulthood and the ability to procreate. It is also when the Lord approaches every person to choose or reject Him as their Heavenly Father. Barna states that this is the time of the highest probability of accepting Jesus as Lord and Savior. I made my commitment to the Lord in this stage.
- The age of discipleship (learning, training) (20+); and, finally,
- The age of the fully trained for priesthood (25-30+), when you are expected to demonstrate the highest level of maturity and professionalism and exercise your spiritual gifts in the fullness of the Spirit, through situationally-sporadic 'fillings'. Jesus was filled to begin his ministry at age 30.

The Lord doesn't ask children to carry out tasks that require the maturity of adulthood as He knows that we go through development phases. Responsibilities are added as we grow and move from one level of maturity to another. When the indwelling Spirit sees that we are mature enough to take on the greater responsibilities of ministry, He *appoints* and 'empowers' us to carry them out. This invariably involves speaking in tongues, which is a common aspect of being filled by the Spirit and 'acting like a prophet'.

We are normally afraid of greater responsibility, but we must overcome our fears, fully accept our changing maturity levels and submit to the Spirit-orchestrated assignments that are appropriate to our maturity level. We are called to go "*from glory to glory*". (2 Corinthians 3:18) This is essential for success in life and for our physical, emotional and spiritual wellbeing. It is an essential aspect of true worship, if we want to maintain a healthy, true relationship as part of God's family and for Him to be our Lord. Failure to develop or move from one developmental level to another is pathological whether physically, emotionally or spiritually. Can you avoid moving on to the highest maturity level and living in the fullness of the Spirit by letting fear overcome you and by refusing to grow up? Yes, you can, but not without resisting and disappointing the Spirit. *"Do not stifle the Holy Spirit."* (1 Thessalonians 5:19 NLT) *"All who are guided by God's Spirit are God's children."* (Romans 8:14, GWT) Will you start off well, but finish poorly? I hope not. So, if you are led by the Spirit, then you will also carry out whatever responsibility you are given. You will not disobey or rebel against the Lord. You will accept His empowerment in whatever form it is presented, at the time it is needed, so that you can contribute to the common good, be an effective peacemaker and God's obedient child and faithful witness. The Lord seeks to be able to count on you. *"You are the salt of the earth. But if the salt loses its saltiness, how can it be made salty again? It is no longer good for anything, except to be thrown out and trampled underfoot."* (Matthew 5:13)

I once heard this story about a young man in South Africa during the time of *apartheid.* He was urged by the Holy Spirit to share the Gospel with the young black man who was serving him in a restaurant. He refused as it was not politically correct to do so in public. In disobedience, he compromised by giving him a large tip and waited outside hoping the waiter would come out to thank him. While waiting, he heard what sounded like a gunshot and sounds of a commotion coming from inside the restaurant. He ran in to find the same waiter lying on the ground dead in a pool of blood. You can imagine how that young man felt.

So, don't be afraid. Don't test the Lord by failing to obey Him out of fear or pride. The Israelite leaders were afraid of their assignment to go and possess the land, so they sent spies to check out the magnitude of the job. Then, when they figured that the mission was difficult, they not only rebelled against the

Lord, but also encouraged the people to rebel, as well. Disobedience, unbelief, distrust and rebellion towards the Lord will result in chaos, adversity, pain, suffering and death. (Deuteronomy 1:22-33; Hebrews 3:12-19; 4:1-6) You are '*against*' rather than '*for*' Him, '*scattering*' rather than '*gathering*' (Matthew 12:30) and you risk being rejected as an '*evildoer*' (Matthew 7:21-23) and one of the '*foolish virgins*', who resist the Spirit and is late for the wedding. (Parable of the Ten Virgins, Matthew 25:1-13)

I have battled with fear for most of my life. I have asked the Lord many times to rid me of it. As the years go by, the fear has gotten smaller and smaller until almost disappearing, as now I no longer suffer from stage-fright, which was the norm almost every time I went up to the pulpit. I have, however, come to the realization that it really doesn't matter whether I am afraid or not. In fact, fear can be helpful. What matters is that I obey. The manifestations of the Holy Spirit, when they do occur, are like a comfort blanket to me. They assure me that the Spirit is with me and leading, so I can relax and let the Spirit do His thing. What a privilege and a joy to work with my Heavenly Father in bringing transformation to the land! Thank you for healing and empowering me, Lord. I love you!

Third Purpose of the Anointing is Spiritual Enrichment to be Like Him

Principle: God is holy and righteous; therefore, you must be also.

The Spirit enriches your character to help you attain the image of your Heavenly Father. The Spirit's anointing will help you demonstrate the very traits that show that you are a child of God -- an abundance of spiritual fruit (*love, peace, joy, patience, kindness, goodness, faith, gentleness, self-control). (*Galatians 5:22-23). None of these are optional but are essential to life, not only within the house and the Kingdom of God, but also in the very eco-system, of which we are a part. No wonder Jesus criticized the religious leaders of His day for their behavior, for it more represented the Evil Devil than the kind-hearted Heavenly Father. The Holy Spirit will help you by refining you and purging you of all your unrighteous impurities. He accomplishes this through your desert experiences.

Desert experiences are an important part of this process of molding you into your Father's image.

Purpose 1: To experience the Heavenly Father's nurturing care.

The first year of Israel's desert experience was pre-planned to demonstrate Yahweh's Fatherly care and to teach them to look out for it. He did it to *"humble and to test you so that in the end it might go well with you."* (Deuteronomy 8:16, NIV) As a Father, He guided, taught, satisfied their hunger, quenched their thirst, disciplined and cared for them thus demonstrating His Father's heart. This all gave them an experience that they could remember for the future. So, next time, you find yourself going through a desert experience, don't complain like the Israelites did, but be glad and thankful, for it is an opportunity to experience the Father's touch -- His tender loving care.

Purpose 2: To teach you to trust in the Heavenly Father's care.

Experiencing the Father's care will teach you to trust in Him, even though, you "*walk through the valley of the shadow of death*". (Psalm 23) This will eliminate the fear that comes with scarcity and result in your quiet confidence during adversity. As the people travelled through the desert on their way out of Egypt, the Heavenly Father was there every step of the way, providing miraculously for them -- even providing water out of a rock and manna and quail from heaven. Their shoes did not wear out and the Lord delivered them from all their enemies. *"During the forty years that I led you through the desert, your clothes did not wear out, nor did the sandals on your feet."* (Deuteronomy 29:5) As the Lord is with you, desert experiences are not risking for failure, but rather opportunities to see your Father and your Provider intervene miraculously on your behalf. So, learn to trust in Him and as you do, let Him refine you.

Purpose 3: Refine you

In the **Oxford Dictionary**, refine means: *"Remove impurities or unwanted elements.*

> *"Remember how the LORD your God led you all the way in the desert these forty years, to humble you and to test you in order to know what was in your heart, whether or not you would keep his commands."* (Deuteronomy 8:2, NIV; cf. Zechariah 13:9; cf. Malachi 3:3)

A desert experience is a refining process to make you pure, better able to fulfill your purpose and integrate the whole. This benefits you and the common good in the end as you will acquire more of God's character and be more fruitful.

Silver and gold in their raw state are full of impurities. Thus, the Lord, like the silversmith, is very involved in your refining. He stands there earnestly watching the piece of silver He has placed in the hottest part of the fire. He watches intently because if it stays too long, it will be ruined. He doesn't want to take you out too soon before all the impurities are gone. He must constantly check to see if He can see his image clearly as that demonstrates the purifying process has finished. The refining process has a beginning and an end. You cannot speed up the process. Be patient and wait for the Refiner to say, "It is finished" for *"the one who endures to the end, he will be saved."* (Matthew 24:9-13) As you recall, Jesus was tempted to shorten His own refining in the desert and transform stones into bread so that He could eat and satisfy his raging hunger. His answer to Satan revealed his wisdom: *"No! The Scriptures say, 'People do not live by bread alone, but by every word that comes from the mouth of God.'"* (Matthew 4:4, NLT)

Principle: Be faithful to the end even as God is faithful.

Israel's desert and refining experiences were prolonged because they resisted and complained against God's leadership, even though, it would benefit them hugely in the end. Instead of one year, it became forty years. As they were not completely refined, impurities remained that ensnared them, took away from the glorious life that their Heavenly Father had envisioned for them, and brought strife, turmoil and pain to the Promised Land that was to be like heaven on earth. You are God's project and building; therefore, you must be committed to completing the process even as He is. Do not quit. The Godlier or more Christ-like you are the greater blessing you become. When you are healthy and pure, you enjoy life more, besides being more beneficial to the common good because you promote health and prosperity in the community.

God is far more interested in the being than in the doing. As you submit to the Christ-like-character-building and refining role of the Holy Spirit, it will make you willingly walk in the narrow way and deny the selfish desires of the flesh. As disciples or Spiritual leaders-in-training, you will still be asked by the Lord to carry out tasks while you are in this training and refining process. This is a potential problem as people may see in your imperfections and lack of professionalism, a reason not to accept you or what you are saying. However, in rejecting you, they also reject the Lord who sent you. (Luke 10:16)

So, expect the Lord to utilize the team, including trainees and women, and distribute different gifts to many as are available so that all are edified, and God is glorified. Everything in our ecosystem works synergistically; we too must have a strategy to synergize with one another, all the while having patience, gentleness, firmness, kindness and self-control.

Fourth Purpose of the Anointing is to Foment Intimacy with God

Principle: Every true Spiritual leader has a quality devotional lifestyle

We have a quality devotional life style when we spend time in His presence. **No** spiritual leader can work with the Holy Spirit unless he/she has intimacy with God. It is not only for us to determine when we spend time in His Presence but, more importantly, are we available when He seeks us out "*in the cool of the day*". Or, will He be crying out to us, "*Where are you*?" Genesis 3:8-9 When the Lord searches us out during the night, will you allow the Lord to bond with you and be gracious to you, for He never comes emptyhanded? There is a beautiful illustration of the drama that plays out, many times, in the Song of Solomon: -

> *I slept, but my heart was awake, when I heard my lover knocking and calling: "Open to me, my treasure, my darling, my dove, my perfect one. My head is drenched with dew, my hair with the dampness of the night." But I responded, "I have taken off my robe. Should I get dressed again? I have washed my feet. Should I get them soiled?" My lover tried to unlatch the door, and my heart thrilled within me. I jumped up to open the door for my love, and my hands dripped with perfume. My fingers dripped with lovely myrrh as I pulled back the bolt. I opened to my lover, but he was gone! My heart sank. I searched for him but could not find him anywhere. I called to him, but there was no reply. The night watchmen found me as they made their rounds. They beat and bruised me and stripped off my veil, those watchmen on the walls. Make this promise, O women of*

Jerusalem— If you find my lover, tell him I am weak with love. (Song of Solomon 5:2-8)

Furthermore, it is during these divine visits that the Lord informs us of His peacemaking action plans, strategies, goals and objectives. Look at His complaint:

> *"Have any of these prophets been in the LORD's presence to hear what he is really saying? Has even one of them cared enough to listen? "I have not sent these prophets, yet they run around claiming to speak for me. I have given them no message, yet they go on prophesying. If they had stood before me and listened to me, they would have spoken my words, and they would have turned my people from their evil ways and deeds. Am I a God who is only close at hand?" says the LORD. "No, I am far away at the same time."* (Jeremiah 23:18, 21-23)

The Lord showed His disappointment at those so-called prophets for their failure to honor Him and truly represent His Father's heart. Having a good submissive relationship with our Helper, His Holy Spirit, is vitally important as He has the responsibility of preparing us for Christ's coming and marriage, besides being essential for proper worship, for fomenting intimacy and for successful peacemaking. Resisting His efforts to move (lead), empower and enrich you will result in the Lord stating: *'I tell you the truth, I do not know you!'* (Matthew 25:12) You can argue that you worked on His behalf, *'Lord, Lord, did we not prophesy in your name and in your name drive out demons and, in your name, perform many miracles?* But what really matters, is whether you do *"the will of my Father who is in heaven."* (Matthew 7:21-23)

It is obvious, from all the work of the indwelling Spirit, in and through us, that we have a real treasure, which we must protect and value. Therefore, let the Spirit's God-fearing attitude mold your lifestyle. *"He will be the sure foundation for your times, a rich store of salvation and wisdom and knowledge; the fear of the LORD is the key to this treasure."* (Isaiah 33: 6; cf. Isaiah 11:2-4).

Now that we understand the importance of honoring the Head and of ensuring its integrity, we must agree wholeheartedly, and be entirely aligned, with its leadership.

AGREE WHOLEHEARTEDLY WITH THE HEAD

Principle: Love the Way of Righteousness for it is the way of life. It avoids pain, suffering, trouble and death.

The Lord, on creating the Heavens and the earth, wisely and intelligently designed them in such a way as to embed His rules of engagement in the infrastructure of His creation, thus making Spiritual rules into natural ones. He would then point to nature when He wanted to teach us right from wrong and tell us about His creation of the earth, the heavens and all living things. Read His amazing discourse about the latter in Job 38-41.

> *"But ask the animals, and they will teach you, or the birds in the sky, and they will tell you; or speak to the earth, and it will teach you, or let the fish in the sea inform you. Which of all these does not know that the hand of the LORD has done this?"* (Job 12:7-9)
>
> *"Even the stork in the sky knows her appointed seasons, and the dove, the swift and the thrush observe the time of their migration. But my people do not know the requirements of the LORD." (*Jeremiah 8:7)
>
> *"The ox knows its master, the donkey its owner's manger, but Israel does not know, my people do not understand."* (Isaiah 1:3)

Jesus himself pointed to nature in such parables as the Seed-Sower, the leaven and the fig tree when he wished to explain spiritual truths. So, let's look at nature ...

THE RULE OF NATURAL LAW

The Creator, through the Psalmist, relates truth and righteousness with love and peace:

> *"Loving kindness and truth have met together; Righteousness and peace have kissed each other. Truth springs from the earth, and righteousness looks down from heaven. Indeed, the LORD will give what is good, and our land will yield its produce. Righteousness will go before Him and will make His footsteps into a way."* (Psalm 85:10-13, NAS)

The Creator is revealing an amazing truth that loving kindness and wellness are inextricably tied to rock-solid truth and the Way of Righteousness.

> *"Loving kindness and truth have met together; Righteousness and (shalom) peace have kissed each other"*

Truth is the foundation of the way of right living and love and, therefore, must inform and guide our actions. The result is 'shalom', which means peace and overall wellness, success and prosperity. When you see and understand these things, life will no longer be a mystery or a secret, but will be abundantly clear to you. We must acquire and apply its knowledge in order to experience the joy and peace of overall health and wellness; and your life and wisdom will shine "*like the Sun at noon*". As we will see, God created our world in such a way that truth knowledge and natural law do dictate how life must be lived. Here, I will divide out the rest of these verses into 3 parts and go through them in greater detail.

1. *"Truth springs from the ground, Right living looks down from the skies"*

2. *"Indeed, the LORD will give what is good, and our land will yield its produce."*

3. *"Righteousness will go before Him and will make His footsteps into a way."*

"Truth springs from the ground, Right living looks down from the skies" (Psalm 85:11)

The **Oxford Dictionary** tells us that truth is '*the quality or state of being true*". **Merriam-Webster** defines it as "*the state of being the case; the body of real things, events, and facts; the body of true statements and propositions*." The fact that we can understand life, not only from the Scriptures, but also from observing and studying nature is fascinating. Paul understood this: "*For since the creation of the world God's invisible qualities--his eternal power and divine nature-- have been clearly seen, being understood from what has been made, so that people are without excuse.*" (Romans 1:20)

Scientists have long considered the universe to be fractal, in that, the same patterns that are observed under a microscope can be seen through a telescope. These patterns extend throughout the entire system, from the atomic to the galactic, and as Scripture decrees, from the physical to the spiritual. People who study life sciences and nature benefit from the knowledge, even as I did from studying Medicine. Thus, whether you study the skies or things here on earth, the observation and scientific study of nature teaches the truth about life and how it works. This knowledge can be used to shed light on spiritual principles, to help one live abundantly and love genuinely; and to enjoy life to the fullest, not only in the now, but eternally. Further to this, it can be used to solve life's problems. When the Way is transgressed and imbalance results, this is scientifically measurable, which allows us to understand the details of the transgression and the path of repentance. This helps us restore ourselves or the transgressor back to health and balance. In other words, there is a path of justice for every path of injustice. It also illuminates to us our eternal need to acknowledge and submit to the Head, which is Christ. It is no wonder that companies are learning to invest in truth finding and application, as their chief strategies for success, as they benefit from the profit -- lots of it.

Governments should be guided by truth knowledge when legislating and governing, rather than ignoring and attempting to remove foreordained boundaries, like Judah did (Hosea 5:10); or failing to acknowledge the Creator and Head of Heaven and earth, who not only guides us into all truth, but also helps us reverse the damage, both to ourselves and to the environment; (Hosea 5:7) and delivers us from powerful and evil beings, whose only objective in life is to oppose, oppress and destroy humanity. These are the aliens we should all be worried about rather than supposed ones living in other galaxies. Pride is useless and counter-productive (Hosea 5:5) as it leads to reckless, dangerous and destructive behaviors, besides alienating the only One who can help us. When companies and governments realize that honoring truth, loving-kindness, doing things right and profitability are all tied together, everyone benefits, especially them.

Being Part of an Organized Universal Ecosystem (the Common Good) that Works Together in Divine Synergy

System, as defined by the Oxford Dictionary, is "A *set of things working together as parts of a mechanism or an interconnecting network; a complex whole.*" The Bible says, *"And we know that all things work together for (the common) good."* (Romans 8:28a; NET) In 2001, a thousand scientists at the European Geophysical Union meeting, signed the Declaration of Amsterdam, starting with the statement: *"The*

Earth System behaves as a single, self-regulating system with physical, chemical, biological, and human components". And then from the Business Dictionary.com, we see:

> *"An organized, purposeful structure regarded as a whole and consisting of interrelated and interdependent elements (components, entities, factors, members, parts etc.). These elements continually influence one another (directly or indirectly) to maintain their activity and the existence of the system, in order to achieve the goal of the system." All systems have:*
> *(a) inputs, outputs, and feedback mechanisms,*
> *(b) maintain an internal steady-state (called homeostasis) despite a changing external environment,*
> *(c) display properties that are peculiar to the whole (called emergent properties) but are not possessed by any of the individual elements, and*
> *(d) have boundaries.*
>
> *Systems underlie every phenomenon and are everywhere one looks for them. They are limited only by the observer's capacity to comprehend the complexity of the observed entity, item or phenomenon. Every system is a part of a larger system, is composed of subsystems, and shares common properties with other systems that help in transferring understanding and solutions from one system to another. Systems obey rules that cannot be understood by breaking them into parts, and stop functioning (or malfunction) when an element is removed or altered significantly. Together, they provide a coherent and unified way of viewing and interpreting the universe as a meta-system of interlinked wholes, and of organizing our thoughts about the world. Although different types of systems (from a cell to the human body, soap bubbles to galaxies, ant colonies to nations) look so very different on the surface, they have remarkable similarities.*

In Psalm 104, the Psalmist praised the Creator when he observed this intricate organization of nature, which allows us to better appreciate the Genesis statement: *"God saw all that He had made, and behold, it was very good."* (Genesis 1:31) The entire universe functions as one giant whole. Each component in each sub-system is interdependent with all the other components as each one has a purpose to play in the overall ecosystem. The heavenly bodies, the sun and the moon ordained in their paths, on the one hand, and the Godhead, on the other, rule the affairs of the earth subsystem. While the former utilizes an assortment of rays, the latter has a host of angels at His service who work behind the scenes to benefit us and ensure the integrity of the ecosystem.

Remember we read in Job, *"Do you know the first thing about the sky's constellations and how they affect things on Earth?"* (Job 38:33, The Message) This entire ecosystem makes up the Kingdom of God and it encompasses heaven and earth with Yahweh as its Head, Chief Cornerstone and Chief Benefactor. As you recall from Step Two, God is at the top of the stairs that spans heaven and earth. The angels are traversing back and forth, and God and His created nature bless humanity, and even more so, those who are systemically aligned, integrated and make positive contributions.

> ***"Indeed, the LORD will give what is good, and our land will yield its produce."* (Psalm 85:12)**

Seeing that the entire ecosystem functions as one whole, you must …

Care for the Common Good as It Cares for You

The common good is what is good for everyone in an ecosystem economy. Everyone benefits from the quality life that the common good provides us. As everyone have responsibilities and purposes in the ecosystem, then everyone benefits when every component does their job for the common good. Ideally, everyone contributes faithfully to the common good.

"But seek first the Kingdom of God and his righteousness, and all these things will be added to you." (Matthew 6:33, ABPE) God and nature do their part independent of the irresponsibility of some. ***God is good because he works for the common good*** – *"for He causes His sun to rise on the evil and the good and sends rain on the righteous and the unrighteous."* (Matthew 5:45) The trees and vegetation consume the carbon dioxide we and other living things produce while producing oxygen that is vital to our survival. The entire functioning ecosystem, like the mother's pregnant womb, is a home in which we thrive, multiply and live. Similarly, it is to our collective and individual benefit when you fulfill your purpose and carry out your responsibilities because ***"all things (do) work together for good..."*** (Romans 8:28, NET*)* Each person's contribution towards the common good is important and, indeed, can be vital to the survival of others. Imagine a mother's responsibilities towards her unborn or newly born child or, if we fail to take care of the environment; there is no room for failure, for whatever reason.

Forces Exist in the Ecosystem that Bind Us Together

Astronomy and cosmology reveal truths about life. We can learn a great deal from the fixed order observed in the heavens. Look at how the galaxies are grouped together like clans, tribes and nations. The star with its planets and moons is like a family. Stars die and are born. The structure of the solar system is so strong that it keeps each component in place. The electro-magnetic forces exert such an attractive force that it keeps each planet in its orbit. These bonds can be shaken, but not broken; because, if any 'flee' from its orbit, the endangerment to self and others would be astronomical. In other areas of the ecosystem, there are forces built into its infrastructure that become evident when one leaves the boundaries of the Way. Homeostatic-restorative forces exist that strive to maintain in and return everything and everyone to the Way of Righteousness, in order to maintain wholeness, synergy and balance. However, these forces can and are overwhelmed when forces to the contrary 'push' them to the breaking point, in which case, the restorative forces then change the goal to recycling the non-conforming element. Order is restored one way or the other.

Besides the physical bonds, there are emotional ones that literally 'urge' us to behave in a manner that safeguards the ecosystem and the common good. Bonds of love move us to consistently carry out our communal responsibilities, which produce reciprocal feelings and thanksgiving in the beneficiaries. When we add the spiritual dimension of the Holy Spirit, these bonds become an unshakeable commitment. Together, these forces produce the unity, team and community that we have come to appreciate, which benefit everyone. Peace, wellness and joy, which are the result of our staying together within the boundaries of the Way, are, in themselves, reasons to stay in it, because their loss, in addition to pain, suffering and adversity, are potent forces that dissuade us from wrong behavior.

Such is the power of group dynamics in our universal ecosystem, in teamwork and in family, as it works to keep each member integrated. As well, it contributes to proper interdependent behavior that forces each to accommodate, align and stay within the boundaries. It opposes individualism and selfish/ egocentric behavior that are contrary to the whole, as behaviors, outside the boundaries, stress the bonds of peace and disturb and detract from the joy of living that the community shares.

We Either Work for the Common Good or We Work Against It

Inherent to all systems is interconnectedness. Every (legitimate) component has a role and purpose in the ecosystem so altogether everyone works for the common good of the whole. Teamwork is the means of success, wellbeing and survival. Hence, any malfunctioning or non-contributing part works against the other components and the overall ecosystem. In the ecosystem, we either work for the common good or we work against it. It is for this reason that the Lord said, "*Whoever is not with me is against me, and whoever does not gather with me scatters.*" (Matthew 12:30) By-standing, neglect, incompetence or incomplete actions work against the ecosystem and its collective good; one cannot remain on the fence -- *"So then, while we have opportunity, let us **work for the common good** of all people, and especially to those who are of the household of the faith."* (Galatians 6:10)

We Do Not Belong to Ourselves

Who owns your body? Do you have absolute rights over your body? No! In our interdependent and synergistic ecosystem world, we do not belong to ourselves but to the common good. Once you are born, you become part of the community to fulfill your role and purposes and to contribute to the common good like everybody else. You cannot control your '*own destiny*' nor is it in your '*power to determine what will happen*'. (Jeremiah10:23, NET*)* These determinations are fixed in nature as pre-determined by the Creator. Your responsibility, therefore, is to look after yourself, exercise self-control and remain within the boundaries of natural normalcy, so that you can be a consistent contributor to the common good.

Now that you better understand our ecosystem -- that all things, including you and I, are part of a whole that work together for the common good of all; that if I do not work for the common good, I actually work against it; that there are forces that bind us together; and that you do not belong to yourself, but to the community -- you can see why systemic or Kingdom values are so vitally important and why individualism, greed and egocentrism do not have a place in nature nor should they have a place in society. We must all work for the common good for it works tirelessly for everyone's welfare. The health of the entire ecosystem exercises far greater benefit towards its individual components than vice versa. 'We' and 'Us' are more important values than 'I' and 'Me'. Interdependence trumps independence. Team is in, individualism is out. The Musketeers had it right when they adopted the motto: *"One for all and all for one".* They understood that the collective wellbeing depended on their teamwork. Divided they fell. United they stood tall and unbeatable. They lived.

***"Righteousness will go before Him and will make His footsteps into a way."* (Psalm 85:13)**

In order for this to work, each component of the ecosystem such as you and I must behave in a prescribed manner.

One Way to Live -- a Thousand Ways to Die

Principle: Everyone, including you, benefits when you walk in the Way of life and righteousness.

As you observe nature, you will notice that everything has set foreordained boundaries and purposes. There is a normal range for everything in nature. This is a key principle in our systemic, synergistic world and is a well-known Christian principle. The Creator made the earth, the seas and the atmosphere and systematically populated them with living things, ultimately creating an intelligently-designed ecosystem. From the Oxford Dictionary, we can read that an '*ecosystem*' means: *"A biological community of interacting organisms and their physical environment."* This physical environment, our planet, is just as alive as the flora and fauna that call it home. Each living thing was created to fulfill a purpose or purposes in the ecosystem. Lastly, God created humans, as the centerpiece of His creation, and placed them in this ecosystem to look after it and to rule over every living being. (Genesis 1:26-31; 2:15)

Each component must remain within the Creator's prescribed and fixed parameters of being and behavior in order to fulfill their foreordained purposes, so that the whole can function synergistically. The life of the entire ecosystem is dependent upon each part remaining within its respective boundaries and functioning in their prescribed manner. Fortunately, the boundaries of all the noble parts are fixed in nature. The sun stays on its course. The earth, planets and moon run in their respective orbits, without wavering. God remains steadfast in His purpose, as Head, and so should all humans whom He created in His own marvelous image.

> *"Praise him, sun and moon. Praise him, all shining stars. Praise him, you highest heaven and the water above the sky. Let them praise the name of the LORD because they were created by his command. He set them in their places forever and ever. He made it a law that no one can break."* (Psalm 148:3-6 NASB; cf. Psalm 104; Jeremiah 31:35-36)

Principle: The normal range of everything is pre-set and unchangeable.

The normal range of human blood electrolytes and a host of other normal components of our bodies are fixed. They cannot be changed. They are the same in any part of the planet and will be, as long as the Sun, moon and stars remain. In fact, God ties the presence of this fixed order to the existence of Israel as a nation. Israel, today, despite all their mistakes, remains part of God's overall plan.

> *"This is what the LORD says: The One who*
> *gives the sun for light by day, the fixed*
> *order of moon and stars for light by night, who stirs*
> *up the sea and makes its waves roar, Yahweh of*
> *Hosts is His name: If this fixed*
> *order departs from My presence this is*

the LORD's declaration -- then
also Israel's descendants will cease to be a
nation before Me forever." (Jeremiah 31:35-36, HCS;
cf. Jeremiah 33:20-21,25; Psalm 89:34,37)

Look at the amazing statement God makes about humanity's quest for knowledge and how this relates to Israel's existence, as a nation, and to God's care for the Jews:

"This is what the LORD says: If the
heavens above can be measured and the
foundations of the earth below explored, I will
reject all of Israel's descendants because
of all they have done — this is
the LORD's declaration." (Jeremiah 31:37, HCS)

Fortunately, I believe, science is still far from figuring out these hidden things.

Therefore, life is predictable because of this permanent fixed order. It allows us to make laws, rules and regulations based on these set parameters. We know how things in life are supposed to behave to fulfill their purpose and responsibilities in the ecosystem. The terms that God uses to describe this fixed order and its boundaries and rules are righteousness and justice. While these terms are mostly used interchangeably, righteousness refers to the normal range or narrow way, whereas justice refers to the boundaries beyond which mechanisms are unleashed to return any errant component back to the Way. Justice is deemed victorious when it succeeds in returning the errant one back to normalcy or in restoring order. Jesus will ultimately "*cause justice to be victorious*". Matthew 12:20

Amazingly, long before the advent of modern science, Jesus made this enlightening statement about the way of righteousness and justice:

"Enter through the narrow gate; for the gate is wide and the way is broad that leads to destruction, and there are many who enter through it; but the gate is small and the way is narrow that leads to life, and there are few who find it." (Matthew 7:13-14, NASB; cf. Deuteronomy.5:32*)*

Life will flourish and thrive within this confined, narrow way of life, while it will suffer outside of it, on either side. For example, if the earth gets too near the Sun, everything and everyone on Earth would burn to death and be destroyed. If it goes too far, you will freeze to death. Your blood sugar must be within the normal range for you to live. If there is hypo- or hyperglycemia (deficiency or excess, respectively), your health and quality of life becomes diminished, and you can die, if it is not corrected soon. If your finger is yanked out of its normal range, you will immediately feel pain and it will break, if it is too far outside the normal range.

If you transgress the boundaries of normal behavior, you will suffer adversity. Therefore, pain, malfunction, ineffectiveness, loss of ability to fulfill one's purpose, loss of quality of life, death and destruction are all symptoms of our being outside our normal or optimal range. This is what the Bible calls *sin* and *evil*. Life loses its quality proportionate to the degree that it is off track. Thus, the way of righteousness offers the highest quality of life, which is complete wellness, as this ensures synergy and the integrity of the whole.

Let us look at the following schematic which shows the narrow way with its foreordained boundaries:

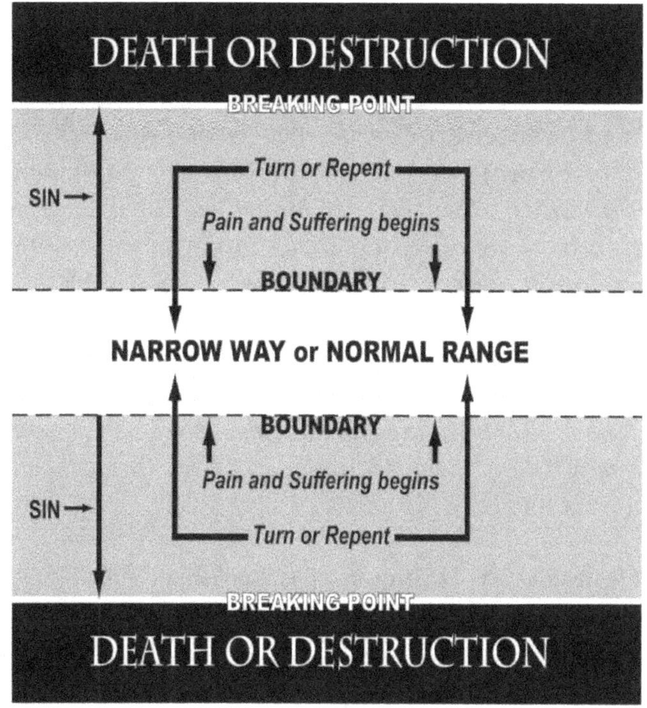

The breaking points, on either side, make up the boundaries of the broad way. On either side, as one abandons the boundary-confined narrow way, there is the onset of pain, suffering and malfunctioning. Pain and suffering increase the further one distances oneself from the boundaries of the narrow way until the breaking point is reached and the part no longer fulfills its purpose. Death and destruction ensue. The values of both the normal range and the breaking points for each element and behavior are fixed in nature.

The Bible used many words and synonyms to refer to this way of life and are invariably translated as *road, way, highway, ordinance, decree, statute, fixed order, pathway, path, course*.

The Way of life: "*The path of life leads upward for the wise; they leave the grave behind.*" (Proverbs 15:24, NLT)

The Way of Righteousness: *"In the way of righteousness is life, and in its pathway, there is no death."* (Proverbs 12:28, ESV)

The Road to Success: *"Keep the charge of the LORD your God, to walk in His* ***ways****, to keep His* ***statutes****, His* ***commandments****, His* ***ordinances****, and His testimonies, according to what is written in the Law of Moses, that you may succeed in all that you do and wherever you turn."* (1 Kings 2:3, NASB)

The Way of the Lord: *"For I have chosen him, so that he may command his children and his household after him to keep the* ***way*** *of the LORD by doing righteousness and justice, so that the LORD may bring upon Abraham what He has spoken about him."* (Genesis 18:19 NASB)

The Highway of Holiness: *"A* ***highway*** *will be there, a* ***roadway****, and it will be called the* ***Highway*** *of Holiness. The unclean will not travel on it, but it will be for him who walks that* ***way****, and fools will not wander on it. No lion will be there, nor will any vicious beast go up on it; these will not be found there. But the redeemed will walk there, and the ransomed of the LORD will return and come with joyful shouting to Zion, with everlasting joy upon their heads. They will find gladness and joy, and sorrow and sighing will flee away."* (Isaiah 35:8-10, NASB)

The Way of Peace and Wellness: *"The way of peace (wellness) they do not know, and there is no justice in their paths; they have made their roads crooked; no one who treads on them knows peace,"* (Isaiah 59:8, NASB) The Hebrew word, '*shalom*', which is usually translated as peace, includes the following meanings -- wellness, health, overall wellbeing, wholeness; peace, prosperity. It is life in all its fullness; abundant or quality life. *"I have come that they may have life and have it to the full."* (John 10:10)

You are able to withstand life's trials when you walk in it: *When the storms of life come, the wicked are whirled away, but the godly have a lasting foundation."* (Proverbs 10:25)

You avoid adversity: *"The road of right living bypasses evil; watch your step and save your life."* (Proverbs 16:17, MSG) and *"Why then are you transgressing the commandment of the LORD, when it will not succeed (bring benefit)?* (Numbers 14:41, NASB)

Note: Webster's Revised Unabridged Dictionary states that 'to transgress' means: *To overpass a prescribed limit or boundary; to break a law; to sin.*

You are not lost or confused: *"... for the LORD knows the way of the righteous, but the way of the wicked is being lost." (*Psalm 1:6)

Hiking to the top of Gavea Rock, Rio de Janeiro, Brazil

I once went with a group of young people to the top of the Pedra da Gavea (Gavea Rock). This mountain, located in Gavea, in the southern part of Rio de Janeiro is so named because at its top is perched a huge rock, square in shape, which can be seen from almost any part of Rio. At the foot of the mountain is a huge forest through which we could traverse to get to the top. There is a main road going up this mountain, which stops just short of the rock. It's quite common to find cars with hand gliders tied down to the roof making their way up this road as it is an ideal take off location for hand gliders. However, we desired the thrill of trekking through the forest, so we avoided the road and went up using the more exciting trail through the Tijuca Forest (Botanical Gardens and Conservation Park), another one of Rio's popular tourist attractions.

We quickly found the trail located in the heart of the forest just off the asphalt road. At times, the trail opened into a clearing, but for the most part it was a narrow path. Anyone thinking of leaving the trail would have to face, not only the thick bush that formed natural boundaries on either side of the path, but also the risk of getting lost if they strayed too far off the beaten trail. Quite a few stories abound of trekkers who got lost, which led us to stay close to one another and never venture off the main trail.

It wasn't long before we were at the top of the rock overlooking one of the most beautiful cities in the world. What a view, but scary nonetheless as a sheer drop confronted us on three sides of the huge rock. We watched as a young man prepared his hand glider and then ran off the top of the rock into the strong, invisible but reliable hands of the wind. After a good time of gliding through the air, he would later land on one of Rio's famous beaches, the Ipanema Beach, popularized by the famous Brazilian song played in the Bossa Nova rhythm, "*The Girl from Ipanema*".

There are benefits to remaining on the main road to get to the destination, rather than taking a less established trail going through the thick bush and getting injured or lost or even losing one's life, as many had done over the years. Our Heavenly Father created a highway for all humanity that is based on truth knowledge and maintains balance and synergy in the ecosystem. In it, we thrive, multiply and live forever. This road is full of life: it breathes and produces a quality life; it is the abundant and glorious life He promised; and no death is found on it.

This way of righteousness has boundaries, which confine and separate it from the multitude of paths and trails that Jesus referred to as the broad way that lead to dysfunction and ultimately death. Beaten paths are created simply by many people walking on them. Their existence doesn't mean that they are based on truth, are safe or are effective at preserving equilibrium or safeguarding the common good. It only means that people have chosen to create and utilize it. The rules of justice identify the behaviors that transgress. For this reason, God gave us the Ten Commandments and all the other rules (ordinances, statutes, laws) which tell us when we have transgressed the boundaries of life, have fallen from grace and from the abundant (quality) life and have entered the broad way. These paths of injustice are also confined by breaking points beyond which destruction or death occur.

According to the Scriptures and to nature, we can all enjoy a rich and satisfying life now by simply remaining within the Creator-prescribed way of life. However, this fact is tempered by the understanding that, because we live in an ecosystem, we can still suffer the consequences of the transgressions of others and even of past generations. In other words, bad things can and will still happen to good people; even if they obey the rules of engagement that God and nature require.

As we are a team, and for the sake of the common good, we become responsible to 'urge' transgressors to repent. This community-mindedness will contribute to our overall wellbeing. Besides, these adversities can ultimately contribute to trying us, molding us and proving us so we become 'pure gold' and come out as overcomers. As we saw before, our Heavenly Father is our refuge from the storm of life's adversities and does promise that life will become everlasting and truly abundant, without the tears and sorrow that result from transgressions; if we abide in His love and in the narrow way.

DO EVERYTHING AS TOLD --WITHOUT ADDING OR SUBTRACTING

Restorative Justice: Natural, Divine and Legal

Principle: As an ecosystem, all the components of life, whether spiritual, biological or physical, must be in perfect balance or synergy.

Balance or equilibrium is necessary for the perfect functioning of each component at the microscopic level and of the whole ecosystem at the macroscopic level. Synergy, and thus wellness, result when balance is attained and maintained. Balance is the bull's eye. In nature, it is called a balanced ecosystem. In medical terms, it is called homeostasis.

Homeostasis is the physiological process by which the internal systems of the body (e.g. blood pressure, body temperature, and acid-base balance) are maintained in equilibrium despite variations in the external conditions. Homeostasis is lost, however, when the variations exceed their tolerance level. Disease, adversity, inability to thrive and eventually death and or destruction would ensue, if balance is not restored quickly.

Perfect balance occurs when each component can fulfill its set, fore-ordained purposes and remain or behave within their set, fore-ordained boundaries. This balance is accomplished and maintained through nature's restorative mechanisms, which include sharing, and giving and receiving, on the one hand, and neutralizing, isolating, quarantining and recycling, on the other. The Creator placed, in us/ in nature, a restorative mechanism that returns a part to normal every time it transgresses the boundaries of the normal range. In other words, whether it's a physical element or a person that got onto a wayward path (injustice), a restorative path (justice) intervenes. Thus, justice restores order from disorder and balance from imbalance. The Word says, *"I will correct you with justice. I won't let you go entirely unpunished."* (Jeremiah 30:11c, GW cf. and 10:24)

Intercellular Dynamics: An Example of Biological Interdependence and Sharing

Every component of life -- internally, at the biochemical level, and, externally, at the interpersonal or ecosystem levels -- must share its resources with one another, if all are to fulfill their purposes and live optimally. In our bodies, each cell does not possess everything it needs to survive. Some elements are in excess and some are in deficiency; and both these states are detrimental to cellular health. Fortunately, there are transport mechanisms in place that allow cells to share across their respective walls, so that together they arrive at a state of balance. Each cell has gaps in its walls through which ionic exchange can occur, so that whichever one had an element in excess, can share it with another that has it in deficiency, and vice versa. Outside the cell walls there is an extracellular (also called intercellular) space, which functions as a pool into which all the elements in excess go. These travel throughout the body via the lymphatic and blood vessels. Cells, when in need, can and will take from this pool. Thus, cells share their excess to avoid being internally poisoned and, at the same time, contribute to the welfare of other cells and organs and to the common good. This way, the cells can all remain in perfect balance and health. When the entire body is in homeostasis, no cell has excessive or deficient amounts of any element for too long due to this non-stop, continuous sharing. This is the essence and work of community. In a crisis, however, less important organs, such as, the skin and muscles have a curtailed access to the intercellular space and its resources, thus favoring the noble organs.

Just as our body is continuously rebalancing itself throughout the day, we ourselves must also carefully and tirelessly do the same, fearing the effects of imbalance. Society and government have an important responsibility to ensure balance through the equitable sharing of, and access to, resources and the prompt restoration of 'malfunctioning' elements through quarantine, isolation and other restorative justice measures. These ensure the health of the entire community.

The well-known life principle, "*You reap what you sow*" is a true statement. You reap abundant life when you remain within the confines of the normal range of life; and reap adversity, pain and sorrow and even death, if you stray too far. It is, therefore, not only in your best interest to remain within the narrow way, but it is also in the best interest of the community and of nature. It's your responsibility to first re-balance your own life, then to work with others and with the Holy Spirit to re-balance the world.

Now that you have seen nature's corrective measures at work, let's look at how the biblical ordinance of tithing promote equilibrium.

Equilibrium Occurs Through the Ordinance of Tithes and Offerings

The interdependent and balancing mechanisms observed at the intercellular level shed light on the Biblical ordinance of tithes and offerings that have the purpose of sharing resources and putting food on the table of God's ministers and the needy.

> "*Bring all the tithes into the* ***storehouse*** *so there will be enough food in my Temple. If you do," says the LORD of Heaven's Armies, "I will open the windows of heaven for you. I will pour out a blessing so great you won't have enough room to take it in! Try it! Put me to the test!*" (Malachi 3:10, NLT)

The **storehouse** has the same function as the 'extracellular space'. We are to set aside a tithe (or tenth) "*of all that you give me*" to give to the Lord's workers -- whose only source of income is the ministry: pastors, missionaries, ministry workers (the noble organs) (Numbers 18:21-24, 26-28) -- and to the poor (the skin and muscles). (Deuteronomy 26:12) The priests and Levites managed a central storehouse from which distribution took place, but the people could give directly to the Levites and poor in their towns. Offerings were also given to the ministers, and special offerings were collected for building, renovations and other ministry expenses. (Exodus 30:12-16; 2 Chronicles

24:6) All undesignated offerings would also be allotted to building and ministry expenses, once everyone had enough. This was to ensure that tithes were not used for other purposes other than putting food on the tables of the workers and giving to the poor. In times of crisis, as in the body, the ministry workers would get first access to the storehouse.

Today, there is no physical central storehouse and no central distribution center. Each church has become a localized central storehouse for each congregation, but not without problems. The responsibility to rightly distribute the tithes and offerings has fallen upon those who manage the congregations. While the apostles and elders managed the city churches of their time, pastors and church boards, today, have taken on the onus of administrating the distribution. In the Parable of the Faithful Steward, Jesus warns all managers to be careful to distribute the tithe equitably so that all ministry workers are adequately fed, as they are the primary beneficiaries:

> *"And the Lord replied, "A faithful, sensible servant is one to whom the master can give the responsibility of managing his other household servants and feeding them. If the master returns and finds that the servant has done a good job, there will be a reward. I tell you the truth, the master will put that servant in charge of all he owns. But what if the servant thinks, 'My master won't be back for a while,' and he begins beating the other servants, partying, and getting drunk? The master will return unannounced and unexpected, and he will cut the servant in pieces and banish him with the unfaithful."* (Luke 12:42-46, NLT)

Unfortunately, global and local missionaries have not had the same access to tithes as pastors do and here are some of the reasons:

First, missionaries are generally not seen as entitled to the tithes and special offerings are sought for these. Missionaries or apostles (sent ones) are ministry workers and, therefore, are entitled to the equitable distribution of the tithes.

Second, tithes have been used for things other than the remuneration of ministry workers. They are applied to general ministry expenses, which include mortgages, rents, utilities, etc., and even building renovations and building funds. Missionaries only get the left-overs, if any, or hope for dedicated offerings.

Third, an erroneous teaching has been given to congregations that their entire tithe belonged in the church where *"they were being fed on a regular basis"*. In other words, each local church sees itself as a central storehouse. The giving of tithes to ministry workers outside the congregation has been frowned upon and made difficult by internal church policies and constant reminders from the pulpit. Members sometimes are asked to sign an agreement to bring all their tithes to the church.

This led to yet another error: **other ministry agencies other than churches have been designated as 'Para-churches' without the entitlement to receive tithes.** *Para-churches* are organizations that '*come alongside churches*' to engage in Kingdom business. The traditional church appreciates the ministry of these para-churches and, in fact, utilizes them as outlets for ministry. The Biblical truth is that any gathering of the Elect is considered a Church (*"For where two or three gather together as my followers, I am there among them."* (Matthew 18:20*)* In fact, missionaries are apostles, whom the Lord has called, appointed and sent on missions. However, they must raise their own support through crowd funding to fulfill God's Great Commission as they are not guaranteed a salary as pastors are. Mission organizations, like OM, are not considered as churches so are not entitled to collect tithes; even though, they are scripturally and legally able to. As churches assumed the responsibility to collect and distribute tithes, their leaders became responsible before the Lord (*Parable of the Unfaithful Steward*) to do so faithfully and equitably, which has not always been the case. Missionaries and other para-church ministers have not been able to access the tithes in an equitable manner.

The proper practice should be for pastors to encourage their congregations to give their tithes to any worker engaged in ministry as led by the Spirit. Mission organizations should be able to receive tithes like churches do, so as to be able to pay salaries, benefits and pensions to their workers in order to correct a grave injustice. Now, they rely solely on offerings and sponsors. Whenever a believer is called to work in the harvest on a fulltime or part-time basis, they should have an easier access to the tithes of the people as all the priests and Levites did when tithing was first introduced by our Lord.

It is the Holy Spirit who calls, appoints and commissions workers so they have as much right to the tithe as pastors do. It is for **all** the latter and the former that the Lord instituted tithing to ensure they were adequately cared for. You cannot say to the newly called worker: *"If the Lord has called you then He will provide your wages*". The Lord, over three thousand years ago, already provided this mechanism of tithing and offerings for this very purpose. There is no other mechanism available from the Lord other than what has already been created. Many churches aim to allocate 10% of their income towards missions and some even aim for more, but this practice still falls far short of what the Lord told us to do. One hundred percent (100%) of tithes must be allocated towards remunerating the workers. When tithes are insufficient, then offerings can be sought.

Tithes and offerings allow for equilibrium to occur so that everyone has enough rather than some have too much, and some have too little. As we saw in intercellular dynamics, everyone should have easier access to the resources in the 'extracellular space'. The Early Church had it right when they implemented this principle of sharing soon after its inauguration:

> *"And all the believers met together in one place and shared everything they had. They sold their property and possessions and shared the money with those in need. They worshiped together at the Temple each day, met in homes for the Lord's Supper, and shared their meals with great joy and generosity— all the while praising God and enjoying the goodwill of all the people. And each day the Lord added to their fellowship those who were being saved."* (Acts 2:44-47, NLT)

What a testimony to the world when they witness this sort of common unity in Christendom! What joy our Lord will have when He returns and finds all His workers being adequately cared for!

Now, let's look at the role that forgiveness and reconciliation play in promoting equilibrium and wholeness.

Equilibrium via Forgiveness and Reconciliation

The Lord told the Israelites to "*not despise an Egyptian, because you resided as foreigners in their country.*" (Deuteronomy 23:7) Any Israelite would have felt justified in hating the Egyptians for mistreating them. Future generations would also feel the right to harbor resentment against them for the same reason. The Lord, though, knew that these feelings were detrimental to community and would disrupt not only the interpersonal balance, but also the balance at the internal level. Harboring these toxic sentiments would raise interpersonal barriers, which would prevent sharing, giving and taking – "*I do not want anything from you*"; *"I will not give you anything"; or, "I will not have anything to do with you"*. Perfect balance can only occur when we are willing to share, give or take from others. Furthermore, the anger and bitterness that stem from withholding forgiveness will eventually disrupt the internal equilibrium, stress the internal organs and lower the body's immunity, which in turn results in a variety of physical and mental illnesses. Thus, forgiveness and reconciliation promote equilibrium and restore wellness and community.

Now, we will look at the other side of the coin of nature's restorative mechanisms.

Poisons Disrupt Equilibrium

Principle: No poisons must be found in an ecosystem as they upset the perfect balance or order in nature.

God created powerful restorative forces to spring into action whenever any element is outside its normal range. Like the forces that seek to restore elastic to its resting state when it is stretched, such are these restorative forces that transform, neutralize, isolate and/or remove what is disjointed, detrimental or useless to the ecosystem. Jesus pointed this out when he reminded us that *"You are the salt of the earth. But if the salt loses its saltiness, how can it be made salty again? It is no longer good for anything, except to be thrown out and trampled underfoot."* (Matthew 5:13) Transgressions of nature's narrow way, which disrupt its perfect balance, will unleash these restorative mechanisms to either restore the transgressor to the Narrow Way or, in the case of failure, they will continue working to recycle the element to dust. "*By the sweat of your brow you will eat your food until you return to the ground, since from it you were taken; for dust you are and to dust you will return."* (Genesis 3:19) The increase in sin, despite these restorative forces being unleashed, has led to the reduction in humans' life span. While people lived to almost a millennium in Adam's time, it was capped at a hundred and twenty years (Genesis 6:3*);* most people now live only on average 70 to 80 years, "*by reason of strength*". (Psalm 90:10)

We are all aware of what poisons can do to us. No one would willingly choose a glass of cyanide over a glass of water. Cyanide is a foreign element and has no function in our bodies.

Similarly, 'foreign' behaviors are disruptive both to our society and to nature: *"A man must not defile himself by having sex with an animal. And a woman must not offer herself to a male animal to have intercourse with it. This is a perverse act."* (Leviticus 18:23) The Hebrew transliterated word, *tebel,* usually translated as 'perversion', or 'incest' also means *'confusion, violation of the divine order or violation of nature's order,* according to the TDOT (Botterweck and Ringgren). The synonym 'defiled' can also be translated as *'polluted'* or *'poisoned'*. Any foreign element or perverse behavior leads to dysfunction in the ecosystem.

There is zero tolerance towards some poisonous elements. The human body's answer to any poison is to quarantine, isolate and/or eliminate it so as to prevent it from harming the body. An element in excess will function as a toxin to the body; hence, the need to keep it strictly within the normal range. An organ that is under- or hyper-functioning can be a liability to the entire body and will, in most cases, need the urgent intervention of physicians and surgeons to restore or excise the diseased and disjointed organ and replace it with a transplant, when possible. The Lord was adamant at prohibiting tattoo markings on one's body because it would lead to immune deficiencies and a host of other diseases -- *"Do not ... put tattoo marks on yourselves. I am the LORD."* Lev.19:28 The Lord knew that the body's immune system would try to quarantine and eliminate the foreign body (ink), which would lead to immune deficiency disorders.

Whenever you suffer food poisoning, the body will immediately react with vomiting to eliminate the perpetrator. Similarly, bad behaviors, whether of the excessive nature (rage, homosexuality, witchcraft) or of the deficient kind (by-standing, neglect, insufficient nurture, motivation or guidance) will have a similar dysfunctional and negative effect upon the body, community or land and must, therefore, be curtailed and eliminated.

Look at the dilemma it causes the Lord:

"The Kingdom of heaven may be compared to a man who sowed good seed in his field. "But while his men were sleeping, his enemy came and sowed tares among the wheat, and went away. "But when the wheat sprouted and bore grain, then the tares became evident also. "The slaves of the landowner came and said to him, 'Sir, did you not sow good seed in your field? How then does it have tares?' "And he said to them, 'An enemy has done this!' The slaves said to him, 'Do you want us, then, to go and gather them up?' "But he said, 'No; for while you are gathering up the tares, you may uproot the wheat with them. 'Allow both to grow together until the harvest; and in the time of the harvest I will say to the reapers, "First gather up the tares and bind them in bundles to burn them up; but gather the wheat into my barn." (Matthew 13:24-30, NASB)

Tares were noxious weeds that, at a certain point in their development, looked just like wheat. While we are not concerned when a few blades of grass are removed with the weeds, the Lord shows His concern about wanting to avoid collateral damage to the innocents when evil people are '*rooted out*'. The suggestion is to leave them to the 'final harvest of Divine Justice' when everyone will be sorted out. This is not to say that nature's and society's legal justice system should not continue their work. Nature's Justice is always working and will be doing so as long as this Solar Order is in place. It is, however, slow, giving people the chance to repent and rehabilitate.

While extra caution is warranted with people, no such concern must be given to poisonous behavior and false ideas; these must be avoided, quarantined, isolated and eliminated just like what the immune system does in our body system. Otherwise, they will harm us and the entire ecosystem. Failure to do so will be disastrous, whether it is to a body system, to a society or to the land. Take, for example, the false idea that "there is no one perfect". This false idea that no one can be perfect has been ingrained in us throughout our lives. It tells us that we don't have to try hard to get rid of our bad habits for we will not succeed. As a result, society is made up of people who expect others to accept them the way they are. They even created labor unions to protect your interests should your employer try to get rid of you. The Lord, however, knowing that the ecosystem requires perfection, tells us to "be perfect therefore as your Heavenly Father is perfect." (Matthew 5:48) The purpose and work of the Holy Spirit is to refine and purge us of all our sinful ways until we are holy, that is, pure just like He is; (1 Peter 1:16) for "*without holiness no one will see the Lord*". (Hebrews 12:14)

Effects of Immorality on Nature and Climate Change

When we continually transgress against nature's boundaries, it has a negative effect on the planet. God warned the Israelites: *"All these detestable activities are practiced by the people of the land where I am taking you, and this is how the land has become defiled. So do not defile the land and give it a reason to vomit you out, as it will vomit out the people who live there now."* (Leviticus 18:27-28 HCSB) Our collective survival depends on this or else nature will '*vomit us out*' and put others in our place. When referring to the reason for the adversities that Israel was facing, God said through Jeremiah, *"My people do not know the requirements of the Lord."* (Jeremiah 8:7b) It could also be put like this: "*My people do not know life's (or nature's) requirements.*" The Creator lays out the charges against the people and by them explains what really hurts the land -- our bad behavior and our reckless ignoring of knowledge – complacency:

> *"Hear the word of the Lord, you Israelites, because the Lord has a charge to bring against you who live in the land: "There is no faithfulness (truth), no love, no*

acknowledgment of God in the land. There is only cursing, lying and murder, stealing and adultery; they break all bounds, and bloodshed follows bloodshed. Because of this the land dries up, and all who live in it waste away; the beasts of the field, the birds in the sky and the fish in the sea are swept away. My people are destroyed from lack of knowledge. "Because you have rejected knowledge, I also reject you as my priests; because you have ignored the law of your God, I also will ignore your children." (Hosea 4:1-3, 6)

After listing many forms of sexual immorality, including bestiality, homosexuality, adultery and incest, He goes on to say,

"All these detestable activities are practiced by the people of the land where I am taking you, and this is how the land has become defiled. So do not defile the land and give it a reason to vomit you out, as it will vomit out the people who live there now. Whoever commits any of these detestable sins will be cut off from the community of Israel. So obey my instructions, and do not defile yourselves by committing any of these detestable practices that were committed by the people who lived in the land before you. I am the LORD your God." Leviticus 18:27-30.

Our bad behavior does have consequences in the ecosystem. They have negative cascading effects that ultimately harm the environment.

The proper application of knowledge is very important and failure to do so is disastrous. God even criticizes the priests because their role was to instruct the people and be role models of right living. Instead their immoral behavior demonstrated a rejection or ignoring of that knowledge, which was not only foolish, but detrimental to society and to nature -- to society, because they were supposed to be role models and, as teachers, they were giving false instruction; and to nature, because they not only engaged in the same abominable behavior but encouraged the people to continue in wrongdoing, which all together had a harmful effect on nature. Today, we are witnessing this same behavior by a segment of the Church, as is evidenced by the sexual scandals and politically correct sanctioning of same-sex marriages, etc.

Nature's inevitable response would be to *'vomit them out'* just as the body does when it ingests spoilt food. Look at this prophecy of Isaiah from the early 700s BCE:

> "*Earth is polluted by its very own people, who have broken its laws, disrupted its order, violated the sacred and eternal covenant. Therefore a curse, like a cancer, ravages the earth. Its people pay the price of their sacrilege. They dwindle away, dying out one by one.*" (Isaiah 24:5-6 MSG)

Today, the news is filled with the signs and concerns about Global Warming and its effect upon nature and all humanity. Everyone is experiencing the instability that one can observe in the form of earthquakes, tsunamis and extreme weather turmoil. In 2016, Canadians experienced the warmest winter ever. Since Al Gore came out with the documentary, 'An Inconvenient Truth', it has been on everybody's minds. Governments are scrambling to come up with an effective strategy; and scientists are doing the same trying to pinpoint the blame and so arrive at the solution or solutions.

Everyone agrees that humans have wrecked the earth and the environment. The question is, "In what way?" This is an important question because if the problem(s) is (are) adequately analyzed then the solution(s) will also be adequate; the alternative is troubling. Scientists acknowledge the natural cycles of global warming and cooling. We might be going through one of those warming cycles. However, aren't human irresponsibility, foolishness and greed also part of the problem? Couldn't human foolishness be contributing and adding to global warming? As for the Lord, He would say "Yes!" He should know for He created it! In those days, there was no real pollution in the magnitude that exists today for people to blame; deforestation certainly was not at the level it is today; but witchcraft and sexual immorality were just as rampant as today.

Have we reached the tipping point? I hope not! If we haven't, is it reversible? I believe so because if a significant percentage of people repent of wrongdoing and commit to unselfish love, there will be a net positive benefit to everyone. It is not wise for governments to institute carbon taxing while promoting and decriminalizing, in the name of freedom of expression and human rights, the very behavior that will break the earth and cause it to '*vomit*' us out. Carbon taxing will be ineffective and wasted when we must pay for the consequences of those very bad behaviors upon lives, families, society and the environment.

Humans have violated nature by their egotistic, self-serving and greedy attitudes. They have disobeyed the rules of engagement that have existed since humans came into existence and broken off the much needed and mutually beneficial relationship between them, the created ones, and their Creator; or, put in other terms, between sons and daughters and their Heavenly Father, the Head. His Fatherly role and purpose are to teach His children the right way and to raise them to be successful and highly productive adults. For the most part, humans have chosen to ignore, reject and remain orphans of their Heavenly Father. They have instead become angry at Him and His children for admonishing and encouraging them to turn away from their destructive behavior. Men and women, governments and scientists have gone so far as to deny His existence and are currently engaged in wiping out all references to Him in all areas of our lives. They count His rules and statutes as religious garbage, myths and fairy tales and have refused His instruction and help. They have in fact made Him, the Creator, a *persona non-grata* in human affairs and in His own land.

Rev. Joe Wright, senior pastor of the 2,500-member Central Christian Church in Wichita, delivered this opening prayer at a session of the Kansas House of Representatives in January of 1996 using a version of the Prayer to Change a Nation first written and delivered by Bob Russell in 1995 at the Kentucky Governor's Prayer Breakfast in Frankfort, Kentucky:

> *Heavenly Father, we come before you to ask for your forgiveness. We seek your direction and your guidance. We know your Word says, "Woe to those who call evil good". But that's what we've done.*
> *We've lost our spiritual equilibrium. We have inverted our values.*
> *We have ridiculed the absolute truth of your Word in the name of moral pluralism.*
> *We have worshipped other gods and called it multiculturalism.*
> *We have endorsed perversion and called it an alternative lifestyle.*
> *We have exploited the poor and called it a lottery.*
> *We have neglected the needy and called it self-preservation.*
> *We have rewarded laziness and called it welfare.*
> *In the name of choice, we have killed our unborn.*
> *In the name of right to life, we have killed abortionists.*
> *We have neglected to discipline our children and called it building self-esteem.*
> *We have abused power and called it political savvy.*
> *We have coveted our neighbor's possessions and called it taxes.*
> *We have polluted the air with profanity and pornography and called it freedom of expression.*
> *We have ridiculed the time-honored values of our forefathers and called it enlightenment.*

Search us, oh God, and know our hearts today. Try us and show us any wickedness within us. Cleanse us from every sin and set us free. Guide and bless these men and women who have been sent here by the people of Kansas, and that they have been ordained by You to govern this great state. Grant them Your wisdom to rule. May their decisions direct us to the center of Your will. And, as we continue our prayer and as we come in out of the fog, give us clear minds to accomplish our goals as we begin this Legislature. For we pray in Jesus' name, Amen.

In our synergistic ecosystem, each legitimate component fulfilling its natural purpose(s) and responsibilities, will contribute to a state of equilibrium by remaining within its set parameters in order to produce optimal results for the common good. Removing an element or introducing a foreign element or altering the behavior of an element will create imbalance and malfunction. This means that you cannot change the parameters to whatever suits you or some segment of society as this only harms the common good. Changing the rules of engagement just to satisfy a culture, a religious cult, a lobby group or some uncaring individual will only disrupt the balance to the detriment of the entire community. Human rights can never be detached from human responsibilities. Your right to be part of the community is contingent on your consistently carrying out your responsibilities. This is your contribution to the equilibrium in the ecosystem. No one has the right to disrupt the balance in the community. Balance can still be disrupted even if your anti-ecosystem behavior is behind closed doors or in the privacy of your home. Such is the nature of a systemic community.

Also, as humans are responsible for taking care of the earth and all other living beings, it is obvious that we must collectively embrace this important charge and carry out our duties with care and wisdom. If society sees it more as an encumbrance and goes about its business without integrity, it will no doubt stand by and witness the transformation of the land from highly productive to a howling wilderness overgrown with thorns and bristles, as is the case of vast areas of the earth today. As temperatures rise, water levels drop, animals become extinct and their lush habitats disappear at an alarming rate, antibiotic resistance rises, and never-before-seen-diseases appear, it's time for society to acknowledge its place in the universal ecosystem, and again take up the reins of its responsibility and correct its course.

An Unholy Alliance

Humans are not only to be blamed, however. It is apparent from the Scriptures that the Lord had commissioned the angels to help and encourage humans in their stewardship responsibilities of the earth. While most were faithful servants of the Lord, some did rebel and actively sought to undermine God and His creation by tempting and corrupting humans' stewardship and by creating an unholy alliance with them.

Today, we are witnessing the evidence of their poisonous and corrupting influence with the growing fascination with the occult -- from video games permitting players to role-play the evil villain, to books popularizing voodoo among the younger generation, such as, the Harry Potter series, and to movies in which evil triumphs, such as The Exorcist. Jesus mentioned the troubling practices of churches that not only tolerate, but also teach tolerance of witchcraft and sexual immorality, specifically mentioning the former churches in Pergamum and Thyatira (Revelations 2). *"I will make war against them with the sword of My mouth,"* (Revelations 2:16) and *"I will kill her children with pestilence"* (Revelations 2:23), Jesus warned all those who engage in such practices, if they do not repent soon. To engage directly or indirectly with the enemy of us all is not only naïve and foolish, due to its poisonous effect upon every part of our lives and upon society, but it is also treasonous and rebellious against our Heavenly Father.

Government leaders and legislators must pay special attention to all these things as failure to act quickly and appropriately, whether due to political correctness, fear of people or otherwise, can bring irreparable harm to society. They are elected to be the 'fathers' and 'mothers' of the 'home' and to create a safe environment for everyone, in accordance with the truth knowledge of Natural Law. Society is already at or near the tipping point from which there will be no turning back. Human rights include the right to a safe and healthy environment. This cannot be promoted by leaders allowing irresponsible behaviors that transgress the laws of nature and hurt both the community and the environment. Human rights do not include the right to be irresponsible members of the community seeing that we are all part of the ecosystem with the responsibility to live within the normal range, maintain balance within the ecosystem, and protect the common good. The practice of ignoring the existence of boundaries in nature and giving in to the reckless and anarchist desires of rich shareholders -- who rely on the relaxing and removal of those very boundaries to satisfy their own greedy and voracious appetite for more wealth -- lead to disequilibrium at all levels and across all spheres of life, with the resulting effect of increasingly negative and disruptive social and environmental ills; and the increase in government spending to 'fix' those ills.

Consumerism

Church leaders must be aware of all the poisonous ideas that harm the Body of Christ and displease our Father. One such troubling idea is the consumerism/prosperity doctrine. Church leaders are being taught through leadership summits that they can learn from the secular business sector; assimilate their business/leadership philosophies into the Church; treat their congregants as consumers; and create Walmart-type conglomerates. This is a dangerous and poisonous doctrine as congregants are not consumers who 'buy' services from their service provider, the Church, nor are they always right.

Congregants are God's children who are taught, guided, cared for, advocated for and protected; they are groomed to 'pastor' people and to walk on an unchanging way of righteousness, which does not change with each blast of the winds of political correctness.

Church leaders are not under obligation to follow business management manuals of best practices or to bow down to the god of money. Their only allegiance is to the Heavenly Father, Jesus Christ and the Holy Spirit. One cannot assimilate Walmart-type business and leadership philosophies, whose biggest objective is to earn profit, even at the expense of the 'consumer', without alienating the One who has humbled Himself to come alongside us to help us grow and mature. "*And so, dear brothers and sisters, I plead with you - Don't copy the behavior and customs of this world ... Then you will learn to know God's will for you, which is good and pleasing and perfect.*" (Romans 12:1-2, NLT)

Sexual Immorality

Another poisonous idea is tolerance towards homosexuality and Same-Sex Marriage. The ongoing trend by society and by governments to ignore the God-ordained, as well as, nature's own boundaries, as they apply to sexual relationships and lifestyles, has already resulted in systemic disequilibrium. The resulting dysfunction -- with its exponentially rising costs in lives and healthcare dollars, not to mention the cries of the millions of AIDS orphans who are being barely cared for by aging grandmothers or by other older siblings in Africa, does not demand tolerance, but intolerance. We must see these harmful behaviors for what they are; they are poisonous. If a poison is not viewed as poison, how will it be treated appropriately? If a sickness is not regarded as sickness; how will it be adequately dealt with by physicians and therapists? If a government does not deal appropriately with these things, but instead legislates the 'normalcy' of unnatural and harmful behaviors; then it effectively pulls the rug from under the feet of its own citizens to treat, detoxify and modify those who practice them. Government legislation to outlaw conversion therapies is wrong and harmful.

The decision of well-intentioned Church leaders to modify their Constitutions to show more tolerance of bad behavior not only demonstrates their ignorance of how nature and life work, but it also shows their rejection of the Gospel and of Jesus Christ whom they purport to represent. Of course, they no longer represent their Lord, but the Adversary – in the church! The dysfunction that is observed in their buildings speaks loudly to the lack of health in their denominations and churches; but repentance will restore them back to the narrow way, where life flourishes. Furthermore, many are also instituting practices that are tantamount to reverse discrimination as those who resist their efforts to change laws and traditions are now being persecuted as intolerant and bigots. This will only add to society's sins and result in greater damnation, not only from nature, but from the Head of this universe.

So, the careful fulfillment of one's purpose and responsibilities by remaining in the normal range and encouraging everyone to do so is what makes a positive contribution to equilibrium at all levels. On the other hand, misbehavior and non-fulfillment of one's responsibilities will contribute negatively. In fact, our wrong behaviors have a poisonous impact on the ecosystem and community so that we become the target of the powerful homeostatic and restorative forces created by God and present in nature.

Restorative Justice in Society

Even as there are homeostatic forces at play in the human body and in nature to restore each element to the pre-set range whenever they are out of bounds, so must society have restorative mechanisms in place for wayward people. Restorative justice has that very purpose. Laws are in place to delineate the boundaries beyond which restorative justice plays its part to share information, guide and teach on the one hand and on the other, neutralize, isolate and restore the wayward person or group to the highway of responsible communal life. The purpose of justice is to correct wrong behaviors and to ensure the common good of all. The dysfunction and pain that occurs upon crossing the boundaries of life have a purpose to warn you of impending doom and to entice you to return to the safety of the narrow way. In other words, regret and remorse are insufficient, but repentance is the only adequate solution. Repentance not only acknowledges the wrongdoing and takes responsibility for the consequences, but it also corrects the wrong behavior, turns it and moves it back toward the normal range. Justice, therefore, is more than punishment for sin, as its main purpose is restorative, to ensure balance in the ecosystem and create optimal conditions for joyful, long and quality living for everyone.

Look at how Christ's ministry is described:

> *"Look at my servant, whom I strengthen. He is my chosen one, who pleases me. I have put my Spirit upon him. He will bring justice to the nations. He will not shout or raise his voice in public. He will not crush the weakest reed or put out a flickering candle. He will bring justice to all who have been wronged. He will not falter or lose heart until justice prevails throughout the earth."* (Isaiah 42:1-4, NLT)

His purpose has always been to lead us to *"... a rich and satisfying life",* (John 10:10, NLT) now and forever. The restorative ministry of the Holy Spirit is to *"correct the world concerning sin and concerning righteousness and concerning judgment"* and to *"lead you into the whole truth."* (John 16:8,12a, ABPE) He is the '*refining fire*' that purges away all the dross of impurities and bad habits, as well as, the enabling spring of life-giving and cleansing streams of water. Certainly, one must acknowledge the restorative work of the Holy Spirit, who releases us from being enslaved to destructive and toxic habits; restores our innate value and general wellbeing; dresses us up for the bridegroom (Matthew 22:12) like kings and queens; (Ezekiel 16:1-14) then, commissions and empowers us to restore others. What an amazing work of restorative justice!

Parents also have an important leadership role to steer their household back into the way of righteousness and to wholeness. Teaching, guiding, disciplining and other restorative actions are important means to this end and must never be neglected or taken away for the common good is at stake. It is a matter of life and death for children, who are neither sufficiently developed, nor knowledgeable, to make wise decisions. They are dependent on the restorative actions, primarily of their parents, but also of their teachers and the rest of the village. The pastoral role of God's representatives can also be understood in this light. They are anointed for this very purpose to help their Heavenly Father carry out His restorative responsibilities in the world. It is for this reason that Jesus and His Holy Spirit were sent. As His children, we are anointed with the same Spirit and, therefore, with the Father's heart.

The Life Meter and Index of Morality

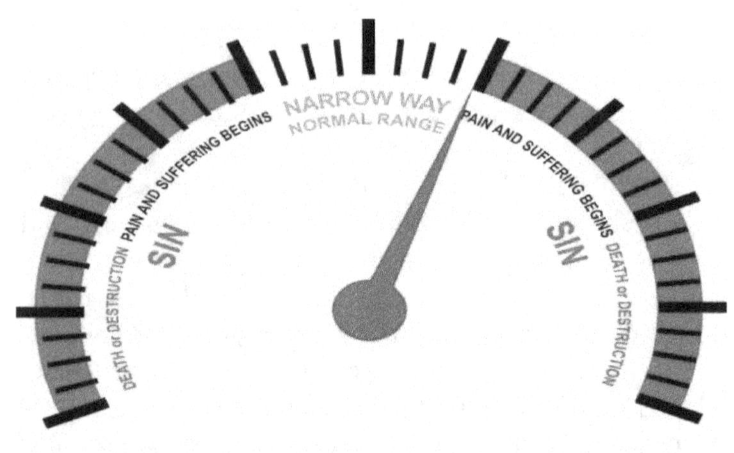

The pendulum must be within the normal range in order to maintain balance and ensure synergy on the one hand and avoid the adverse consequences of nature's restorative justice. The pendulum moves corresponding to our behavior.

Our government representatives must understand this important function of leadership -- their fatherly (motherly) role -- because a lack of understanding, neglect, incompetence or governing to their own liking and not according to the reality of nature's justice, will have disastrous results for everyone. Like nature's justice, human legal justice has a very important role in ensuring the common good of all. The Executive, Legislative and Judiciary arms of government must ensure that the pendulum of the index of morality remains firmly within the normal range.

Every legislative and executive action that promotes immorality will swing the pendulum into the realm of natural imbalance and adversity and towards the breaking point; if not beyond. So, I become very concerned, and so should you, when governments are keen to ignore nature's set boundaries and move legal boundaries by decriminalizing perverse behavior. This only endangers the peace and wellness of society, takes away from the joy of community and breaks the common unity of humanity. These legislators place the human rights of the few over those of the majority, irrespective of the consequences to the whole. Nature's justice, though, is carved in stone and immutable, so the consequences are unavoidable.

When unbalancing and dangerous behaviors fall outside the boundaries of the legal justice system, they are still subject to nature's justice. This doesn't stop just because a government decides to change the rules of engagement and ignore it. Political correctness and human rights based on false grounds, faulty reasoning and 'corroborated' by dishonest science will have adverse consequences for all of society due to the systemic nature of the world in which we live in -- *"they sow the wind and they shall reap the whirlwind."* (Hosea 8:7, ESV)

Therefore, when the pendulum on the index of morality moves further away from the narrow way of quality life for everyone, through such actions as, assisted suicide, euthanasia, same-sex marriage, the elimination of traditional gender boundaries, etc., we can expect an increase in:

- Personal and collective despair and more suicides, which we are sadly witnessing among our indigenous and entertainment communities;
- Mental health disorders;
- Social turmoil;
- Natural turmoil with climate change;
- Government parenting, as more children are brought into care;

- Increased secondary care spending primarily, but also primary prevention and tertiary research spending;
- Persecution and prosecution of well-meaning members who acknowledge and respect Natural Law and Justice. They are persecuted for being intolerant and not adhering to society's counterfeit values.

"The love of many shall grow cold", (Matthew 24:12) Jesus warned, as the new norm is gross indifference exemplified by new legislation that allows for assisted suicide; euthanasia; late-term abortion; increased community care for mental health patients, criminals and general patient care; endangering the lives and welfare of children and women by eliminating the traditional gender boundaries, allowing unisex and transgender bathroom use, allowing closet pedophiles to adopt children, and reducing the legal age of accountability; as well as, the curtailing of serious restorative justice measures for convicted felons and transgressors.

Does the Death Penalty Have a Place in Our Society? The death penalty does have its place, seeing that it has a prominent place in nature. It certainly has a role when serious capital crimes have been repeatedly committed and when all restorative actions have failed. However, in the past and present, it has been severely abused to the point of some governments utilizing it as a means of getting rid of political opponents, religious 'apostates', people with disabilities, ethnic minorities -- ethnic genocide. This is a mockery of true justice.

RESTORATIVE JUSTICE: DIVINE

Nature's justice is an extension of God's justice and rule. It is temporary, applying only to our physical world. This allows Him to withhold intervention until the end. (Matthew 13:24-30) Similar to nature, His justice is restorative and inevitable. While Nature's justice can be considered one layer of restorative justice, His divine interventions can be considered an additional layer. By His grace, He has purchased, with Jesus' blood, all who have accepted His offer of salvation. The blood covers over our sins, removing them *"as far as the east is from the west"* (Psalm 103:12), and allowing His Holy Spirit to dwell among us sinful people to restore us to the Way of Righteousness and refine us to His holy standard. We are under grace so long as we continue to collaborate with His Holy Spirit so that He can complete His work of sanctification in us.

Under the terms of the New Covenant in the blood of Jesus, no longer does the majority have to suffer for the sins of one person; each person will suffer for his or her own sins:

> *"In those days people will no longer say, 'The parents have eaten sour grapes, and the children's teeth are set on edge.' Instead, everyone will die for their own sin; whoever eats sour grapes--their own teeth will be set on edge."* (Jeremiah 31:29-30)

This is in sharp contrast to nature's justice wherein we continue to suffer the consequences of nature's imbalance, which, over millennia, has resulted in hereditary disorders due to genetic mutations. Children continue to suffer the consequences of their parents' sins. For instance, children are still born with familial hereditary disorders and suffer from FAS/FASD (Fetal Alcohol Syndrome/ Fetal Alcohol Spectrum Disorder) because of their mothers' drinking alcoholic concoctions during pregnancy. Alcohol damages the brain of the developing fetus, especially, during the first month of pregnancy. It is for this reason that the Lord admonished Samson's mother, *"She must not eat grapes or raisins, drink wine or any other alcoholic drink, or eat any forbidden food."* (Judges 13:14, NLT)

It is important to take advantage of these restorative attempts by repenting and submitting to the Spirit's refining actions for, should these fail, there is only a fearful awaiting His final solution to restore order, which will have eternal repercussions. Unfortunately, like the Israelites who created an added layer to the temple -- beyond the walls of the temple and the altar of repentance – there is a similar segment of the 'church' today who refuse to repent and submit to the Spirit -- "*They will act religious, but they will reject the power that could make them godly.*" (2 Timothy 3:5)

In the time of the end, He will come to complete His Divine Justice:

> "*Then the kings of the earth and the great men and the commanders and the rich and the strong and every slave and free man hid themselves in the caves and among the rocks of the mountains; and they said to the mountains and to the rocks, "Fall on us and hide us from the presence of Him who sits on the throne, and from the wrath of the Lamb; for the great day of their wrath has come, and who is able to stand?*" (Revelation 6:14-16)

While God has delayed the completion of His justice in order to await those who are to repent, there will come a time when…

> "*The Kingdom of the world has become the Kingdom of our Lord and of his Messiah, and he will reign forever and ever." And the twenty-four elders, who were seated on their thrones before God, fell on their faces and worshiped God, saying: "We give thanks to you, Lord God Almighty, the One who is and who was, because you have taken your great power and have begun to reign. The nations were angry, and your wrath has come. The time has come for judging the dead, and for rewarding your servants the prophets and your people who revere your name, both great and small— and for destroying those who destroy the earth.*" (Revelation 11:15b-18)
> "*He who testifies to these things says, "Yes, I am coming soon." Amen. Come, Lord Jesus.*" (Revelation.22:20)

So, **are we subject to the law of justice** seeing that Paul made such comments as *"But if you are led by the Spirit, you are not under the law..."* (Galatians 5:18) *"but under grace "?* (Romans 6:14) The answer is yes, for Paul also said, "*You have been set free from sin and have become slaves to righteousness."* (Romans 6:18) Righteousness, as you have seen, is required under the law, both in this Solar order and in the Divine Order. Jesus dispels any misunderstanding by affirming,

> *"Do not think that I have come to abolish the Law or the Prophets; I have not come to abolish them but to fulfill them. For truly I tell you, until heaven and earth disappear, not the smallest letter, not the least stroke of a pen, will by any means disappear from the Law until everything is accomplished. Therefore, anyone who sets aside one of the least of these commands and teaches others accordingly will be called least in the Kingdom of heaven, but whoever practices and teaches these commands will be called great in the Kingdom of heaven. For I tell you that unless your righteousness surpasses that of the Pharisees and the teachers of the law, you will certainly not enter the Kingdom of heaven."* (Matthew 5:17-20)

The rules of justice exist because of the fixed order of creation and, therefore, can only be cancelled by its destruction. So, there will be a time when the written code of the physical laws required by the Natural Order, such as, right sexual behavior, normal blood sugar, etc. will be superseded by the resurrection to our new immortal bodies and life in our new heavenly home. This written code or letter of the Law will be removed and all that will remain is the Spirit of the Law.

The Spirit moves every one of us to holiness and loving-kindness. The sole purpose of the laws was to make us *"'Love the Lord your God with all your heart and with all your soul and with all your mind.' This is the first and greatest commandment. And the second is like it: 'Love your neighbour as yourself';* (Matthew 22:37-39) and "*He has told you, O man, what is good; and what does the LORD require of you, but to do justice, and to love kindness, and to walk humbly with your God?"*(Micah 6:8, ESV) It was for this reason that the Lord despised the peoples' hypocrisy because they obeyed the letter of the Law, but disobeyed the Spirit of the Law. *"I hate all your show and pretense -- the hypocrisy of your religious festivals and solemn assemblies."* (Amos 5:21, NLT) While our Natural Order is temporary; the Spirit of the law is eternal.

Paul was right, however, to say that "*you are not under the Law*" because he was referring to the section of the written code of the Law regarding temple rituals, such as, circumcision and ritual washings, which had now been superseded by the New Covenant of the blood of Jesus. He was also right to affirm that the laws only apply to the transgressors and not to those who obediently and wisely walk in the Way. The latter are under the grace of the Lord due to their obedience and so experience the joy and benefits of God's wonderful promises, while the former are under the Law and experience all the force of its restorative-homeostatic-recycling function. The Law only kicks in when we cross the boundaries of the way of life. It is our reality. We cannot avoid it. It is as sure as the sun rises every morning and it is evidence that God is in control, for He created it, and no one can escape its long arms. As we can surmise, though, from our understanding of the Natural Order, God's grace is now constrained by it while we are under its rule because its systemic nature means that we will still suffer the consequences of the imbalance that is the result of collective sin. While we may not sin, we still suffer the consequences of others' sins. In other words, bad things still happen to good people.

Why Bad Things Happen to Good People?

I hope you have already understood why bad things happen to good people. Let us look, though, at it all again. Job's story is the perfect example of bad things happening to very good people. He lost everything: all his wealth (and he was wealthy!), his children and his health. The only things that remained were what was left of his life, his wife and his faith in God. He had all the reasons to be quite upset and he was. He complained to God and everyone. He was embittered and angry. His friends answered him, but they could not alleviate his pain and suffering. Finally, God answered. You should read the full extent of His answer in Job 38-41.

In God's rebuttal of Job, He said he had to first acknowledge that God had done a great job creating the world with such order as to be mathematically devised. *"The morning stars sang together and all the angels shouted for joy"* (Job 38:7) and He, Himself, concluded that it was "*very good*". (Genesis 1:31) There was nothing that could have been done to make it better. Second, he had to also acknowledge that he did not know enough to judge the Creator. I, myself, have learned never to criticize God for what He has done. It doesn't matter how intelligent and knowledgeable I am; it is nowhere near His. So, I always humble myself before Him. However, what I have discovered so far that has amazed me, is not only how intelligently designed our universe is, but also how much love, teamwork and interdependence are its values; and these are not optional, but essential.

We are all part of this ecosystem, interdependent and interconnected. Like a well-oiled machine, it is self-regulating to maintain balance and synergy and, in so doing, allows you and I to live a quality life. When anyone or anything behaves outside the fixed order, disorder results, which affects the rest of the ecosystem; this includes you and I, the animal Kingdom, the flora and the environment. While I mostly suffer from the error of my ways, you and I do suffer as well from the errors of the ways of the people around us, especially, if they exert leadership over us, as those in government do.

Herein, though, lies the beauty of God's creation. Restorative mechanisms are immediately unleashed all around, whenever disorder is detected. Sensors throughout the ecosystem sound the alarm whenever the boundaries of normalcy are breached and unleash the restorative responses. All these have one purpose -- to restore the wayward component back on track. There is a path of justice for every path of injustice. This is the essence of justice. The pain and suffering that arise from transgressing the boundaries of normalcy are strong motivational factors to get the perpetrator(s) back on track through repentance. The pain and suffering that you and I suffer when others sin, are strong motivational influences upon us to prevent and/or correct the disorder; encourage others to repent and align with the established divine and natural order; be peacemakers; and love others rather than ignore their suffering. The ecosystem exists to create a common good for all, which we all have the responsibility to protect and maintain. We are truly a global family and one another's keeper. Therefore, we must watch out for one another. What you do affects me and what I do affects you. No one owns their own destiny. We are all important parts of the whole.

Unfortunately, a lot of noise is coming from human rights activists and libertarians, who feel that they have the human right to do whatever they want. They ignore the fact that they are part of a systemic whole with a natural order, which when disrupted, will not only affect them adversely, but also the rest of the ecosystem. Humans, as administrators of the ecosystem, must care for it well and protect the natural order as failure to do so will have disastrous consequences for everyone, including the good and innocent victims. It is a tragic calamity to witness children being aborted in a cold-blooded manner even after birth (third-trimester, partial abortions, etc.); those born with sequelae of Thalidomide treatment and alcohol abuse by pregnant mothers; people suffering from radiation, biochemical and biological poisoning; and countless other scenarios.

In the face of so much pain and suffering many question the wisdom of God's creation. Is it fair, though, to blame the Creator? No! God created an intelligently-designed, self-regulating ecosystem, which motivates all to love and to care for one another, together, as one global family. This promotes love, family, teamwork and interdependence. What wisdom! Instead, selfish and egotistical people, either destitute of truth knowledge or who simply choose to intentionally ignore it, have not only disrupted the order, but also applauded those who do. No wonder, the Lord saw all this and regretted having made humans. He, as our Creator and Heavenly Father, is the most saddened by all this pain and suffering. He dreads the coming Day of the Lord when He will have to put an end to all this and destroy *"those who destroy the earth."* (Revelation 11:18)

Is there a solution? Yes! We are to only accept God's ordained and chosen Savior and Lord and follow His lead back to wholesome and responsible living. Humans must take up the mantle of caretakers of God's ecosystem with all seriousness, wisdom and faithfulness. Governments and their legal justice systems must align their system with nature's, to reflect true justice, and so restore transgressors and reward faithfulness, not the other way around. Prevention is a key strategy. I lovingly teach and guide my children diligently to prevent trouble. If mistakes happen, and they are bound to happen, then I lovingly and wisely guide them back to the safety and security of the narrow way. Governments and private companies would be wise to invest heavily in primary preventative and tertiary measures as it costs less to do so than to deal with the exponentially rising costs of secondary treatments. When natural and other calamities hit, how will we be able to survive? It is wise, therefore, to prevent them from happening by promoting and fomenting the Spirit of the Law embedded in the natural order. The Lord created it, and all those who listen to Him and value the quality of their lives, must champion it.

The Currency of Life -- Love

The concept of team is so prevalent throughout the ecosystem that the only currency available is love. It is for this reason that Jesus summarized all the laws into one word -- love:

> *"'Love the Lord your God with all your heart and with all your soul and with all your mind.' This is the first and greatest commandment. And the second is like it: 'Love your neighbor as yourself.' All the Law and the Prophets hang on these two commandments."* (Matthew 22:37-40)

In a team, each component is important, valuable and some even essential. Together, the entire ecosystem works tirelessly to produce and sustain life of which we are the primary beneficiaries. As each component faithfully fulfills its important responsibilities in the ecosystem, demonstrating their love for you, it is in your best interest to value and love each component, more so the noble parts. Most of all, we are to love the Head, the Lord God -- this is vitally important. He is our Heavenly Father who cares for us. He proved His love for us by sending His Own Son to pay the price of our sins and to give us a second chance at life. Even as I care for, watch over and seek the welfare of my children, so does He; reciprocating His love, therefore, is not only right and just, but essential.

You also have important responsibilities that benefit others and the whole, so carrying them out completely and faithfully, are your acts of love. Thus, love is action. It is not just in words only. The Church in Ephesus was chastised for this very reason: *"Yet I hold this against you: You have forsaken the love you had at first."* And they were told to "*Consider how far you have fallen"* and to *"Repent and do the things you did at first."* (Revelation 2:4-5) You cannot say that you love if you do not do the deeds that demonstrate love. In fact, the absence of the deeds is hating. The Church was commissioned to demonstrate this love through evangelism, local and global missions and taking care of the ministers, missionaries and the needy. A church that does not engage in the basic deeds of love does not fulfill its purpose; hence, Jesus' warning: *"If you do not repent, I will come to you and remove your lampstand from its place."* (Revelation 2:5)

A nursing child owes its very existence to its caring mother. Truth has determined the way of righteousness in which this mother must walk. It determines what the mother's purposes are towards the suckling child -- at the child's birth, it is to feed her child life-giving milk from her life-springing breasts every two hours or when the child requests, even though they might be hurting; child-proof the house to keep the child away from danger; as well as, clothe, clean regularly, guide, teach, advocate for and nurture the child till adulthood. Only in this way can it become a whole responsible citizen and reliable member of the community. Love is being there when someone needs you in the same way that you want them to be there for you when you need them.

Today, we live in a society in which we discriminate against one another for many trivial reasons, such as, skin color, ethnicity, nationality and disability. Scientists have already proven that there is only one race in the world, not a multiplicity of races. We are all shades of color, determined by the amount of melanin in our skin, living in one global village. So, we have no right to discriminate against others because of the amount of pigment in their skin or ethnicity. We are all distant cousins and relatives.

In Jesus' time, the Jews discriminated against the Samaritans. So, Jesus, on explaining what it meant to '*love your neighbor'*, told the story of the Good Samaritan, in which the religious Levite and Priest ignored the plight of a wounded man, passed him by and went about their business. When, however, the Samaritan came along and seeing that the man needed help, he immediately went and tended to his injuries, took him to the inn and paid to have him cared for. The Jews, as God's children, were expected to be compassionate, but the Samaritan was not. He, though, turned out to be kind, loving and compassionate fulfilling his community responsibility towards the wounded man while the others looked the other way. No wonder Jesus said that your righteousness must surpass that of the Pharisees and Scribes, if you are to be saved.

It was late 2011, when the story broke of the little Chinese girl who wandered into the street and was twice run over by two vehicles. No one stopped the girl from wandering unto the street and when she was run over the first time, no one ran to her aid. She lay bleeding on the narrow street for about seven minutes, while more than a dozen people walked or cycled by before she was run over by the second vehicle. Only after that did a woman run up to the dying child and summon help for her; but it was too late, as little Wang Yue, lovingly referred to as Yue Yue, later died of her injuries in the hospital. The many people who could have saved that child were useless bystanders in a malfunctioning and non-existent 'community'.

The news spread across the world like wildfire. It was a typical case of culpable by-standing, willful blindness and gross indifference. Chinese TV later tried to correct this image by showing another episode when someone was injured, and many people immediately ran to the person's aid. Society had supposedly learned a painful lesson, but too late for the little two-year-old Yue Yue. You must always give of yourself at the right time in order to fulfill your purpose in the community. You are of no use to anyone if you see the need but do not move an inch to help; only hoping that someone else does or helping when it is too late. There is a right moment and a right place to carry out your community responsibilities. Love is to do what is expected of you at the right time and at the right place.

The sun shines and the rain falls on the just and the unjust. Jesus died for us all while we were still sinners. Jesus said, *"But to you who are willing to listen, I say, **love your enemies**! Do good to those who hate you. Bless those who curse you. Pray for those who hurt you."* (Luke 6:27-28) Jesus surprised many by this command, but in an ecosystem, this is easily understood. Our Heavenly Father, as Creator, has built loving-kindness into the ecosystem. Every legitimate component has intrinsic value and important functions and purposes in the ecosystem and must, therefore, be valued and loved for their important and essential contributions. Even your enemies have important responsibilities in life, which, when carried out, benefit even you. So, it is counter-productive for you to take away their God-given value or to reject their role in life. Grudges due to past offences are the most common reasons for being called an enemy. Jesus reminds us that we are not here to be a judge -- leave that to God. We do, though, have a duty to help one another and restore the disjointed one, whenever the need arises, at the right time and at the right place.

You cannot love without adhering to truth and acting wisely. It's wise to follow the norms laid down by our Creator -- norms established in nature and in our DNA and referred to in the Scriptures. The Holy Spirit and your observation of nature will guide you to all truth. Success can only be reached, and hence, you can only love, if you apply truth knowledge. Don't add to it or subtract from it. In other words, don't '*cut corners*'. *"So be careful to obey all the commands I give you. You must not add anything to them or subtract anything from them.*" (Deuteronomy 12:32, NLT)

The Juice Lady, Cherie Calbon, emphasized the essence of this in her testimony, when the Lord revealed to her that His army of followers were weak, because they didn't walk in God's righteous Way and had poor eating habits. They were perishing for lack of knowledge. He, thus, moved her to study Nutrition, share her findings and help all those who would listen.

So, to love, you must act morally -- that is, within the boundaries of the narrow way of life and righteousness. Breaking the laws signal that you have transgressed the boundaries of love and entered the broad way of hate. This defines love and how to love. Anything else is hate. Love ensures, maintains, sustains and promotes a life of wholeness. Wellness, peace, happiness and abundant life are the results of lovingly adhering to truth and carefully walking the way of righteousness. Moral with immoral living, (at times, loving, at times hating), hot with cold, has a net of lukewarm living and a net effect of provoking vomit and disgust. This was God's complaint against the Church at Laodicea:

> "*I know all the things you do, that you are neither hot nor cold. I wish that you were one or the other! But since you are like lukewarm water, neither hot nor cold, I will spit you out of my mouth! You say, 'I am rich. I have everything I want. I don't need a thing!' And you don't realize that you are wretched and miserable and poor and blind and naked. So I advise you to buy gold from me -- gold that has been purified by fire. Then you will be rich. Also buy white garments from me so you will not be shamed by your nakedness, and ointment for your eyes so you will be able to see. I correct and discipline everyone I love. So be diligent and turn from your indifference.*" (Revelation 3:15-19)

Love is the essence of systemic or Kingdom life, because it promotes wholeness -- equilibrium in yourself, in your neighbors and in your community. People love by sharing their resources with one another. In other words, "*you are your brother or sister's keeper*". Your money is our money. Use money to carry out your responsibilities. Don't waste or save it at the expense of carrying out your responsibilities towards yourself, your family, the community and God. As you have a responsibility to put food on the table of your fellow siblings and workers in Kingdom business, don't save up surpluses at the expense of your duty towards them. This is displeasing to our Lord. Give of your firstfruits to God as this is an act of love towards Him. But, don't neglect helping your needy parents or others. Jesus corrected the religious leaders because they taught that it was okay to neglect their needy parents, while being meticulously faithful in giving tithes and offerings to God. (Mark 7:11-12)

You cannot ignore what goes on around you as it will affect you one way or another. The health of the community is important to you because when it is healthy, you are positively affected and when it is not you are adversely affected. You cannot just look after yourself or your family and ignore the common good. It is not enough for you to walk within the normal parameters of life. In fact, you cannot walk within the way of life without caring for others; you must be concerned where the others around you are walking. It only takes one person to decide to cross the boundaries of normalcy, go out and buy a gun or explosives and then carry out a murderous act right in your neighborhood. That single act could affect you or your loved ones directly. Therefore, you must care about what goes on around you. You must be, like the Heavenly Father, an advocate for wholeness, righteousness and justice in the world. You must be a tool of restoration in your household, neighborhood, city, the entire nation and to the ends of the earth. It is your God-given purpose in life to be an agent of transformation.

Immediately after Creation, God told Adam and Eve to *"Be fertile, increase in number,* ***fill the earth, and be its master***.

Rule *the fish in the sea, the birds in the sky, and all the animals that crawl on the earth."* (Genesis 1:28, GWT) As heads, their responsibilities and purpose in life were to "*govern and rule*" their land with love, wisdom, diligence and courage. That was the command the Lord also gave the Israelites -- to take possession of the entire land He was giving them and to rid it of all the abominations that were being committed there. As landowners, they had a duty to take care of their land and keep it clean and healthy. Yes, you have a responsibility to take care of the land in which you live. Your purpose in life is not just to make and raise a family, own property(ies) and take care of your own, but also to take responsibility and to take ownership of what goes on around you. You must take ownership, clean up and control every sphere of society: family, religion, government, the arts, media, business, and education. As part of humanity, you have a responsibility to govern well, not poorly, carelessly, neglectfully, incompetently or *laissez faire* (let it be).

You must be strategic and synergistic in transforming your neighborhood and country, and wisely engage in each sphere of society, to have maximum effectiveness at reaping the full benefits. The Lord told Moses, Joshua and all the people that they must work together as one to '*possess the land*' until everyone found '*rest*'. As you take more responsibility for what goes on in your communities, you must come together with others to analyze needs, weaknesses and strengths, to strategize, plan, create short and long-term objectives and goals and implement those plans. Wonderful things will happen that will benefit the common good. A healthy community contributes to a healthy you and healthy families as well as to your peace and happiness.

There are many success stories of what happens when people do come together to tackle complex community problems engaging our Father's help. As people unwaveringly adhere to fundamental truths by diligently following the rules of engagement, vexing problems are solved, and lasting peace ensues. Get a hold of the series of Transformation videos that portray glimpses of what can happen when every one of God's wise counsels are diligently followed. It can be accessed by contacting The Sentinel Group and Transform our World or Transform Now.

You love by carrying out your responsibilities in the community. Love fulfils the law. The entire ecosystem, the common good and the Kingdom depend on it. **Someone** cared enough to save you and restore you at Gilgal. At Bethel, you learned that that **Someone** was the Heavenly Father. In fact, you saw that love was the language spoken in His house and Kingdom just as He had poured it out on Jacob, Elisha and on all of us. Now that you have learned that language, you must use it to cleanse and restore the people and land by applying the lessons of peacemaking you learned at Jericho.

At the Jordan River, you learned that the entire universe is built in such a way that you are obliged to care in order to live, thrive and survive. It's the currency of the entire ecosystem. The way of righteousness goes hand in hand with the way of tender loving care. It is the core reason and justification for restorative justice. As there is a path of restorative justice for every path of injustice, you are called to give the transgressor the opportunity to repent and return. Justice is not just punishment, but encouragement to return to the normal way – back to wholeness.

Love is '*the bond of unity*', (Colossians 3:14) the glue that holds us and the entire universe together. It is the currency that identifies God's children and is the currency of His Kingdom. You cannot enter the Kingdom of heaven without it. However, you cannot take care of others or those of your community without first taking care of yourself. Jesus told us to "*Love your neighbor as yourself*" and to *"Watch and pray so that you will not fall into temptation. The spirit is willing, but the flesh is weak."* (Matthew 26:41) You cannot take care of others or of the community or be of use to our Heavenly Father, if you are weak.

Therefore, **SELF- CARE** is essential.

Submit to the Head: God is the Head therefore align with His Reign and submit.

Eliminate bad behaviors/ habits/ addictions: They are poisonous to you and others.

Love to do what is right. It is wise to follow God's and nature's rules of engagement.

Forgive self and others. Forgiving, forgetting and reconciling benefit you and the community. It restores lost equilibrium.

Contemplative Spiritual Disciplines: Prayer, Scripture reading, Study and Meditation.

Activity: Regular daily outdoor physical activity, such as, walking and running, have enormous benefits.

Rest: Enough nightly rest, appropriate for your age, is highly beneficial.

Eat healthy. Follow nutritional rules based on truth knowledge.

As you live by grace, do not tire at *"doing what is good. At just the right time we will reap a harvest of blessing if we don't give up."* (Galatians 6:9, NLT) Yes, there is a lot of work in caring and loving. So, work at it without tiring, even despite opposition. As you live by God's grace, you are to use this same grace, that is, His Holy Spirit's help to care for others. It is for this very purpose that God gave you His Spirit to help you carry out all your caring responsibilities with consistence, power and wisdom. We read in Matthew, "*Do to others whatever you would like them to do to you. This is the essence of all that is taught in the law and the prophets.*" (Matthew 7:12)

So, what '*works*' was Paul referring to when he said, *"for it is by grace you have been saved, through faith -- and this is not from yourselves, it is the gift of God -- not by works, so that no one can boast."* (Eph.2:8-9) Paul and Jesus lived in the time of the second temple with all its rituals prescribed by God through Moses: circumcision, animal sacrifices, ritual washings of hands and of utensils and all the other Temple practices, which the Pharisees, the religious leaders of the day, not only expanded on and rigorously practiced, but also enforced on everyone. These were the 'works' the Lord was referring to. Look at what He thinks of them:

> *"The multitude of your sacrifices— what are they to me?" says the LORD. "I have more than enough of burnt offerings, of rams and the fat of fattened animals; I have no pleasure in the blood of bulls and lambs and goats. When you come to appear before me, who has asked this of you, this trampling of my courts? Stop bringing meaningless offerings! Your incense is detestable to me. New Moons, Sabbaths and convocations— I cannot bear your worthless assemblies. Your New Moon feasts and your appointed festivals I hate with all my being. They have become a burden to me; I am weary of bearing them. When you spread out your hands in prayer, I hide my eyes from you; even when you offer many prayers, I am not listening. Your hands are full of blood!"* (Isaiah 1:11-15)

What He really wants is genuine loving care; it's what He and His Kingdom are all about. He built everything in such a way that we would all have to love. These are the works God wants us to do:

> *"Wash and make yourselves clean. Take your evil deeds out of my sight; stop doing wrong. Learn to do right; seek justice. Defend the oppressed. Take up the cause of the fatherless; plead the case of the widow."* (Isaiah 1:16-17)

I hope by now that you understand how essential love is in nature and in the Kingdom of God. It is the currency of life. You cannot do anything in life: buy or sell, marry, raise a family or work without love for it's the currency of teamwork, interdependence and community. It's the currency of righteousness and the reason behind God's restorative justice. It's the currency of the Kingdom of God. Love in all its forms – responsible-ness, patience, kindness, goodness, meekness, gentleness, self-control, and integrity buy life in all its fullness. It buys happiness, peace, and hope, as well as abundant and eternal life. What wisdom to build the world in such a way that love becomes the currency of life that buys you peace, joy and prosperity! Wow!

CONCLUSION

A THEOLOGY OF PAIN AND SUFFERING

What does it all mean?
Many Parts, One Whole, One Team
Many Subsystems, One Ecosystem
Many Interdependent Parts, One Interconnected Ecosystem
Many Parts, Many Purposes, One Common Good
Heaven and Earth, One Kingdom of God

We live in a universe that is a self-regulating, positive- and negative-feedback-based ecosystem with many interconnected parts each with its own purposes, rights and responsibilities. The ecosystem encompasses heaven and earth, everything and everyone therein, with Yahweh, as its Head and Sovereign Ruler. The systemic nature of our natural order reveals a model that ties together truth, righteousness, lovingkindness and overall wellness. It is a model that maintains and assures wholeness and synergy. In this model, morality becomes not just an option, but essential to quality living, survival and the common good. It allows the Almighty God to reign despite the presence of evil and decay.

The changes that occur when one transgresses the boundaries of the Way of Righteousness and marches defiantly to the breaking point are mathematically formulaic and calculable. In Medicine, the progression of disease can and is both mapped out and measurable. To match these paths of injustice, the Creator intelligently designed restorative paths of justice to restore order to this apparent chaos. These paths of justice will either restore the repentant soul to the Way or recycle the unrepentant to dust. One way or the other, order is restored. What an amazing Creator to design such an intelligent Natural Order in which He reigns despite the appearance of chaos.

Are the Scriptural principles aligned with the systemic reality of life? Yes! The Ten Commandments are perfectly aligned with it. All the Biblical laws, statutes and ordinances make perfect sense when there is a systemic order in place because they reveal the boundaries beyond which equilibrium is lost and restorative mechanisms are unleashed. They are virtual boundary markers that help us stay on the highway of life, protect the common good and foster wholeness. Yes, there is a common good that everyone must strive to protect, as it benefits us all.

Each component, including each human being, has a right to be a valuable part of the whole, and as such, has responsibilities to contribute towards the common good. You do not belong to self, but to the common good -- to faithfully and steadfastly fulfill your purposes and responsibilities. Sharing, giving and receiving are essential acts of systemic, community or Kingdom life because they ensure balance, synergy, and wholeness. Community, teamwork, interdependence and seeking the common good are essential while individualism, independence and selfish egocentrism are counterproductive, dangerous and must have no place in the world.

The set parameters that exist in nature create a confined highway in which life flourishes. In fact, life will gradually lose its quality once you go beyond its boundaries. Pain, suffering and dysfunction begin, once you cross the border of rightness, and will increase in magnitude until the breaking point is reached and, death and/or destruction ensue. Some things are repairable, while others are not. There is a window of opportunity for people to repent and be restored to wholeness as well as a point of no return. Sin or evil is being out of bounds, outside the normal range, and missing the mark.

All the laws, statutes and ordinances show you how to live, love and do things the right way. There is one way to do it right and a thousand ways to do it wrongly. Wrong ways of doing things are ineffective and lead to dysfunction. Optimal results are only accomplished when things are done the right way. This is of vital importance whether one is building a bridge or a house, rearing a child or governing a nation. The failure to build according to the rules will result in the failure of the bridge or building to withstand stresses, such as, those caused by hurricane-force winds and earthquakes. Similarly, failure, with regards to rearing children or ruling a nation, will also result in broken lives and societies.

The Danger of Man-Made Traditions

Traditions are an important part of our lives but can often detract from our wellbeing as individuals and institutions. According to the Oxford Dictionary, a tradition is "*A long-established custom or belief that has been passed on from one generation to another.*" Obviously, traditions that foster wholeness, that is, those based on truth, will promote healthy living, thus enhancing our lives. For example, brushing and flossing our teeth are healthy traditions and so is the worship of our Lord, seeing that He is the Head. Jesus was however concerned with man-made traditions that fall outside of God's commands:

> *"He replied, "Isaiah was right when he prophesied about you hypocrites; as it is written: 'These people honor me with their lips, but their hearts are far from*

me. They worship me in vain; their teachings are merely human rules.' You have let go of the commands of God and are holding on to human traditions." And he continued, "You have a fine way of setting aside the commands of God in order to observe your own traditions! For Moses said, 'Honor your father and mother,' and, 'Anyone who curses their father or mother is to be put to death.' But you say that if anyone declares that what might have been used to help their father or mother is Corban (that is, devoted to God) -- then you no longer let them do anything for their father or mother. Thus you nullify the word of God by your tradition that you have handed down. And you do many things like that." (Mark 7:6-13)

The Pharisees and Elders were notorious for creating additions, subtractions and amendments that were counterproductive due to the end result -- disjointedness and disorder. They created so many traditions that people were also sidetracked from obeying the real rules. Human traditions are rules made by humans, not God. As with any rule, people are annoyed, get angry and are willing to divide, separate, harass and even kill when these rules are broken; even though, they may even go against God's rules. This is a perverted version of justice that hurts the common good and angers God, as they are not aligned with God's and nature's justice. Besides, upon obeying them, they waste our precious time and energy, weaken our heart and keep us from doing what is God's perfect will for wholeness and the common good. No wonder Jesus condemned these man-made traditions. So, do yourself a favor and keep it simple; don't waste energy on them. You will not have enough energy to demonstrate real love. Man-made traditions that do not fulfill the law of love are like noxious weeds and poisons in our ecosystem -- they sap your strength and energy, so you neglect the real business.

Thus, to experience abundant life, **life is a balancing act**. As the whole earth ecosystem constantly, re-balances itself to remain in the normal range for maximal effectiveness, you too must do the same in those areas where you have control. As Jesus exhorts us, you must deny your urges to cross the boundaries and sin. If you have already crossed, be smart, exercise self-control and bring yourself back on track. If you are weak, ask the Heavenly Father and He will help you. Nature, society and you will immediately reap the benefits of a restored balanced lifestyle. Therefore, it is essential that you identify any poisonous element or behaviors at once and take the appropriate treatment for it, to correct, quarantine, isolate or eliminate it.

It is unfortunate that there is a campaign in society to decriminalize or legitimize behaviors that are known to be dangerous, wrong or unnatural. A case in point is homosexuality. Devious sexual behaviors can cause immune disorders, HIV/AIDS and other scourges that are decimating populations even today, not to mention the financial strain that these place on countries' health care systems. No one should be given the right to hurt others, even if they are practicing their devious behaviors in the intimacy of their own homes and behind closed doors. One of a government's responsibilities is to protect society. A government is wrong when it legislates, decriminalizes and legitimizes dangerous behaviors under the guise of human rights. Such actions are foolhardy and self-destructive and place an intolerable strain on society and societal institutions. An ecosystem, including people, society and the land, do have a breaking point. Nature becomes corrupt and poisoned, so much so that we are sadly experiencing the effects of climate change, which is creating even more dysfunction, pain, misery, death and destruction. You sow the wind and you inevitably reap a whirlwind.

As God's ordinances are embedded in nature, Christian and moral values become natural and so enable us to be well. The fact that God encourages all people to acknowledge and obey them demonstrates His love, as He knows that failure to do so will result in the world's loss of quality of life and destruction. Any loving father would do the same to protect his children. It is foolish, then, to ignore them just because the Bible and the Church defend them. It is not a religious or faith-based act to follow God's and nature's rules of engagement, but a wise one. The Moral Index of society must remain within the boundaries of the Normal Range for the common good, for the enjoyment and quality living of everyone, and to flourish. This is a major responsibility of every individual, institution and government. Your actions, or failure to act, can and do move the needle of the Moral Index.

Leaders, whether political, corporate or ecclesiastical, will do well to take Divine and Natural Law and Orders into consideration, when they legislate policies and laws. Even though we are diverse in our beliefs and cultures, there is only one God and Head and one Natural Order for all. Truth knowledge is defined by what aligns with the Natural Order, therefore, all beliefs and cultures, and hence laws and policies, must adapt and come into alignment with it. Those religious or cultural beliefs that do not align must be considered unnatural and hence incompatible with the common good. Multiculturalism and religious freedoms enshrined in constitutions make no sense in light of nature's immutable laws, which are based on love and on protecting the common good. Even Christianity must align with the natural and divine orders.

Love seeks the common good of all well-meaning people. Countries and individuals alike cannot seek the common good, if they allow those who are not well meaning, to have their way. This only opens the door and allows them to harm the common good. Policies must encourage justice-minded and well-meaning people, while discouraging evildoers and wickedness. These same policies must deal appropriately with the latter, seeking a full restoration to wholeness and normalcy. Restorative justice must, thus, be an important component of government policies, even as it is in nature. These laws must not be mere words in a policy manual but must be backed up by meaningful and appropriate actions. Primary prevention is always less costly than secondary reactions because, without adequate preventive and restorative measures, their increasing cost to society will be exponential, both in monies and otherwise.

What about those who cannot be rehabilitated and say they have a human right not to be? No one has the human right to hurt themselves and the common good. The systemic nature of life requires us to deal appropriately with those who insist on hurting the common good, that is, correct, guide, teach and rehabilitate, on the one hand, and isolate or quarantine and/or give the death penalty to, on the other. The latter must be a last resort after repeated restorative failures. Fortunately, multiple layers of restorative justice exist that have been in place since birth. If one does not control oneself, then one's parents will have to exercise control over the person. If they can't control the rebel, then the legal restorative justice system should. The moment we sin, we immediately come under nature's curse and its justice mechanisms come into play to control the wrongdoer, one way or the other. If the offender fails to repent, then the Almighty God will control them in Hell forever.

Jesus' summarizing the laws into one word -- love, was because love is the only way to be perfectly balanced and synergistic in the ecosystem. Love fulfills every law, brings us into wholeness and protects the common good. Love does no harm. The law in fact defines what love and hate are. We are called to do things in the proper way and obey the rules of engagement in order to love and not hate. Hate is the lack of love and can be passive or active. Altering any parameter is harmful because it leads to dysfunction and hurt, imbalance and hate -- synergy is lost. Disobedience, rebellion or rejection of any rule is the same as hate because it harms and endangers self, others and the common good. Living in the way of righteousness or within the normal range demonstrates love; while it is hateful to live outside of it. It's a matter of love to build rightly and an act of hatred to ignore and disobey the rules. Love is carrying out all your responsibilities with care -- being complete in doing so is love in action, while incompleteness can be perceived as hatred, due to the bad results. Great benefit comes about when you operate within the optimal range and a loss of benefit and toxicity outside of it. In other words, do yourself a favor and live within the boundaries**.** Love yourself and others by living righteously. Right living is showing your love towards your Heavenly Father. The entire ecosystem is founded on love, the currency of life and of the Kingdom of God.

Life is a **matter of choice, even if this choice is mostly an illusion**. This is because most of the essential events are involuntary, run on auto-pilot and are fixed in our genes. The rest are voluntary, but just a little less important than those on auto-pilot. However, even here, innate forces move us towards behaving in the prescribed way. For example, eating is a choice, but try going without eating for too long. The pain and discomfort that result will force you to eat to ease and eliminate the pain. The forces of group dynamics in team and family also encourage and urge us to act in a manner becoming the common unity of societal and Kingdom life. The forces of restorative justice present in nature and society have powerful molding effects upon our behavior.

Life is like a maze where the course is already mapped out for us with some options to choose from, which is where the problem begins. One can still choose to live happily or to overcome natural, societal and spiritual forces and suffer and die. A person suffering from anorexia nervosa can still starve herself to death. A teenager can run away from the wholesome life at home and live as a homeless bum on the street. A born-again believer can turn his back on our Heavenly Father, run away like the prodigal son and end up in Hell.

Life is a matter of **faithfulness in carrying out one's responsibilities and fulfilling one's purposes.** We are interdependent on each other carrying out their responsibilities. We are dependent on the sun's ability to fulfill its purposes to the earth and all its inhabitants. A new born child is totally dependent on the parents, especially, the mother, to provide vital care. The injured person just ran over by a car and lying in a pool of blood, but still alive, is dependent on the members of the community to carry out their responsibilities and help in a timely manner. All of us are dependent on each other's sharing their resources so that we can have the vital resources we need to live, grow and prosper.

We are also dependent on the earth's resources being there, available and still in their pristine, pure and original state -- water, fruit and vegetables, the right air mixture, the animals and trees and forests to provide essential resources, all the minerals, etc. Then, whenever there is an imbalance in the ecosystem, we are dependent on the scientists' ability to figure out the problem, find the right solution and restore balance. Humans have the responsibility of caring for and managing this earth and its environment. If wisdom prevails and all are faithful, then they will fulfill their purpose, and everyone will live happily.... Tragically, this is not the case. Since the first human beings graced this earth, a succession of bad decisions and wrong choices have been made, some in ignorance and some with malice, which only resulted in failures, tragedies, suffering, death and destruction, as one after another, people failed to fulfill their responsibilities toward self, one another, the environment and God.

Life is **being submissive to the Head, the Almighty God**, who purposed to create us in His own image, just a little lower than the angels, and with a little freedom to make our own life choices. He is Head of the entire universe, Sovereign over heaven and earth. It is to our benefit that He rules because He is righteous and just. Fortunately for us, His compassionate nature led Him to fulfill the role of our Heavenly Father, so He made a paternalistic covenant with everyone. This covenant involves rights and responsibilities and is highly beneficial to us. He has rights and responsibilities and so do we. Even as He is faithful, so must you and I be. He placed the first people in a garden, with everything they needed to grow and multiply. He even created feedback mechanisms, both negative and positive, to rebalance the ecosystem. He saw that everything He had accomplished was very good, and then stood back and waited to see what the outcome would be. He soon regretted His decision to create humans, for besides failing to fulfill their responsibilities toward one another, some were actively seeking the other's failure and even death. Cain committed the first crime, killing his own brother and things went downhill, exponentially, from thereon.

As the head has a great responsibility to lead us to wholeness in the way of righteousness and to enable us to follow the rules laid down in Scripture and in our chromosomes (DNA), we are to rule with logic and reason based on truth knowledge and impassioned by our emotions. Proper leadership will never transgress the boundaries of right living. For this reason, one of the Lord's first concerns was to institute a plan to set up proper leadership: one that is aligned with the Head of the universe, is wise, understanding and knowledgeable of the Natural and Divine Orders, as well as, with the same Fatherly heart as the Heavenly Father Himself. Proper leadership will always strive to protect the common good and, in so doing, restore the wayward ones to the Way. Knowledge of the truth benefits us all, so you must yearn for it, align with it, apply its principles, so that life will work for you and you will thrive. Ignore or reject it and you will experience the sad consequences -- loss of quality of life and you will produce rotten fruit, no fruit or noxious weeds. It's a no brainer. Choose life and reject pain and suffering. Once you have accepted Jesus as your Lord and Savior, you are transformed and restored to live in the Kingdom of God. You live now in His House and in His Kingdom and you are, therefore, subject to His rules.

Everything you have learned about living in this book teaches you how to live in His Home and Kingdom. As nature's values are also Christian and Kingdom values, commit to live by them wholeheartedly. These values are eternal even extending into life in Heaven. It is foolish not to follow them. Be confident in loving and following truth and in being wise. There will be those who oppose your following the truth because they do not want you to exercise self-control for the sake of the common good and they do not care for the innocents who are hurt by their egocentric behavior. They spread fake news and champion dishonest 'science' that falsely 'corroborates' their falsehoods. Don't be discouraged by these forces but be bold in standing up for the truth and….

CHEW as you GO

Principle: You can only be transformed and transform your community when you choose wholeness and to fully align yourself with God's and nature's standards of right living.

Catch every one of the Lord's wise and life-giving counsels.

Hold them dear to your heart. Embrace every counsel. You will need it for your own life and for your restorative function in the world.

Envision all He is giving you. Meditate on it. Kick it around in your head as you go about your life.

Watch out as you go about applying everything to your life, household and community.

"My son, pay attention to my words; listen closely to my sayings. Don't lose sight of them; keep them within your heart. For they are life to those

who find them, and health to one's whole body. Guard your heart above all else, for it is the source of life. Don't let your mouth speak dishonestly, and don't let your lips talk deviously. Let your eyes look forward; fix your gaze straight ahead. Carefully consider the path for your feet, and all your ways will be established. Don't turn to the right or to the left; keep your feet away from evil." (Proverbs 4:20-27, HCSB; cf. Deuteronomy. 4:1, 5-10)

After first aligning with the truth and applying it to your own life then you go and transform the world.

Principle: You cannot be a force for transformation, if you yourself are not first transformed

Give away what the Lord has given you. Share it with your children, companions, friends and everyone who will listen. Post it on the internet. Write a book and then,

Overhaul, restore and invigorate your community. Transform your world. Go with confidence in the power of and led by the Holy Spirit, together with your other like-minded brethren and be a blessing to all the families of the world. The Lord is with you even as He was with Elisha.

> *"The LORD will always lead you, satisfy you in a parched land, and strengthen your bones. You will be like a watered garden and like a spring whose waters never run dry. Some of you will rebuild the ancient ruins; you will restore the foundations laid long ago; you will be called the repairer of broken walls, the restorer of lives."* (Isaiah 58:11-12, HCSB)

The land will thank you;
The oppressed people will thank you; and,
God will thank you.

Oh, how I love all you've revealed;
I reverently ponder it all the day long.
Your commands give me an edge on my enemies;
they never become obsolete.
I've even become smarter than my teachers
since I've pondered and absorbed your counsel.
I've become wiser than the wise old sages
simply by doing what you tell me.
I watch my step, avoiding the ditches and ruts of evil
so I can spend all my time keeping your Word.
I never make detours from the route you laid out;
you gave me such good directions.
Your words are so choice, so tasty;
I prefer them to the best home cooking.
With your instruction, I understand life;
that's why I hate false propaganda.
By your words I can see where I'm going;
they throw a beam of light on my dark path.
I've committed myself and I'll never turn back
from living by your righteous
order.
(Psalm 119: 97-106, MSG; cf. 2 Samuel 22)

THE LAST STEP AND FINAL WORD

I hope that reading this book has been a blessing to you as it has been to me in preparing it. Wholeness will be perfected at the resurrection, in Heaven, when *"we will all be changed – in a flash, in the twinkling of an eye, at the last trumpet. For the trumpet will sound, the dead will be raised imperishable, and we will all be changed."* (1 Corinthians 15:51b-52)

Now, you are aware of God's plan to restore you, the land and the entire world to wholeness; a plan that was fore-ordained since Creation. Gilgal, Bethel, Jericho and the Jordan River are steps in His restorative plan. Each is an important step towards the goal of wholeness and full restoration. No one can be a successful peacemaker in the community, if they do not go through these stages. The minister or pastor must first be healed, be fully dressed in the identity of God's son or daughter and work with, not against, the Father's Holy Spirit, before becoming a successful minister.

Furthermore, success in life and in ministry depends on one's willingness to obey the requirements of life as set out in the Scriptures and in nature. As God is the Creator, He embedded His values into His creation, therefore, you will see that you cannot accept or reject the one without accepting or rejecting the other as both God and nature have the same requirements. Like Israel, we are to uphold the symbols of truth, as represented by the Ark of the Covenant, throughout our lives and ministry. We must know and demonstrate that:

God is Head

God is Head and, therefore, you must be led by His Holy Spirit. It is a requirement for salvation, as stated by the Scriptures: *"For those who are led by the Spirit of God are the children of God"* (Romans 8:14); and, is an obvious requirement for ministry. You have learned how important it is to wait on Him, recognize those He sends and put in place policies and strategies that ensure His continuous leadership in your life and organization.

Your Willingness to Live and Minister by the Rules

You must be willing to live and minister by the rules as exemplified by the Ten Commandments and substantiated by the existence of the Natural Order. Repentance is an important aspect of acknowledging, living and constraining oneself and one's organization to act within the confines of God's and nature's boundaries.

- This Natural Order, and hence God's Kingdom, is systemically interdependent, functioning in synergy, thereby requiring unity at all levels.

- The Natural Order demands moral living and loving-kindness to maintain balance in the ecosystem and as the means of abundant life and happiness. In other words, following the principles will result in growth and success while rejection, altering, adding or subtracting, will lead to stunted growth and even death.
- Transgression of its rules will disrupt balance and unity (synergy), work against the Lord and the common good, and unleash the restorative forces of justice.
- The presence of the latter does not indicate chaos nor take away from God's sovereign rule, but instead demonstrates His wisdom in creating a self-regulating, positive-and negative-feedback-based system which is able to restore the wayward element, person or institution to the Way or, in failing to do so, recycle it to dust, in order to maintain the integrity of the common good (wholeness).
- The presence of these restorative mechanisms in nature, in reaction to transgressions, exemplifies how society must respond to transgressors, whether they are your children, citizens or corporate institutions. You must offer a restorative pathway for every injustice.
- Earth, a living planet, is our home, and like in our other home, we have rights and responsibilities. We have the right to enjoy its rich resources, but with it come the responsibility to use those resources wisely, as failure to do so is detrimental to everyone. As such, we have the responsibility to know and understand its limitations, its rules of engagement and the boundaries of acceptable behavior. Governments need to be proactive to make this information part of their core curriculum in their educational institutions so that, eventually, it would become common knowledge among the general population. Natural Law should be required knowledge of every elected politician. Similarly, the Church has the responsibility of ensuring that its leaders are also

educated and that its Bible schools have Natural Law as a core curricular subject in order to foster wellbeing.

- Truth demands that wisdom be applied always. Ignorance is not bliss nor is failure to apply knowledge. Wrong behavior, whether by ignorance or willful disobedience, disrupts the order and unleashes restorative mechanisms. While there are those who disdain the truth, who are unwilling to discipline themselves for the sake of the common good, even going so far as to changing laws and traditions to allow for greater liberty for their selfish, un-natural and unbalancing desires, we -- you and I must stand firm in the defense of truth and the common good.
- While globalization is systems-based, we must stand up for one that is rules-based -- not any set of rules, but the one created by our Creator, with Him as its Head, and aligned with nature.

You will Cherish Each Experience of the Father's Heart

Revelations, whether they be in the form of guidance, teaching, nurture, comfort, provision, protection or joy, only serve to enrich your relationship with your Heavenly Father and enable you to bond with Him. Meditate on your Spiritual experiences and on those of others as they demonstrate His care for you and that He is with you always.

'Put this Money to Work until I Come Back'

In the Parable of the Ten Minas, Jesus commanded, *'Put this money to work until I come back'.* (Luke 19:11-26*)* In this parable, one was fruitful 10-fold, another 5-fold and the other, 0-fold, but Jesus said that we should expect productiveness to be as much as a 100-fold. (Matthew 13:8) We must be obedient and fruitful to the extent that our Heavenly Father expects us to be and not rebel against His leadership. He is King, has the power to enforce His sovereign authority, and will do so, sooner or later. So, let's put our strengths and talents to work and, especially, let the Holy Spirit move and carry us for our own benefit and for the common good. Don't be found together with the disobedient, the cowards, the mockers and the rebels. Especially, don't pretend that you submit when your heart is not in it to do so. Rather, open your heart and submit wholeheartedly to His leadership, especially, to His Holy Spirit's urging, moving and carrying you forward.

Guard your heart against the lusts of the eyes and ears and from fear. Avoid uncaring, unconcerned selfish ambition and egocentrism; laziness; resentfulness, bitterness; as well as, useless traditions, which not only sap your strength, but keep you from fulfilling your purposes and carrying out your responsibilities in the community of God's Kingdom. These are the things that weaken your heart and take away your confidence, so guard it well as it is the power behind your will. Even if you have everything else, but you have a weak heart you will not have the energy or power to accomplish anything. Life is not worth living, if you cannot experience the joy, peace and general wellness that stem from doing your part in the Kingdom. You will be full of death rather than full of life.

Elisha demonstrated lack of confidence soon after Elijah went up in the chariot of fire when he tried to part the waters of the Jordan River, like Elijah had done earlier. He did not trust in the Lord to do this miracle on his behalf hence his cry: *Where is the Lord, the God of Elijah?"* (2 Kings 2:14) Confidence is developed as you bravely allow the Spirit to move and carry you; as you follow the Spirit's rules of engagement learnt at Jericho; as you adhere to the best practices of the Way of Righteousness, which you saw previously as being also nature's best practices; and as you protect your heart from lusts, unforgiveness and fear.

Today, at all levels of society, a very vocal minority disdains truth and are unwilling to discipline themselves for the sake of the common good; even going as far as to effect changes to laws and traditions to allow for greater liberty for their selfish, unnatural and unbalancing desires. These rebellious forces are defiantly consolidating against the God of Israel. They reveal their utter disdain for moral values, even counting them as religious garbage, despite the fact they are also the same values required by our Natural Order -- values, which are critical to our collective welfare and survival. Refuse to join them or to conform with the changes being implemented that ignore age-old truths. They will meet their end soon.

> "*The kings of the earth, the princes, the generals, the rich, the mighty, and everyone else, both slave and free, hid in caves and among the rocks of the mountains and cried out to the mountains and the rocks, "Fall on us and hide us from the face of him who sits on the throne and from the wrath of the Lamb! For the great day of their wrath has come, and who can withstand it?"* (Revelation 6:15-17)

Rather, you and I must stand firm with our Lord in the defense of truth and the common good and you will be a part of that

> *"great multitude that no one could count, from every nation, tribe, people and language, standing before the throne and before the Lamb. They were wearing white robes and were holding palm branches in their hands."* (Revelation.7:9)

Your purpose in life is to work with God and with the rest of the ecosystem for the common good of all -- to be a blessing to all the families of the earth. We must work together to restore our broken and fallen world to the way of righteousness. This is the work of restorative justice. We each have the responsibility, both as an individual and as a corporate body, to effect justice in the world under the Spirit's leadership and coordination. Doing it well by respecting the order is, therefore, of prime importance. Lives depend on it.

God sent the Israelites to the Promised Land at one of its worst times, when it needed and longed for redemption and renewal. Similarly, Jesus, our Savior, came to the same land when it was suffering under the violent occupation of the pagan Roman Empire. We, therefore, are to possess the land, not just the land of Israel, but the entire earth and restore its rebellious people and corrupted land to its rightful King and Owner, the Almighty God, and to His righteous ways. This is your purpose in life to walk in synergy with your Heavenly Father and with the rest of His creation in His Kingdom.

I truly hope this book has allowed you to catch God's vision of life and the hidden secrets of its restorative paths. Cherish the vision dearly, and wholeheartedly apply it throughout your life, so that you can be a blessing to all the families of the earth and a joy to your Heavenly Father. Acquire a love for learning and wisdom. Remember, though, that truth knowledge has no benefit if it collects the proverbial dust in your mind and is never applied or only applied inconsistently. Apply it always and be wise for it's the only life worth living! Obey His command to "*put this money to work until I return*". *"Yes, I am coming soon", says Jesus. Amen. Come, Lord Jesus".* (Revelation 22:20)

May He find you so doing when He returns. Have a blessed life and be an amazing blessing to us all. Amen.

Bibliography

1. A Greek-English Lexicon of the New Testament and Other Early Christian Literature, 3rd Edition; based on Walter Bauer's work and on previous editions by W.F. Arndt, F.W. Gingwich and F.W. Danker; Revised and edited by F.W. Danker; The University of Chicago Press; 2000
2. Chasing the Dragon, Jackie Pullinger, Andrew Quicke; Hodder & Stoughton; 1980
3. Dictionary of Jesus and the Gospels by Joel B. Green, Scot McKnight, I. Howard Marshall; IVP; 1992
4. Douay-Rheims Bible, Courtesy Berean Bible.com © 2013, 2014
5. GOD'S WORD®, Copyright 1995 by God's Word to the Nations.
6. Holman Christian Standard Bible®, Copyright © 1999, 2000, 2002, 2003, 2009 by Holman Bible Publishers.
7. Holy Bible, New International Version®, NIV® Copyright © 1973, 1978, 1984, 2011 by Biblica, Inc.®

8. Illustrated Dictionary & Concordance of the Bible; Gen. Ed. Geoffrey Wigoder; G.G. The Jerusalem Publishing House, Ltd.; 1986
9. Mosby's Medical Dictionary, 9th edition. © 2009, Elsevier.
10. NET Bible copyright © 1996-2006 by Biblical Studies Press
11. New American Standard Bible Copyright © 1960, 1962, 1963, 1968, 1971, 1972, 1973, 1975, 1977, 1995 by The Lockman Foundation, La Habra, Calif.
12. New Heart English Bible, Edited by Wayne A. Mitchell, Public Domain 2008-2018
13. The Brown-Driver-Briggs Hebrew and English Lexicon; Hendrickson; 1999
14. The Equipping Pastor: A System's Approach to Congregational Leadership by R. Paul Stevens and Phil Collins; Rowman & Littlefield Publishers; 1993
15. The Girl in the Picture: The Story of Kim Phuc, the Photograph and the Vietnam War by Denise Chong; Penguin Books; 2001
16. The Hiding Place by Corrie Ten Boom, Elizabeth & John Sherrill; Bantam Books; 1974
17. The Holy Bible, English Standard Version®) copyright © 2001 by Crossway Bibles, a publishing ministry of Good News Publishers.
18. The Holy Bible: International Standard Version® Release 2.1, Copyright © 1996-2012 The ISV Foundation
19. The Holy Bible, New Living Translation, copyright ©1996, 2004, 2007; Tyndale House Publishers, Inc., Carol Stream, Illinois 60188.
20. The Message (MSG), Copyright © 1993, 1994, 1995, 1996, 2000, 2001, 2002 by Eugene H. Peterson
21. Theological Dictionary of the New Testament; Editors: G. Kittel & G. Friedrich; Abridged in One Volume by Geoffrey W. Bromley; Eerdsmans;1985

22. The Original Aramaic New Testament in Plain English-with Psalms & Proverbs, Copyright © 2007; 8th edition Copyright © 2013
23. The Throne Zone: A Worship Revolution by Keith Duncan; Copyright by Keith Duncan; 2007
24. Total Quality Ministry by Walther Kallestad & Steve Schey: Augsburg Fortress: 1994
25. Various Internet Articles including Wikipedia Encyclopaedia
26. Webster Bible Translation, Courtesy BereanBible.com, © 2013, 2014

www.ingramcontent.com/pod-product-compliance
Lightning Source LLC
LaVergne TN
LVHW010052170826
845678LV00012B/2118